How Christianity Transforms
Human Thinking and Creates
World Prosperity

How Christianity Transforms Human Thinking and Creates World Prosperity

Volume I: Foundations of Thinking

Christianity, the Antidote to Malevolent Human Thinking And the Keys to the Good Life

C. H. Kirchner

April 2024 First Edition

Truth Publications
https://xnthinking.com

I

Preface Vol I: Foundations of Thinking

Genesis 1:27-28 says that God designed the world for humanity to use, enjoy, and have a fruitful life. The theme of God's desire for human prosperity runs throughout the Bible and that prosperity is initially stated as material prosperity because that could be easily understood. As mankind's history unfolds and is documented, the definition of prosperity would be expanded with the Hebrew word "**shalom**".

שָׁלוֹם *šālôm 237x peace, safety, prosperity, well-being; intactness, wholeness; peace can have a focus of security, safety which can bring feelings of satisfaction, well-being, and contentment.*

The two Volume set traces how Christianity emerged from Judaism to conquer the Roman Empire by friendly persuasion and change the malicious, self-serving, and malevolent thinking of mankind to create a dynamic prosperity, the Good Life, for the Western World.

Volume I defines the prosperity promised by God to both Jews and Christians. It examines the current worldwide prosperity and how Christian thinking has impacted prosperity around the world. Human thinking is driven by built-in genetics, human consciousness, and human religions and their thinking. These are mankind's fundamental drivers for thinking that lead to the malevolent life. Christian thinking, as an antidote to malevolent thinking, comes from the wisdom and knowledge of the Bible and provides us with God's view of a Philosophy of Life that produces shalom prosperity. Volume I will examine these forces, how they develop and dominate life, and how Christian thinking can be traced from Abraham and Judaism.

Volume II addresses the historical transition from Judaism to Christianity as God's plan for mankind and assesses key aspects of Christian theology and the Philosophy of Life that impact prosperity. It then traces the rapid transition of the Roman Empire to Christianity and and how Christianity launched the explosion of education, the arts, and then science that led to our current Western World prosperity. How modern science sees a Creator behind the design of the world and life is the consequence of this scientific journey.

The premise of this story is that Christianity is the cause of the Western World's prosperity, and to evaluate this premise we will examine several aspects relative to this question. First of all, what exactly do we mean by prosperity? Secondly, what do current evaluations of prosperity around the world tell us? Thirdly, given that how people think and act can impact prosperity significantly, what are the fundamental drivers of human thinking and responses to life? Are there forces at work that control or modify human thinking and societies and cultures that can create winners and losers? And how does Christianity stack up against all of the world's philosophies, especially other religions?

Certainly, prosperity is not all about money. Several aspects of prosperity have to do with how one thinks about life and deals with life. We're calling this thinking aspect a philosophy of life and to examine this impact on prosperity we will examine the beginnings of mankind's thinking and how it developed through a dynamic event called consciousness, becoming self-aware. Another factor in thinking is how genetics plays into the thinking of a culture and passes down that common culture from generation to generation.

The third aspect of our evaluation will be the impact of religion on mankind's thinking. Most people in the world view religion as an integral part of everyday life. It flavors all of mankind's thinking and thus influences prosperity.

There are four important impacts of human thinking then, genetics, the advent of becoming conscious human beings, and the Theology and Philosophy of Life from the religion of choice and whatever secular thinking and philosophy might develop. Thus we will examine religions around the world, especially Christianity to look for factors that would promote prosperity, or detract from it.

The differences between religions may seem to be small and inconsequential when looking at the big picture of Theology, worship, and rituals, but these small differences can play a big role in the outcome. Everyone in the Western World who follows sports knows that the difference between winning a world championship or a major golf or tennis tournament can be very subtle in terms of the play. Games and matches all hang on precision accomplishments at the right time. The difference between winning and losing can seem very slim. One team or player only has to be a little better than the opponent to become a winner over and over again. This is what we will find with prosperity as well. The devil is in the details and it is in the details where Christianity provides some key differences in Theology and Philosophy that make a big difference in the outcome.

Acknowledgments

This book began some 10 years ago as an apologetic for my beliefs about Christianity, and to confront the challenges from the diverse popular Christian media, and from my brother Bob, both of whom saw Christianity from different perspectives than mine.

Before one starts writing, key aspects of the book should be identified, the story to be told, the storytelling approach, and the audience. I did none of these things, I just began writing some things down and tried to frame them in an unusual setting such as letters from one person to another, or advice from an old guru. I went through this stage with many restarts over a number of years, all the while collecting information and writing it into chapters of the book. As I accumulated more information I would see the need to reorganize the information and the approach to present it.

Much of the story seemed to revolve around what was happening with Christianity itself as people seemed to be less interested and church attendance was down significantly all around the world. This led to examining the objectives of Christianity and then to the notion that it had perhaps been too successful. People were too prosperous and no longer needed the comfort of religion to help keep them going. (Drugs, alcohol, and ego satisfaction being other sources of comfort.) Other possibilities were that life had become too busy and Sunday was the only true day of rest. Or that the Churches, each in their own way, had lost sight of their mission, which, for all Christians, is the Great Commission, Matthew 28:16–20.

Eventually, the focus of the book became exploring the detailed objectives of Christianity itself, and that expanded into Judaism as the precursor to Christianity. This resulted in a good deal of Biblical research going back to Genesis. If I were to discuss the objectives of religion and Christianity I'd have to examine where and why it all got started as well as the results, as we see things today.

One aspect I wanted to avoid was criticizing various Christian denominations, pointing out where I thought they had gone off the rails. This is always an easy trap to fall into and results in the alienation of just about everyone. The truth is none are perfect, but most are trying. So I have fallen back to the best approach, which is to present the truth of the objectives of Christianity, as best I can determine from the Bible. Certainly, I have stomped on some toes in this process but at least the criticism is masked in what I consider to be the Bible's take on things, with lots of documented references and texts.

I hope also to have clarified sufficiently that there is more than one way to do things, and secondly perhaps, that more than one way, better matches variations in human nature. There is no absolute right way to accomplish the Christian Mission when dealing with human nature, or variations in natural environments.

In telling a story you want to have it laid out in some logical order and after about 10 years of writing and rewriting I was getting close. My wife, Pat, and I, and my brother and his wife, happened to be on a one-week vacation cruise out of Seattle in June of 2023 and I carried my laptop trying to put the final touches on the manuscript which had grown to over 600 pages and two volumes. Every morning on the cruise I would get up early and head to the coffee bar with my laptop. One morning a fellow passenger had noticed all my serious work and asked what I was doing so earnestly. I admitted I was writing a book and he immediately asked me a question that I had not asked myself, what was the book about? Fortunately, I'd already had two expressos and a surprising answer popped out of my head, something along the lines of "How Christianity was the cause of World prosperity". He thought that was an interesting topic and we chatted a bit for several days about it.

I had never thought about the book in the sense of who the audience might be, what might attract a reader, or even what the title of the book should be. So my expresso-charged brain had given me a good start at a title, and the audience, as someone interested in Christian-focused books or philosophies. At that point, I realized I was further from the finish line than I thought. I would need to do some reorganization and perhaps add a bit more information on Christian Theology and Philosophy to support my supposition than I had included thus far.

I had written the story more from a historical standpoint and had not addressed perhaps the key questions of interest to Christians. That is, what is there about Christianity that causes the prosperity I was claiming, and does the Bible really claim prosperity is God's desire for us? I had been addressing the evidence but not the desirability from God's perspective, nor the potential causes, both critical missing links.

Fortunately, I had most of the material researched and written, what was required was a reorganization and the addition of a bit more of the Christian Theology and Philosophy that addresses the weaknesses in content pointed out above. So where I was hoping to have it printed last summer, it took me a little longer to make that happen.

So I have to give a big thanks to Tom Howard at Harding University for asking me that key question I had neglected to ask myself. And thanks also to my brother Bob for raising all those questions about Christianity and being willing to discuss them at length. And thanks to Diane, Bob's wife, and my wife Pat, for enduring some of those discussions over dinner. (With apologies to nearby diners as well.) Thanks also to Pat, and daughters Gwen and Gail who helped with clarification, editing the content, and especially removing my sarcastic comments and insider jokes that no one would appreciate. And a special thanks to "The Man", who spent his entire life teaching the value of the content of the Bible and especially noting that God has a "greater grace" available for his people.

About the format

All pictures and quoted text, which are generally indented and italicized, are referenced to a source. Most are either public domain or Wikipedia Commons authorized to use. Biblical Quotes are from the New American Standard (NASB) Bible. All quoted text and pictures are considered "fair use" as educated opinions and ideas valuable to the analysis and worthy of being explained or shown directly as written.

The general approach in research books and papers is to limit references to numbers you have to then look up in the back of the paper or book to see the source. Then you have to go find the source which may be difficult. Here, a partial text of expanded sources and references is included in sufficient detail so that you can view and evaluate the corroborating evidence within the context of the discussion. This makes it easier for the reader to judge the veracity of the argument being made.

Wikipedia is an excellent source of first-line information and a great place to begin research as it precludes most biased financial interests or advertising from getting in the way of facts. It also uses all contributors as fact-checkers so its veracity is probably as good as you can get, especially in historical and scientific areas. You always have to consider that the writer of any text can be biased and this is especially true in areas of controversy such as cutting-edge science, politics, religion, and philosophy. I've pointed out at least one area where politics may have biased a historical reference.

When included, references are in italicized text. The internal reference numbers of all quoted text have been removed to aid comprehension. These are numbers for further reference, about a name or subject, that is listed at the end of the source article. Also, note that Wikipedia's dynamic editing continually changes the referenced material so quoted text may have been changed in later editions of Wikipedia articles.

Comments?

Coming

https://xnthinking.com

Villa of the Nile Mosaic, Lepcis Magna, Tripoli National Museum, circa 1st century

https://commons.wikimedia.org/wikiFile:Villa_of_the_Nile_Mosaic_fishermen.jpg
Marco Prins. CC0. via Wikimedia Commons

SECTION A: DEFINING PROSPERITY

1. Living the Good Life

The first-century picture above certainly looks like the good life to any fishing enthusiast but the story behind it is probably more of a job to catch dinner for the family than a hobby. It all depends on how good the fishing becomes and how great the catch. Food for individuals in Roman times was not readily available to the peasants and the Roman government had to scramble to keep the city supplied with enough grain to feed the masses.

What everyone wants is a prosperous life, but what few consider is exactly what that means. Probably most people subscribe to Frank's definition, Sinatra that is, who said it all in a song, "I Did it My Way". Now that's a great song, one that expresses an idea close to our hearts. We all might dream about a life that we control and manage that turns out to be the envy of the world. That's what the song suggests. But you have to consider that Charles Manson lived his life that same way, as did Ted Bundy, Jeffrey Dahmer, and John Wayne Gacy. So perhaps "Doing it **my way**" is not a great recipe for living a life that is the envy of the world. Your way also has to be the right way.

We also have great thinkers and philosophers throughout the ages who are studied for their unique thinking, Some may be great thinkers in psychology or psychiatry. They develop their theories about life, based on scientific research of people's thinking, actions, and life consequences. But those trained by such studies, have many different views of life and have dispensed with some less than satisfactory advice. Dr. Spock's controversial advice on child rearing comes to mind. There are also self-help books that give us steps to success in many different fields. We can also conclude life decisions from novels and all manner of storytelling productions. But to separate the good and bad advice given in these forms requires us to first have some sense of the merit of those choices.

Mickey Mantle, the baseball player, in his 60s and dying of liver disease from a life of hard drinking often quipped, "If I'd known I was gonna live this long, I'd have taken a lot better care of myself," a line popularized by football legend Bobby Layne *("Mickey Mantle Quotes". Baseball-almanac.com.)*. The point is, "doing it my way" is winging it. Living life without a good compass to point you in the right direction, is maybe not the best prescription for life. "My way" is perhaps good advice when considering what productive field you choose for your life's work, but even there you have to know what you enjoy doing.

There are a hundred and one sources of influence that encircle us daily from friends who have something we don't have, to family traditions, or the lack thereof, to a peer group of tattooed drug dealing gang bangers or characters we see in movies or on television. As teenagers, we are usually locked to our parents and if they are on the ball, we're sheltered or guided away from exposure to the bad options in life. But maybe not. The biggest problem is that some paths are a dead end, a do-over is not possible and once you go too far down that path, your life is set in concrete and a dumpster fire is your future.

The other factor that jumps out as you observe the lives of others is that often what they have doesn't make them happy. So what's up with that? If I won the lottery and had a grand mansion with all the toys I wanted, or enough clothes and shoes and jewelry or grandkids to fill the bedrooms I'd be happy but those who have all that they desire often are grumpy, unhappy people.

So there are two aspects of prosperity, **what we have and what we think about it.** It's complicated. More complicated than anything we can reason or figure out on our own. And we have a great cloud of witnesses who testify as to the difficulties in "doing it my way".

The supposition we are working on is that prosperity in the Western World is driven by ideas promoted by Christianity, in contrast to the rest of the world, which has other sources of influence. Now we know that within the Western World, there are many whose life is a dumpster fire and who happen to be Christian at least in some fashion or another. So there's much more going on than simply being a nominal Christian that family heritage can provide.

The mystery is how a society of Christians where some individual lives may be a disaster compared to the ideal life also produces collectively great prosperity of opportunity at least for most all the members of that society. Why are we, in the Western world, so prosperous, and those in other parts of the world lacking in prosperity? To relegate the answer to luck or lack of resources begs the question and buries our heads in the sand. And to lay it at the feet of Darwin's evolution (we got smarter) doesn't track the ability of second and third-generation immigrants to become fully capable and involved in Western prosperity.

To examine this question we're assuming that the availability of natural resources is not a driving factor since for hundreds of years societies have used commercial trading to obtain the materials and goods they needed. Secondly, climate can be favorable as well as detrimental and does not materially impact the possibility of prosperity in most locations around the world. We tend to think that the United States has both an abundance of natural resources and a favorable climate, and it does. But you should also note that some Western European countries have both cold climates and are lacking some natural resources that have to be obtained by trade. Try working along the East Coast of the United States during the summers before air conditioning, especially in Washington DC. Or consider that most everything has been invented by some Scottish person from the north of England. Go ahead, look it up.

The colonial rule the West has imparted on various segments of the third world and the wars in Europe fought over interpretations of Christianity seem to belie the idea that Christianity is behind these successes, however. The Western World is not without its faults and failings, for its people are mere humans and human nature is prone to get into arguments and disagreements with both relatives and neighbors.

However, the spread of Christianity across the Roman world was swift and almost universal because its basic tenets are rather simply explained. It was not until the explosion of education in the 12th century and the invention of the printing press in the 16th century accelerated reading among the general population, that the full Judaeo-Christian Theology and Philosophy of Life would become widely available and somewhat known and understood. It was this broad understanding of Christianity that motivated the great leap into science and technology that spread through the Western World and revolutionized life. It is also the story of world-leading advances in economics, the arts and architecture, and quality of life.

The assessment is therefore that:

Christianity provides the best Philosophy of Life to live the "Good Life".

Philosophy may seem like a strange term to apply to religion but that is really what Christianity preaches.

> ***philosophy: a theory or attitude held by a person that acts as a guiding principle of behavior.***

The connection of religion with a philosophy of life is actually a well-accepted idea in pop culture. There's a popular song by the Alternative Rock Band REM called "Losing My Religion". It's not really about religion proper but about religion as a Philosophy of Life and how life keeps pushing us to abandon our own philosophy, or perhaps break out of our personality limitations, to be, or be with, the "cool kids" for example. The result, expressed by the lyrics of "Losing My Religion" is the fog of not knowing what to do in life, being pulled in directions you are not able to control. Going back to the fisherman analogy, it's a rowboat without a rudder, you've lost control of your direction in life, and in a boat without oars, you have no power to move in any direction.

Losing My Religion

Losing My Religion lyrics © Night Garden Music

> *That's me in the corner*
> *That's me in the spot-light*
> *Losing my religion*
> *Trying to keep up with you*
> *And I don't know if I can do it*
> *Oh no I've said too much*
> *I haven't said enough*

Songwriters: Peter Lawrence Buck / Michael E. Mills / William Thomas Berry / John Michael Stipe

This is the temptation that we in the Western World have to face every day because we have the freedom politically and economically to examine and test the waters of change. It is a challenge for us in our individual lives as we confront the sirens of influencers calling us to follow their meaningless or destructive ideas. Similarly, there are the sirens of societal change that seek to have us abandon our philosophy of life to follow some just cause and change the world.

These challenges become difficult when the siren, the influencer, or the politician gives us an enticing reason to follow them. Every day we are challenged to change our personal lives by the personalities and slick advertisements that tempt us to try something new or different. Perhaps we're getting used to that distraction, we just ignore everything that wasn't already on our list of potential changes or we turn off or tune out most of these personal sirens. But some will catch our attention and tempt us. So we need a sound baseline to guide our judgement.

The greater challenge lies in the siren song of social change that impacts how our society functions. This becomes especially difficult when politicians, power politics, and money are involved. The goal or prize becomes so great that no ruse or fabricated story or timeline can be too outrageous to discourage a false narrative from being used to sell us the idea. These false narratives can begin as "Trojan Horses", something that seems to be legitimate on the surface, but is just a lie, that once we accept it, sets off a pattern of change that can not be reversed and can doom our prosperity.

> The **Trojan Horse** was a wooden horse said to have been used by the Greeks during the Trojan War to enter the city of Troy and win the war. The Trojan Horse is not mentioned in Homer's Iliad, with the poem ending before the war is concluded, and it is only briefly mentioned in the Odyssey. But in the Aeneid by Virgil, after a fruitless 10-year siege, the Greeks constructed a huge wooden horse at the behest of Odysseus, and hid a select force of men inside, including Odysseus himself. The Greeks pretended to sail away, and the Trojans pulled the horse into their city as a victory trophy. That night, the Greek force crept out of the horse and opened the gates for the rest of the Greek army, which had sailed back under the cover of darkness. The Greeks entered and destroyed the city, ending the war.
>
> Metaphorically, a "Trojan horse" has come to mean any trick or stratagem that causes a target to invite a foe into a securely protected bastion or place. A malicious computer program that tricks users into willingly running it is also called a "Trojan horse" or simply a "Trojan".
>
> The main ancient source for the story still extant is the Aeneid of Virgil, a Latin epic poem from the time of Augustus. The story featured heavily in the Little Iliad and the Sack of Troy, both part of the Epic Cycle, but these have only survived in fragments and epitomes. As Odysseus was the chief architect of the Trojan Horse, it is also referred to in Homer's Odyssey.[1] In the Greek tradition, the horse is called the "wooden horse"
> https://en.wikipedia.org/wiki/Trojan_Horse

The problem of course is that if you don't know how you became prosperous, you are doomed to lose that prosperity to the endless hordes of those who wish to take it away from you. This attack can come from your family, friends, employment, and from your government. It is from your government that the Trojan Horse is likely to be the most dangerous and at the same time most insidious. That such an attack on prosperity is eminently viable, should not be surprising given that excellent examples of the loss of prosperity have already occurred in the Soviet Union,

Communist China, Nazi Germany, Cuba, and Venezuela. Today the rich and famous are already colluding with unelected world political figures to create the crises needed to force people into accepting a critical transfer of power to those same unknown political figures accompanied by a significant loss of prosperity for everyone unless you are truly rich and famous as well.

The playbook is straight out of "1984", creating a crisis, real or imagined, and enforcing nominal-sounding solutions that, step by step, make everyone slaves to the government. This is done by controlling key elements of life, your food, your energy, your housing, your access to travel, and even your access to your own money. These controlling restrictions are already being discussed and when the government has control of these aspects of your life you are indeed a slave. The United States has already agreed to accept the World Council of Health's pandemic instructions.

What we are all faced with is a cascading array of positive and negative ideas, suggestions, desires, wants, and needs that drive our decision-making and actions every hour of every day. Your life is the result of the total of all those influences that are converted into actions. What this means is that you are not in control of your life if you allow your life to be run by the wrong influences or desires. These are the fundamental forces that drove history up until Rome and they are still in force today, amplified by modern forms of a "Me first" ideology.

These forces of human nature are powerful enough to derail your life in a heartbeat. They create a fog around life that confuses your thinking. A fog that messes with your decision-making and keeps tripping you up, messing with your life decisions. Understanding all these forces is key to being able to deal with them. What you also need is a firm foundation for how to live a prosperous life, you need a firm grasp on the right Philosophy of Life. This of course is our premise, Christianity provides that Philosophy; to be justified.

Children fishermen. Engraving by A.I. Zubchaninov, drawing by A.P. Koverznev, 1875

From the series «The Peasant Life». Vsemirnaya Illustration Magazine (The World Illustration Magazine), 1875. V. XIV. - S. Petersburg: Hermann Hoppe Publishing, 1875 Public domain

2. Shalom: Whole Life Prosperity

From the beginning, prosperity has been a symbol of Judaeo-Christian Thinking. This prosperity is defined by the Hebrew word **shalom (שָׁלוֹם** *šālôm)* and the equivalent Greek word **eirene (εἰρήνη eirēnē)**. Both words are often translated as peace, meaning both a state of mind and a physical safety from the world's violence. There is also a concept of material prosperity in the form of an abundance of what one needs for a good life, not necessarily being rich.

This concept of prosperity, as an abundance of needs for a good life, is first stated by Moses in Deuteronomy 28:1-14 as God's promise to the Hebrews as they are about to enter the Promised Land. This promise comes with conditions, however. "If you obey God's commandments or words", with the implication that the conditions are both individual and national. There is a promise of both national and personal blessings characterized as material prosperity.

Deuteronomy 28:1-6 (NASB) 1 "Now it shall be, if you diligently obey the LORD your God, being careful to do all His commandments which I command you today, the LORD your God will set you high above all the nations of the earth. 2 All these blessings will come upon you and overtake you if you obey the LORD your God:

3 "Blessed shall you be in the city, and blessed shall you be in the country.

4 "Blessed shall be the offspring of your body and the produce of your ground and the offspring of your beasts, the increase of your herd and the young of your flock.

5 "Blessed shall be your basket and your kneading bowl.

6 "Blessed shall you be when you come in, and blessed shall you be when you go out.

What Moses did not say is, that if we pray to God, He will bestow blessings on us. He's not going to bless us with prosperity just because we ask. The message is that here are the principles and rules for a prosperous life, BUT it's up to you to take advantage of this wisdom to obtain your prosperity.

This is the "teach a man to fish" approach to prosperity. This approach to prosperity is then carried forward from Judaism into Christianity and a new symbol arises that ties prosperity to Christianity, the symbol of a fish. Fish as a symbol of prosperity is a running theme through the Gospels.

Jesus states his purpose for Christians is the abundant life

- John 10:10, "I came that they may have life, and have it abundantly". This is the tip of the iceberg, God's stated objective. There is much more to be said about the abundant life elsewhere in the New Testament.
- Jesus tells his disciples, some of whom are fishermen, "I will make you fishers of men". (Mark 1: 16-18).
- In John 21:11, fishing is expanded to the idea of prosperity. The disciples had been fishing all night but caught nothing. Jesus then

instructed them to cast the nets on the other side of the boat, and they drew in 153 fish.

- On a national level, the example is in John 6:1-14, the feeding of the five thousand. A large crowd assembles to hear Jesus speak. The crowd was a mix of people who were curious about Jesus because of the sick being healed, they were not necessarily followers. So perhaps this also accounts for prosperity for non-Christians living in association with Christians.

- By the second century AD, a fish symbol quickly became both emblematic of Christianity and a secret symbol of identity in a world where Christians were periodically persecuted for treading on sacred Roman religious traditions. The secret symbol was used when two people met. One would draw one of the curves of the fish in the ground and if the other were a Christian he would draw the opposite curve completing the image and denoting that he was also a Christian.

The prosperity idea is later promoted by the real-time prosperity of Christian monasteries which did not develop from any desire on their part but from the donations of people and hard work building the monasteries themselves. The prosperity of the kings and local leaders also served to indicate God's favor with his people.

The first thing we must do is define prosperity. First of all, we'll define it from Western Civilization's Christian heritage but that can be a problem. Believe it or not, prosperity is a word that connotes a big con game to many Christians, mostly because it has become synonymous with a spurious considered teaching often called "the prosperity gospel". One version of this says that if you are faithful and contribute money to the church, or your favorite preacher, God will bless you and give you health, happiness, and riches in return. There is a nugget of truth in this theology, God wants us to be prosperous, it's in the Bible. But the false premise is that you will receive riches from God by giving money, to specific churches or organizations. That's human religion's big lie, that you can bribe God and get things from Him. We'll examine that a little later. But prosperity is a legitimate Judaeo-Christian subject so we'll use the Bible to define prosperity from that perspective.

One reason for the negative connotation of the "prosperity gospel" is that it raises a question in Christianity that the critics don't want to address. That is, why are some people wealthy and others poor? Is it just a matter of luck, circumstance, or where you happen to be born, or is there something that can be done to change the prosperity outlook for anyone? Or why can't we share what we have and lift those who are poor out of poverty? Those of us who live in the prosperous West occasionally glimpse out at the world and are so dismayed that we quickly divert our eyes, embarrassed that we seem to have so much and many in the world have so little.

Intuitively we know that sharing our wealth is not the answer.

> *"Give a man a fish and he eats for a day, teach him to*
> *fish and you feed him for a lifetime."*

Many assume this is a phrase from the Bible but it's not. It's been attributed to a Chinese proverb as well as a 19th-century English author among others. But whatever the source, it has a ring of truth about it. The phrase distinguishes between the poor man with nothing to eat and the rich man who has an abundance. Learning to fish takes desire and willingness to learn and the drive or a mental push to make it happen. There is nothing physically preventing the poor man from hiring onto a fishing vessel and learning the trade. However, there can be several forces in play that prevent the individual from taking this action and succeeding.

You might say that you can get the person out of poverty but you may not be able to get the poverty out of the person. True prosperity is not so easily achieved or transferred to others. Prosperity is more than having enough to eat. The world today has an overabundance of food, and, with a few exceptions, that food is distributed to where it's needed when it's needed.

Prosperity has a mental component as well. Less than two hundred years ago, life in London in the mid-1800s for the poor was crude and cold, at least as described by Charles Dickens. It has been natural for us to think of prosperity as economic or material prosperity, the rich v.s. the poor, and while that is part of the prosperity equation that is only one aspect of general prosperity to be considered and probably not the most important. Charles Dickens presents such a contrast in his story, "A Christmas Carol" where one character has maximum material prosperity, but lacks any "spiritual" or immaterial mental prosperity, and a second character has marginal material prosperity, but a high level of "spiritual" prosperity. Spiritual here is not necessarily religious but a sense of an immaterial aspect to life with others that transcends material life.

What everyone wants is the "good life". In a broad sense, we can think of the "good life" as much more than material or economic prosperity, it includes peace and happiness as well. What this means is that we're going to broaden this investigation a bit and take it beyond just economic prosperity, which has a primary connotation of having an abundance of the essentials, plus a few frills in life.

We are also examining prosperity from a Judaeo-Christian perspective because the Western World has achieved a high level of prosperity that falls within this material and "spiritual" definition. The Western World has also become the benchmark upon which human quality of life is measured. We're not saying the Western, Christian-influenced world is perfect or without faults. Nor or we going to argue that life in the West is better than the life of a recluse in a Buddhist monastery for example. Such a comparison becomes a meaningless debate between a physical life in a physical world and a life lived within the inner self. What Christianity proposes is to give mankind the most prosperous enjoyable life possible, the Good Life, but it requires thinking about life in the right way.

Is there such a thing as "the good life"? There are four questions to be explored.

1. *What is prosperity?*
2. *What are the factors that influence physical and mental prosperity in life?*
3. *Does Christianity have a Philosophy of Life that promotes a prosperous life?*
4. *Does the historical record support this?*

To explore the Good Life we will examine mankind's multiple views of life, influences in life, and the driving motivations of civilization. All of this is from the perspective of the effects of these factors on the prosperity of humans living in the material world.

Now we've used the word prosperity more comprehensively than is common, to include economic prosperity, peace, and happiness because we don't have a good English word that encompasses the entire spectrum of what the "good life" entails. There is however a single word in the Bible that seems to fully describe the "good life", the Hebrew word "Shalom".

שָׁלוֹם *šālôm 237x peace, safety, prosperity, well-being; intactness, wholeness; peace can have a focus of security, safety which can bring feelings of satisfaction, well-being, and contentment.*
Enhanced Strong's Dictionary©2011 Olive Tree Bible Software, Inc. All rights reserved

Shalom is also related to a word of importance in Islam. It comes from the Semitic root S-L-M which provides a comparable Arabic word and forms the basis for the name of Islam. S-L-M stands for the letters s, l, m, and the dashes represent the vowel sounds that were not written in ancient languages but understood.

salām (سَلَام) peace. The word إسلام Islām is a verbal noun derived from s-l-m, meaning "submission" (i.e. entrusting one's wholeness to a higher force), which may be interpreted as humility. "One who submits" is signified by the participle مسلم, Muslim (fem. مسلمة, muslimah).
https://en.wikipedia.org/wiki/%C5%A0-L-M

In the book, "Not the Way It's Supposed to Be: A Breviary of Sin", author Cornelius Plantinga described the Hebrew concept of shalom.

"The webbing together of God, humans, and all creation in justice, fulfillment, and delight is what the Hebrew prophets call shalom. We call it peace but it means far more than mere peace of mind or a cease-fire between enemies. In the Bible, shalom means universal flourishing, wholeness, and delight – a rich state of affairs in which natural needs are satisfied and natural gifts fruitfully employed, a state of affairs that inspires joyful wonder as its Creator and Savior opens doors and welcomes the creatures in whom he delights. Shalom, in other words, is the way things ought to be."
https://en.wikipedia.org/wiki/Shalom

The Bible's New Testament Greek word corresponding to the Hebrew shalom (שָׁלוֹם šālôm) is εἰρήνη eirēnē, generally translated as "peace" in the New Testament.

εἰρήνη eirēnē; *probably from a primary verb εἴρω eirō (to join); peace (literally or figuratively); by implication, prosperity: — one, peace, quietness, rest, + set at one again.*
    AV- peace, one 1, rest 1, quietness 1;
    a state of national tranquillity, exemption from the rage and havoc of war, peace between individuals, i.e. harmony, concord security, safety, prosperity, felicity, (because peace and harmony make and keep things safe and prosperous) of the Messiah's peace, the way that leads to peace (salvation) of Christianity, the tranquil state of a soul assured of its salvation through Christ, and so fearing nothing from God and content...
Enhanced Strong's Dictionary©2011 Olive Tree Bible Software, Inc. All rights reserved

So we can adopt the English spelling of shalom and its meaning as a word to represent "the good life". But because the English word prosperity can include a connotation of "the good life", beyond just the idea of economic or material prosperity, we'll continue to use the term "prosperity" in its broadest sense and add the descriptor "economic" prosperity to refer to material prosperity. It should also be noted that economic prosperity is not being super rich but having an abundance of material possessions to make life rich and complex, at least to the level that suits your interests and capacity for enjoyment, and also less frantic.

The real world is not always interesting and enjoyable. We live in a world of friction and turmoil from people all around us and even from those who share our homes. And we also are often faced with problems, debts, and expenses that are difficult to handle. So having that all go away becomes our definition of heaven on earth and it remains a constant but often unrealized dream. The best we can do is to learn to cope with these daily frustrations. But coping for most of us is enduring, grinning on the outside as you secretly grind your teeth. It doesn't lessen the emotional and mental impact, it's mostly a diversion, a mental trick to help us forget, for a while.

Shalom, the good life, is much more than gritting our teeth and suppressing our anger at the "fools" all around us. It's looking at all those fools differently and responding differently, not just overlooking the problems but looking beyond the problems and seeing the beauty of life beyond the immediate problems.

This is the essence of our story then, Christianity, Judaism, and Islam certainly address the concept of Shalom. What remains to be seen is the evidence that their philosophy or other philosophies or religions have any serious impact on the prosperous areas of the world. What we will see is that shalom is more than the luck of the draw, dependent on where and when you're born. It is the product of a philosophy of life, a way of living that promotes prosperity in many different environments.

Now all people in all civilizations develop coping strategies as part of their own philosophy of life. Their coping strategies are developed from both their culture and their inner personal nature or personality determined by their genes. By philosophy, we mean this in the sense of its practical application.

philosophy: a theory or attitude held by a person that acts as a guiding principle of behavior.

So what we want in life is economic prosperity, peace, and happiness; and our approach to achieving what we want is driven by our philosophy of life. These two things, what we want and our approach to getting it is heavily influenced by our environment and culture, however. Our genes, philosophy, and environment become a strange brew of conditions and events that produces a surprising mix of results.

One fundamental view is that genes plus your environment shape your philosophy and therefore your outcome in life. This is a simplistic view where the environment is usually reduced to either rich or poor. The question raised in popular fiction exemplified by Mark Twain's "The Prince and the Pauper" is whether someone from poverty and an inferior upbringing (bad genes and bad/poor environment) can ever work his way out of that handicap. Genetics were unknown scientifically at the time but the effects were understood in a general sense from observations of human nature.   While Shalom; prosperity, peace, and happiness; was the inner desire of everyone, it was felt that prosperity was the providence of the wealthy, the aristocrats, royalty, or the powerful.

When we look at all of mankind and the variations of civilizations scattered around the world we find a wide disparity in this concept of Shalom as defined by the realities of the Western World.   Certainly, many in the West glamorized and idealized native island populations lounging around on warm beaches eating fish picked out of the sea, and drinking coconut milk.   They saw them as having escaped the hassle and stress of Western life and wished they could be there.   But the life choices and rich experiences of the West are missing.   A boy or girl born into the island culture has no future as a doctor or engineer or musician or attending a Yankees game or experiencing a symphony orchestra.   This extreme comparison of the West with a remote island culture does not tell the peace and prosperity tale properly, however.   There is a great disparity between people around the world even when not so isolated and limited by their environment as in this example.   And of course, there are certainly islanders seeking a different life who have migrated to the West and become doctors and engineers, great musicians, and great football players.

The question then returns to what we have defined as what everyone wants, Shalom, peace, prosperity, and happiness, and we have several factors here. First of all, we need a better description of what we mean by prosperity, peace, and happiness in a broader and more general way that goes beyond cultures and societies.

> **Peace** is the absence of conflict and contention that disturbs our tranquility (We're not talking about avoiding enjoyable competitive events or debates / friendly verbal arguments)
>
> **Prosperity** is living comfortably with little worries about the economic future and enjoying your own expectations of the pleasures in life from both work and leisure to the limits your abilities will take you.

What was nominal life like in Europe for the last two thousand years, minus the effects of war and oppressive governments?   Perhaps a good example would be rural farm families in the Southern United States before the mid-20th century.   They had homes with no running water or electricity and only "fire" for heat in the winter. There was little money left over for frills, which might be an occasional baloney sandwich with mayonnaise on white bread, (or maybe an occasional "Spam" sandwich) yet they were certainly prosperous in life in many ways. They had delicious fried chicken for sure. Or perhaps look at life in Europe during the sixteenth century through the eyes of Martin Luther and his followers. Or consider the life of Tevye in the musical production, Fiddler on the Roof. (https://en.wikipedia.org/wiki/Fiddler_on_the_Roof)

Prosperity is not about "ha, ha" happiness but about enjoying life as it comes at us, this is prosperity, being able to have satisfaction with a life well lived. Prosperity is enjoying the life you have within your abilities even if it's not quite up to the levels of material prosperity you see in the movies or imagine about the lives of movie stars.

What we know from life is that having all the aspects of, Shalom, is rather difficult because we often find that striving for one aspect can negatively impact the others. The drive for material prosperity can make peace and happiness more difficult to find. In other words peace, economic prosperity, and happiness don't necessarily go together. You can have, or not have, one with or without the other. And you can have many different ways of expressing this.

An examination of the causes and effects of prosperity and Shalom will require examining the following aspects of life.

1. The distribution of prosperity, peace, and happiness (Shalom) around the world
2. An assessment of genetics, consciousness, environment, and culture as the major factors that contribute to or influence life decisions and therefore determine the outcomes of individual lives with respect to Shalom.
3. An examination of the effect of religion, as the dominant cultural influence on life decisions and therefore prosperity outcomes.
4. An examination of Judaeo Christian philosophy as the religious tradition tied most closely with the Western World and its influence on prosperity and Shalom.

This is not an examination of religions in the traditional sense of comparing and contrasting detailed spiritual beliefs or traditions or rituals. Our objective is to look at how religious philosophies in general motivate personal lives and decisions that may either produce or hinder prosperity among its subjects.

Religion is the "elephant in the room". A dominant influence on life decisions and therefore perhaps personal prosperity, even to those who merely live within its sphere of influence but don't adhere to its tenets of faith. But the superficial view of religions is that they deal only with matters of faith and gods and spiritual worlds, of which science can not testify. As such religion is a matter of individual consciousness and to be left alone, neither criticized nor condemned. Their followers are thought to be righteous in their quest for knowing and interacting with their own, personal god. Certainly, priests, monks, and shamans who purport to know the minds of the gods should be more noble people than those who have chosen to ignore religion.

In the real world, religion provides a significant influence on the views, attitudes, and philosophies of life of its followers. The other great modifier of these views of life can be the government. To this end, the Constitution of the United States directly protects the rights of individuals to practice their religion without restriction or pressure from the government, provided that practice does not conflict with the civil laws of the land. The U.S. government also has some very specific ideas concerning a philosophy of life that are derived from Christianity. Those ideas provide a valuable insight into Christian thinking that contributes to the prosperity of the U.S. and its citizens. We'll look at the United States and its founding principles next.

John Trumbull's painting, Declaration of Independence

3. Government Influence

In consideration of the United States and its status as the economic leader, we'll first look at how its philosophy of life forms a foundation for prosperity. This philosophy of life is reflected most specifically in the United States' founding documents.

The United States Declaration of Independence and the preamble to the U.S. Constitution lay out the master plan for prosperity and happiness. It is derived from hundreds of years of Western critical thinking and analysis influenced by Christian thought and principles and provides a masterful summary of the Christian philosophy transposed to practical terms.

U.S. Declaration of Independence

We hold these truths to be self-evident, that all men are created equal, that they are endowed by their Creator with certain unalienable Rights, that among these are Life, Liberty, and the pursuit of Happiness. That to secure these rights, Governments are instituted among Men, deriving their just powers from the consent of the governed. That whenever any Form of Government becomes destructive of these ends, it is the Right of the People to alter or to abolish it, and to institute new Government, laying its foundation on such principles and organizing its powers in such form, as to them shall seem most likely to effect their Safety and Happiness.

Preamble to the U.S. Constitution

We the People of the United States, in Order to form a more perfect Union, **establish Justice, ensure domestic Tranquility, provide for the common defence, promote the general Welfare, and secure the Blessings of Liberty** to ourselves and our Posterity, do ordain and establish this Constitution for the United States of America.

There are five objectives of the United States Government stated here. These are the five overriding tasks the government has as absolute mandates and ought to be the five principles upon which every decision is made and all actions are taken. All five objectives apply to the citizens of the United States only. The Government is working 100% for the citizens.

The one thing misunderstood is that the Government itself has no rights. It is a tool of the citizens to enforce the five mandates or objectives of the government. In the United States, there is a separation of mandates between the Federal Government and the individual States, but neither has rights that are to be protected. You can't harm, defame, or slander the government, or any employee acting for the government, concerning what the government does. You can violate laws made by the government and be subject to those laws, but the laws, rules, and procedures are what are established by governments to accomplish the five mandates.

Absolute mandates/responsibilities of the United States Government

1. **_Fair Laws:_ Establish justice:** make wrongs between people (and organizations of people working together) right or restored.

2. **_Fair Law Enforcement:_ Insure domestic Tranquility:** enforces the prohibition of citizens having their lives and property directly disturbed by others.

3. **_Military:_ Provide for the common defense:** protects citizens from multi-person threats such as mobs, terrorists, and invading armies where an individual can not defend himself.

4. **_Public services:_ Promote the general welfare:** Provide community services that make life richer and more enjoyable.

5. **_Future Proofed Decisions_: Secure the Blessings of Liberty to ourselves and our posterity:** The mandates are to consider the lives of, and impact on, our future citizens, actions must consider future consequences beyond the immediate remedy envisioned.

Everything the Federal and State Governments do should be done from this standpoint of objectives. The overriding factor is that these mandates are for maximum freedom of the individual, Life, Liberty, and the pursuit of happiness. Who are the people and how does all this apply to people in general? The two dominant ideas that emerge are the rights of individuals to own, control, and use personal property as they see fit to pursue their own interests and benefit, i.e., prosperity, happiness, or even greed, the motive doesn't matter under the law. The important aspect of property rights is the right of individuals to own and possess their own property as they see fit. Ownership can be individuals, associations, businesses, and governments.

Conditions attached to property rights.

1. *The right to own property*
2. *the right to use of property*
3. *the right to earn income from the property*
4. *the right to transfer the property to others*
5. *The right to excludability, to limit use by others*
6. *The right to rivalry, to limit use by competitors*

https://en.wikipedia.org/wiki/Property_rights_(economics)

The principle in terms of creating general prosperity comes from the common root Christianity shares with Judaism. That root is derived from two of the Ten Commandments, numbers 8 and 10.

- **Commandment#8** *Exodus 20:15, Deuteronomy 5;19* **Thou shalt not steal**
- **Commandment#10** *Exodus 20:17, Deuteronomy 5;21* **You shall not covet your neighbor's house. You shall not covet your neighbor's wife, or his male or female servant, his ox or donkey, or anything that belongs to your neighbor.**

These two commandments form the basis for capitalism and free enterprise. To summarize them they say, "Not only do you not steal anyone else's "possessions", but you don't even think about it." And by using the term "steal" it implies you don't deprive your neighbor of the full use of his property. This of course rules out all those economic forms of socialism and communism and now you can see the thrust of the Declaration of Independence and the Constitution is to promote the individual's right to his or her property and their own use of it as they see fit. Don't get tripped up on the definition of property including wives and servants/slaves. That's a common language from three thousand or so years ago that defines families from the father's perspective. Neither Judaism nor Christianity condones slavery and women are completely free, and equal and are recognized as having leadership and management skills equal to men. But note also that by defining wives and servants as property to be left alone, it emphasizes that one should do nothing to impact or harm the family unit, including wives' ownership of their husbands. Reciprocality is an easy assumption given that women have the right of ownership as well as men in the Bible. Perhaps men are called out more often as the example because they require extra attention to rules.

The point here is that capitalism, the right to own and freely use property is a key essential to national prosperity. This right has been in existence for thousands of years but in limited forms and understandings. The Declaration of Independence and the U.S. Constitution are perhaps the highest form of its statement and evolved from many incremental changes to English law and the expanded understanding of the value of ownership, free enterprise, and capitalism by Western thinking.

This is the essence of capitalism, the private ownership of property. Both socialism and communism are alternatives that have limited private ownership either partially or completely, with disastrous results.

Capitalism is an economic system and ideology based upon private ownership of the means of production and their operation for profit. Characteristics central to capitalism include private property, capital accumulation, wage labor, voluntary exchange, a price system, and competitive markets. In a capitalist market economy, decision-making and investment are determined by the owners of the means of production in financial and capital markets, whereas prices and the distribution of goods and services are mainly determined by competition in goods and services markets.

Economists, political economists, sociologists, and historians have adopted different perspectives in their analyses of capitalism and have recognized various forms of it in practice. These include laissez-faire or free-market capitalism, welfare capitalism, and state capitalism. Different forms of capitalism feature varying degrees of free markets, public ownership, obstacles to free competition, and state-sanctioned social policies. The degree of competition in markets, the role of intervention and regulation, and the scope of state ownership vary across different models of capitalism. The extent to which different markets are free, as well as the rules defining private property, are matters of politics and policy. Most existing capitalist economies are mixed economies, which combine elements of free markets with state intervention and in some cases economic planning.

Market economies have existed under many forms of government, in many different times, places, and cultures. However, the development of capitalist societies marked by a universalization of money-based social relations, a consistently large and system-wide class of workers who must work for wages, and a capitalist class that dominates control of wealth and political power developed in Western Europe in a process that led to the Industrial Revolution. Capitalist systems with varying degrees of direct government intervention have since become dominant in the Western World and continue to spread.

Capitalism has been criticized for establishing power in the hands of a minority capitalist class that exists through the exploitation of a working-

class majority; for prioritizing profit over social good, natural resources, and the environment; and for being an engine of inequality and economic instabilities.

Supporters argue that it provides better products through competition, creates strong economic growth, yields productivity and prosperity that greatly benefits society, as well as being the most efficient system known for the allocation of resources.

https://en.wikipedia.org/wiki/Capitalism

Socialism *is a range of economic and social systems characterized by social ownership and democratic control of the means of production, as well as the political theories and movements associated with them. Social ownership may refer to forms of public, collective, or cooperative ownership, or to citizen ownership of equity. There are many varieties of socialism and there is no single definition encapsulating all of them, though social ownership is the common element shared by its various forms.*

Socialist economic systems can be divided into non-market and market forms. Non-market socialism involves the substitution of factor markets and money, with engineering and technical criteria, based on calculations performed in-kind, thereby producing an economic mechanism that functions according to different economic laws from those of capitalism. Non-market socialism aims to circumvent the inefficiencies and crises traditionally associated with capital accumulation and the profit system. By contrast, market socialism retains the use of monetary prices, factor markets, and in some cases the profit motive, concerning the operation of socially owned enterprises and the allocation of capital goods between them. Profits generated by these firms would be controlled directly by the workforce of each firm, or accrue to society at large in the form of a social dividend. The socialist calculation debate discusses the feasibility and methods of resource allocation for a socialist system.

https://en.wikipedia.org/wiki/Socialism

Communism *In political and social sciences, communism (from Latin communis, "common, universal") is the philosophical, social, political, and economic ideology and movement whose ultimate goal is the establishment of a communist society, which is a socioeconomic order structured upon the common ownership of the means of production and the absence of social classes, money, and the state.*

Communism includes a variety of schools of thought, which broadly include Marxism, anarchism (anarchist communism), and the political ideologies grouped around both. All of these share the analysis that the

current order of society stems from its economic system, capitalism; that in
this system there are two major social classes: the working class—who must
work to survive and who make up the majority within society—and the
capitalist class—a minority who derives profit from employing the working
class, through private ownership of the means of production—and that
conflict between these two classes is the root of all problems in society and
will ultimately be resolved through a revolution. The revolution will put the
working class in power and in turn establish social ownership of the means
of production, which according to this analysis is the primary element in the
transformation of society towards communism.
https://en.wikipedia.org/wiki/Communism

To simplify these economic approaches a bit:

Capitalism: Private ownership and control of the property to be used for the owners' benefit and interests

Socialism: Government control over the use of property, ownership may be technically by individuals, but they are told how to use that property and what benefits they can derive.

Communism: All property is owned by the collective population and hence effectively owned by the Government which controls its use and doles out benefits to the population as it sees fit.

Under Communism, only those in government have any measure of prosperity and the general population is more or less a slave without any freedom to pursue their own interests or happiness. Under Socialism, individuals have some measure of freedom to pursue interests and happiness but given that the government controls how property is used, corruption leads to prosperity only for the government officials or key favorites in the general population.

At the end of the Cold War, the Soviet Union's communist dictatorship devolved into a form of crony capitalism with a gangster mentality which kept many, but not all, economic benefits in the hands of the political elite. Economic prosperity in Russia has therefore been slow to develop and spread to the entire population.

Pure Capitalism is the economic approach that frees every individual to pursue his own happiness and benefit fully from his own efforts. But there are rules for how the capitalist or free enterprise game is played, that one could argue can make or break capitalism as we see it. This includes government regulations and also payment of taxes to the government. But the bottom line is that our personal property, including financial wealth, is our own and we control its use. Regulations are generally for safety, quality control, and fairness, and taxes are to run the government which has the responsibility to keep things fair and safe. Most prosperity around the world operates under a capitalist economic system with variations of government regulations, as we shall see.

Because of the success of the US economy, many other countries have adopted similar principles to those presented in the Declaration of Independence and the US Constitution. There is often a big difference in the outcome, however. This is for a significant reason. The United States' documents were the product of their own citizens working through the process of defining the nation's objectives. They were generated through the efforts of leaders from every part of the country including feedback from folks back at home. In other words, the US economic and political concepts were developed from the bottom up. They came from the ideas and thinking of citizens, generated under much duress without any compensation. Much of the thinking was also done at the state legislature levels where these types of ideas were debated and carried into local elections where local citizens debated and made choices to support various ideas.

Further, the ideas were derived from historical events and political thinking in England as it was transitioning from an absolute monarchy to a parliamentary form of government over many hundreds of years. This similar bottom-up approach brought major changes to the English government system and England's concepts of economic freedom and free enterprise. It in turn influenced other countries in Europe along the same lines although it took World War II for many of them to see the light.

In other parts of the world, central and South America for example, where similar concepts of economics and freedom are talked about or somewhat included in constitutions, these concepts are top-down dictates from knowledgeable leadership, but the principles are not inherent in the thinking of the population. This indicates that successful implementation was much easier and more profound in the US and much harder in nations without the groundswell of understanding and support.

The lack of citizen understanding and support also allows political corruption and crony capitalism to take hold more easily. The Table of GDP (US$ PPP) shows a big variation in the Western Hemisphere. We'll examine one example of this a little later which demonstrates this point

Also, note that capitalism by itself does not create prosperity any more than the rules of any sport create championship teams. While the United States fully endorses capitalism, the actual implementation of it and the resultant prosperity requires a multitude of independent teams of citizens.

The philosophy of capitalism must lie in the hearts of the citizens of a country. A national constitution and a Declaration of Independence alone are not enough. For capitalism to work effectively it requires a philosophy of life that promotes it. The easy way to look at these elements is as a sports metaphor. The five essential elements of a winning sports team are as follows.

Sports Metaphor for Winning
1. *Rules and Referees - Consistent rules and laws that recognize property rights and freedom to use the property as the owner sees fit*
2. *Motivation - creating a desire to build, create, and expand the property base, to use one's talents*
3. *Teamwork - seeing the value added by others and being willing to work with others, sharing benefits*
4. *Strategies - looking for ways to do, fix something or do something better, always seeking ways to "win" or succeed.*
5. *Training - continuing expanding knowledge and capabilities*

In the sports world, the competition is to win a game. Players will go to extreme measures to be prepared. Capitalism is a competition to create something new and different that will be of benefit not only to the owners but to the users. It competes with itself to generate something new or better but often competes with other groups in the same arena. This competition against other groups is beneficial by making the results better, and products cheaper. It can get rather vicious, in a sporting sense, no one likes to have their pet ideas lose out in the marketplace. But if the rewards are great, the risk is worthwhile.

Capitalism is the engine that improves life in societies and civilizations. The Rules and Referees are set in place by the Declaration of Independence and the preamble to the Constitution that sets forth the United States as a capitalist country. It does this by clearly proclaiming individual property rights and the freedom to use that property as the owner chooses as an overall principle. For prosperity, however, the owner of a property has to actively make use of this property. Capitalism is the game; and its specific rules, as stated by each country, define how well it works. But the other four ingredients, motivation, teamwork, strategies, and training, are principled and learned experiences for the citizen participants.

All five team ingredients are significant in producing a winning team. And these ingredients must be instilled into the instinctive thinking and reactions of the players as well. It's not enough to post them on the wall or put them on a bumper sticker on your car. This thinking comes to individuals and teams through two avenues, directly through field practices and through game experiences, and indirectly through cultural influences. When you have teams that consistently produce winning results over the years, you are seeing the impact of an overarching winning culture that influences and motivates the current players. This is the voice of players past that says to the current team, "You're now our team, live up to the winning tradition".

The prosperity of the Western World thus is not just what's happening today but also the result of what has happened in the past. The overall moral and lifestyle principles of cultures that produce prosperity are instilled in their culture and have lasting results. The culture of the United States and most of Europe is one built on hundreds of years of tradition rooted in the Christian philosophy of life. It is pervasive and relentless in its influence over everyone, even those who do not profess to be Christians because its ideals are contagious and it is seen as a philosophy that works. We'll see this in a bit as we further investigate prosperity around the world.

So far we have talked about two overall methods of influence, the direct influence we encounter in our daily life experiences, and influences from the lives of those around us. These influences are real-time, real events, guidance, and directions on life from our parents and our friends/ peers and life events. There is also an indirect influence that comes to us through stories (in any form) and education. Indirect influences can be historical, religious, and cultural while direct influences are created by immediate circumstances. Either can be bad or good in terms of the outcome. But even bad events can be an encouragement. A good sports team can learn from its losses. Not necessarily true of someone who becomes immersed in criminal activity or heavy drug or chemical abuse, however.

There is also nothing that demands that the cultural and historical lessons and values handed down to anyone are either wise or effective or provide any benefits to one's personal prosperity, economy, peace, safety, or happiness. This is the old scientific adage GIGO, garbage in garbage out. If your inputs to your work are garbage, i.e., bad data or information, the results of your work will be garbage, bad results, as well. This is the story of world prosperity. We'll see major differences in the prosperity of Central and South American countries. It is evident in the story behind Brazil's low rankings in prosperity which we will examine in detail as a textbook example of losing one's direction.

The Bull attacks hooking up, the Bear slashes down

Bull and bear in front of the Frankfurt Stock Exchange

By the sculptor Reinhard Dachlauer. Photo by By Eva K., CC BY-SA 2.5, https://commons.wikimedia.org/w/index.php?curid=824045 Free use by German copyright law

4. World Economic Prosperity

Economic Prosperity is tracked by international economic and business interests based on financial factors. Money is not happiness but it does expand the opportunities for individuals to prosper in terms of a rich fulfilling life. It buys energy that reduces physical work and it buys enjoyment opportunities with both free time and new activities from which to choose. Economic prosperity is still dependent on how society and individuals approach life, however.

There are several indicators of economic prosperity, two of which are somewhat reasonable indicators, GDP, Gross Domestic Product-per capita, and Gross Domestic Product-PPP (purchasing power parity).

- **GDP nominal** - *total income earned by work in the country in US dollars*
- **GDP-per capita** *can be determined in three ways, all of which should, theoretically, give the same result. They are the production (or output or value added) approach, the income approach, or the speculated*

expenditure approach. It is representative of the total output and income within an economy

- **GDP-PPP (Purchasing power parity)** *"exchange rate" is the exchange rate based on the purchasing power parity (PPP) of a currency relative to a selected standard (usually the United States dollar).* **It modifies GDP per capita by the exchange rate.**

    https://en.wikipedia.org/wiki/Gross_domestic_product
    https://en.wikipedia.org/wiki/List_of_countries_by_GDP_(PPP)_per_capita

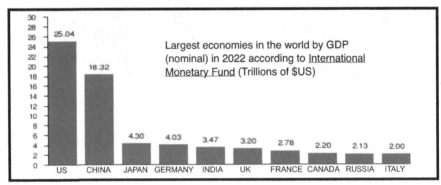

The GDP (PPP) per capita (i.e., GDP PPP per citizen) listing is more relevant than the straight GDP nominal, which lists total GDP per country. The GDP PPP per capita list considers population plus individual prosperity in terms of purchasing power. One striking difference is that China, India, and Japan are in the top 10 of the GDP per

Countries or territories by GDP (nominal) per capita in 2022.

By Allice Hunter and Snowballa68 - Blank map: File:World map (Miller cylindrical projection, blank).svgData from IMF: June 2022 World Economic Outlook Database, April 2022. World Economic Outlook. International Monetary Fund (April 2021)., CC BY-SA 4.0, https://commons.wikimedia.org/w/index.php?

capita list but further down the list when individual purchasing power is considered. The next series of tables shows the worldwide listing of GDP PPP with specific monetary values. The ranking is by the IMF, the major source of economic prosperity information but includes the World Bank and the CIA assessments.

Rank	Country	Location	Source	Pop	IMF Estimate	IMF Year	World Bank Estimate	World Bank Year	CIA Estimate	CIA Year
			GDP per capita (US$ PPP)		IMF		World Bank		CIA	
1	Monaco *	Europe	Tax Haven	39,000	–		190,513	2019	115,700	2015
2	Liechtenstein *	Europe		39,000	–		180,367	2018	139,100	2009
3	Luxembourg *	Europe	Tax Haven	650,000	140,694	2022	118,360	2020	110,300	2020
4	Singapore *	Asia	Tax Haven	5,770,000	131,580	2022	98,526	2020	93,400	2020
5	Ireland *	Europe	Tax Haven		124,596	2022	93,612	2020	89,700	2020
6	Qatar *	Asia	Oil & Gas	2,700,000	112,789	2022	89,949	2020	85,300	2020
7	Macau *	Asia	Tax Haven	657,000	85,612	2022	57,807	2020	54,800	2020
8	Switzerland *	Europe	Tax Haven	8,638,000	84,658	2022	71,352	2020	68,400	2020
9	Isle of Man *	Europe		84,000	–		–		84,600	2014
10	Bermuda *	Caribbean	Tax Haven		–		80,830	2020	81,800	2019
11	United Arab Emirates *	Asia	Oil & Gas	9,900,000	78,255	2022	69,958	2019	67,100	2019
12	Norway *	Europe	Tax Haven	5,367,000	77,808	2022	63,198	2020	63,600	2020
13	United States *	North Am			76,027	2022	63,544	2020	60,200	2020
14	Brunei *	Asia	Oil & Gas	429,000	74,953	2022	65,662	2020	62,200	2020
15	Cayman Islands *	Caribbean	Tax Haven		–		71,594	2020	73,600	2019
16	Falkland Islands *	South Am		3,398	–		–		70,800	2015
17	Hong Kong *	Asia	Tax Haven	7,553,000	70,448	2022	59,238	2020	56,200	2020
18	San Marino *	Europe		34,735	70,139	2022	63,420	2019	60,800	2019
19	Denmark *	Europe	Tax Haven		69,273	2022	60,399	2020	55,900	2020
20	Taiwan *	Asia			68,730	2022	–		24,502	2018
21	Netherlands *	Europe	Tax Haven		68,572	2022	59,229	2020	54,200	2020
22	Austria *	Europe			64,751	2022	55,098	2020	51,900	2020
23	Iceland *	Europe			64,621	2022	55,216	2020	52,300	2020
24	Andorra *	Europe			63,600	2022	–		49,900	2015
25	Germany *	Europe			63,271	2022	53,694	2020	50,900	2020
26	Sweden *	Europe			62,926	2022	54,563	2020	50,700	2020
27	Australia *	Oceania			61,941	2022	52,518	2020	48,700	2020
28	Gibraltar *	Europe			–		–		61,700	2014
29	Belgium *	Europe			61,587	2022	51,968	2020	48,200	2020
30	Finland *	Europe			58,010	2022	51,090	2020	47,300	2020
31	Canada *	North Am			57,812	2022	48,073	2020	45,900	2020
32	Bahrain *	Asia	Oil & Gas		57,424	2022	43,181	2020	45,011	2019
33	Jersey *	Europe			–		–		56,600	2016
34	France *	Europe			56,036	2022	46,227	2020	46,184	2019
35	Saudi Arabia *	Asia	Oil & Gas		55,368	2022	46,763	2020	46,962	2019
36	United Kingdom *	Europe			55,301	2022	44,916	2020	46,659	2019
37	Malta *	Europe			54,647	2022	42,640	2020	44,032	2019
38	European Union *	Europe			53,201	2022	44,491	2020	44,436	2019
39	South Korea *	Asia			53,051	2022	43,124	2020	42,765	2019
40	Guernsey *	Europe			–		–		52,500	2014
41	Kuwait *	Asia	Oil & Gas		50,919	2022	51,962	2019	49,900	2019
42	New Zealand *	Oceania			50,411	2022	44,252	2020	42,888	2019
43	Italy *	Europe			50,216	2022	41,840	2020	42,492	2019
44	Israel *	Asia			50,204	2022	41,855	2020	40,145	2019
45	Japan *	Asia			48,814	2022	42,197	2019	41,429	2019
46	Slovenia *	Europe			48,534	2022	39,593	2020	39,088	2019
47	Cyprus *	Europe			48,443	2022	38,458	2020	39,545	2019
48	Czech Republic *	Europe			47,527	2022	41,737	2020	40,862	2019
49	Lithuania *	Europe			46,479	2022	38,735	2020	37,231	2019
50	Spain *	Europe			46,413	2022	38,335	2020	40,903	2019
51	Saint Pierre and Miquelon *	Caribbean			–		–		46,200	2006
52	Estonia *	Europe			44,778	2022	38,395	2020	36,927	2019
53	Puerto Rico *	Caribbean			42,759	2022	35,279	2020	33,400	2020
54	Greenland *	Caribbean			–		–		41,800	2015
55	Poland *	Europe			41,685	2022	34,265	2020	33,221	2019
56	Hungary *	Europe			40,944	2022	33,084	2020	32,945	2019
57	Portugal *	Europe			40,805	2022	34,496	2020	34,894	2019
58	Bahamas *	Caribbean			40,274	2022	32,454	2020	30,800	2020
59	Faroe Islands *	Europe			–		–		40,000	2014
60	Aruba *	Caribbean			39,508	2022	38,897	2017	37,500	2017

Table of GDP(PPP) per capita by country: from identified sources
https://en.wikipedia.org/wiki/List_of_countries_by_GDP_(PPP)_per_capita

Rank	Country	Location	Source	Pop	IMF Estimate	IMF Year	World Bank Estimate	World Bank Year	CIA Estimate	CIA Year
	GDP per capita (US$ PPP)				IMF		World Bank		CIA	
61	Slovakia *	Europe			38,620	2022	31,832	2020	32,730	2019
62	Guyana *	South Am			38,258	2022	19,706	2020	13,082	2019
63	Turkey *	Asia			37,488	2022	28,120	2020	28,424	2019
64	Latvia *	Europe			37,330	2022	32,019	2020	30,898	2019
65	U.S. Virgin Islands *	Caribbean			–		–		37,000	2016
66	Romania *	Europe			36,622	2022	31,946	2020	29,941	2019
67	Croatia *	Europe			36,201	2022	28,504	2020	28,602	2019
68	Panama *	Central Am			36,085	2022	26,776	2020	31,459	2019
69	Sint Maarten *	Caribbean			–		35,977	2018	35,300	2018
70	Guam *	Oceania			–		–		35,600	2016
71	Greece *	Europe			35,596	2022	28,464	2020	29,799	2019
72	Oman *	Asia			35,286	2022	28,449	2019	27,299	2019
73	Seychelles *	Africa			35,272	2022	25,700	2020	29,223	2019
74	British Virgin Islands *	Caribbean			–		–		34,200	2017
75	Montserrat *	Caribbean			–		–		34,000	2011
76	Malaysia *	Asia			32,901	2022	27,887	2020	28,364	2019
77	New Caledonia *	Oceania			–		–		31,100	2015
78	Kazakhstan *	Asia			30,502	2022	26,729	2020	26,351	2019
79	Russia *	Europe			30,013	2022	28,213	2020	27,044	2019
80	Trinidad and Tobago *	Caribbean			29,884	2022	25,031	2020	23,700	2020
81	Maldives *	Asia			29,133	2022	13,766	2020	19,531	2019
82	Bulgaria *	Europe			28,593	2022	24,367	2020	23,174	2019
83	Chile *	South Am			28,526	2022	25,068	2020	24,226	2019
84	Saint Kitts and Nevis *	Caribbean			27,608	2022	24,537	2020	23,300	2020
85	Uruguay *	South Am			26,663	2022	22,795	2020	21,561	2019
86	Argentina *	South Am			25,822	2022	20,768	2020	22,064	2019
87	Mauritius *	Africa			25,043	2022	20,539	2020	22,870	2019
88	Montenegro *	Europe			24,878	2022	20,567	2020	21,470	2019
89	Northern Mariana Islands *	Oceania			–		–		24,500	2016
90	Costa Rica *	Central Am			24,490	2022	21,032	2020	19,700	2020
91	Dominican Republic *	Caribbean			23,983	2022	17,937	2020	17,000	2020
92	Serbia *	Europe			23,904	2022	19,231	2020	18,233	2019
93	Turks and Caicos Islands	Caribbean			–		22,286	2020	21,100	2020
94	Mexico *	North Am			22,216	2022	18,833	2020	19,796	2019
95	Antigua and Barbuda *	Caribbean			21,890	2022	18,942	2020	18,000	2020
96	Belarus *	Europe			21,686	2022	20,200	2020	19,150	2019
97	Curaçao *	Caribbean			–		21,423	2020	24,500	2019
98	China *	Asia			21,364	2022	17,312	2020	16,117	2019
99	Thailand *	Asia			21,057	2022	18,236	2020	18,460	2019
100	North Macedonia *	Europe			19,726	2022	16,927	2020	16,479	2019
101	Saint Martin *	Caribbean			–		–		19,300	2005
102	Botswana *	Africa			19,287	2022	16,921	2020	17,767	2019
103	Equatorial Guinea *	Africa			19,036	2022	17,942	2020	18,558	2019
104	Turkmenistan *	Asia			18,857	2022	16,196	2019	14,845	2018
105	Georgia *	Asia			18,594	2022	14,863	2020	14,992	2019
106	Libya *	Africa			18,345	2022	10,847	2020	15,174	2019
107	Iran *	Asia			18,332	2022	13,116	2020	12,389	2019
108	Grenada *	Caribbean			18,293	2022	15,893	2020	15,100	2020
109	Colombia *	South America			18,225	2022	14,565	2020	14,722	2019
110	Gabon *	Africa			17,848	2022	15,191	2020	14,950	2019
111	Bosnia and Herzegovina *	Europe			17,471	2022	15,612	2020	14,912	2019
112	Barbados *	Caribbean			17,408	2022	13,577	2020	12,900	2020
113	Albania *	Europe			17,383	2022	13,818	2020	13,965	2019
114	Suriname *	South Am			17,300	2022	17,016	2020	16,525	2019
115	Brazil *	South Am			17,208	2022	14,836	2020	14,652	2019
116	Azerbaijan *	Asia			17,153	2022	14,452	2020	14,404	2019
117	World				–		17,110	2020	17,500	2017
118	French Polynesia *	Oceania			–		–		17,000	2015
119	Moldova *	Europe			16,719	2022	13,002	2020	13,050	2019
120	Cook Islands *	Oceania			–		–		16,700	2016

Table of GDP(PPP) per capita by country: from identified sources
https://en.wikipedia.org/wiki/List of countries by GDP (PPP) per capita

	GDP per capita (US$ PPP)				IMF		World Bank		CIA	
Rank	Country	Location	Source	Pop	Estimate	Year	Estimate	Year	Estimate	Year
121	Saint Lucia *	Caribbean			16,509	2022	12,944	2020	12,300	2020
122	Armenia *	Asia			15,818	2022	13,284	2020	13,654	2019
123	Saint Vincent and the Grenadines *	Caribbean			15,505	2022	12,770	2020	12,100	2020
124	Sri Lanka *	Asia			15,387	2022	13,225	2020	13,078	2019
125	South Africa *	Africa			15,361	2022	12,096	2020	12,482	2019
126	Peru *	South America			15,035	2022	11,879	2020	12,848	2019
127	Egypt *	Africa			14,928	2022	12,608	2020	11,763	2019
128	Indonesia *	Asia			14,535	2022	12,074	2020	11,812	2019
129	Dominica *	Caribbean			14,491	2022	10,435	2020	9,900	2020
130	Paraguay *	South Am			14,430	2022	13,013	2020	12,685	2019
131	Ukraine *	Europe			14,325	2021	13,057	2020	12,810	2019
132	Kosovo *	Europe			13,964	2022	11,368	2020	11,368	2019
133	Palau *	Oceania			13,652	2022	18,316	2019	17,579	2019
134	Fiji *	Oceania			13,598	2022	11,601	2020	13,684	2019
135	Mongolia *	Asia			13,350	2022	12,101	2020	12,317	2019
136	Algeria *	Africa			13,002	2022	11,268	2020	11,511	2019
137	Bhutan *	Asia			12,967	2022	11,508	2020	11,832	2019
138	Vietnam *	Asia			12,881	2022	8,651	2020	8,041	2019
139	Ecuador *	South America			12,664	2022	10,896	2020	11,375	2019
140	Tunisia *	Africa			12,300	2022	10,262	2020	10,756	2019
141	Cuba *	Caribbean			--		--		12,300	2016
142	Lebanon *	Asia			12,035	2020	12,289	2020	14,552	2019
143	Anguilla *	Caribbean			--		--		12,200	2008
144	Iraq *	Asia			12,141	2022	9,764	2020	10,881	2019
145	Jordan *	Asia			11,861	2022	10,356	2020	10,071	2019
146	Jamaica *	Caribbean			11,802	2022	9,222	2020	8,700	2020
147	American Samoa *	Oceania			--		--		11,200	2016
148	Nauru *	Oceania			10,750	2022	14,100	2019	11,583	2019
149	El Salvador *	Central America			10,581	2022	8,499	2020	8,100	2020
150	Namibia *	Africa			10,448	2022	9,382	2020	9,637	2019
151	Eswatini *	Africa			10,411	2022	8,854	2020	8,622	2019
152	Philippines *	Asia			10,393	2022	8,390	2020	8,908	2019
153	Guatemala *	Central Am			9,911	2022	8,854	2020	8,400	2020
154	Bolivia *	South Am			9,856	2022	8,367	2020	8,724	2019
155	Uzbekistan *	Asia			9,243	2022	7,378	2020	6,999	2019
156	Laos *	Asia			9,184	2022	8,235	2020	7,826	2019
157	Morocco *	Africa			9,041	2022	7,296	2020	7,515	2019
158	India *	Asia			8,358	2022	6,454	2020	6,700	2019
159	Saint Helena, Ascension and Tristan da Cunha	Africa			--		--		7,800	2010
160	Cape Verde *	Africa			7,740	2022	6,377	2020	7,172	2019
161	Angola *	Africa			7,360	2022	6,539	2020	6,670	2019
162	Belize *	Central America			7,147	2022	6,456	2020	6,100	2020
163	Nicaragua *	Central America			7,071	2022	5,570	2020	5,300	2020
164	Mauritania *	Africa			6,920	2022	5,257	2020	5,197	2019
165	Tonga *	Oceania			6,783	2022	6,648	2019	6,383	2019
166	Ghana *	Africa			6,754	2022	5,596	2020	5,413	2019
167	Honduras *	Central America			6,740	2022	5,421	2020	5,100	2020
168	Djibouti *	Africa			6,667	2022	5,782	2020	5,535	2019
169	Bangladesh *	Asia			6,633	2022	5,083	2020	4,754	2019
170	Pakistan *	Asia			6,470	2022	6,370	2020	5,820	2019
171	Syria *	Asia			6,374	2010	--		2,900	2015
172	Ivory Coast *	Africa			6,345	2022	5,458	2020	5,213	2019
173	Palestine *	Asia			6,243	[n 2]2022	5,690	[n 3]2020	5,400 / 6,220	[n 4]2020 / 2019
174	Kenya *	Africa			6,061	2022	4,452	2020	4,330	2019
175	Tokelau *	Oceania			--		--		6,004	2017
176	Venezuela *	South Am			5,949	2022	17,528	2011	7,704	2018
177	Samoa *	Oceania			5,935	2022	6,778	2019	6,521	2019
178	Nigeria *	Africa			5,853	2022	5,187	2020	5,136	2019
179	Niue *	Oceania			--		--		5,800	2003
180	Tuvalu *	Oceania			5,798	2022	4,653	2020	4,281	2019

Table of GDP(PPP) per capita by country: from identified sources
https://en.wikipedia.org/wiki/List_of_countries_by_GDP_(PPP)_per_capita

Rank	Country	Location	Source	Pop	IMF Estimate	IMF Year	World Bank Estimate	World Bank Year	CIA Estimate	CIA Year
					GDP per capita (US$ PPP)					
181	Kyrgyzstan *	Asia			5,562	2022	4,965	2020	5,253	2019
182	Cambodia *	Asia			5,493	2022	4,422	2020	4,389	2019
183	Myanmar *	Asia			4,776	2022	4,794	2020	5,142	2019
184	São Tomé and Príncipe *	Africa			4,681	2022	4,274	2020	3,970	2019
185	Tajikistan *	Asia			4,630	2022	3,858	2020	3,380	2019
186	Nepal *	Asia			4,578	2022	4,009	2020	3,417	2019
187	Congo *	Africa			4,578	2022	3,639	2020	3,673	2019
188	Sudan *	Africa			4,442	2022	4,244	2020	3,958	2019
189	Cameroon *	Africa			4,398	2022	3,773	2020	3,642	2019
190	Papua New Guinea *	Oceania			4,299	2022	4,326	2020	4,355	2019
191	Marshall Islands *	Oceania			4,192	2022	4,200	2019	3,889	2018
192	Benin *	Africa			4,137	2022	3,506	2020	3,287	2019
193	Senegal *	Africa			4,093	2022	3,481	2020	3,395	2019
194	Wallis and Futuna *	Oceania			–		–		3,800	2004
195	Zambia *	Africa			3,776	2022	3,450	2020	3,470	2019
196	Micronesia *	Oceania			3,650	2022	3,613	2019	3,464	2018
197	Ethiopia *	Africa			3,407	2022	2,423	2020	2,221	2019
198	Tanzania *	Africa			3,358	2022	2,780	2020	2,660	2019
199	Comoros *	Africa			3,355	2022	3,313	2020	3,060	2019
200	East Timor *	Asia			3,339	2022	3,356	2020	3,553	2019
201	Haiti *	Caribbean			3,189	2022	2,925	2020	2,800	2020
202	Lesotho *	Africa			3,034	2022	2,405	2020	2,704	2019
203	Guinea *	Africa			3,029	2022	2,818	2020	2,562	2019
204	Uganda *	Africa			2,961	2022	2,297	2020	2,187	2019
205	Vanuatu *	Oceania			2,851	2022	2,915	2020	3,153	2019
206	Rwanda *	Africa			2,808	2022	2,214	2020	2,227	2019
207	Guinea-Bissau *	Africa			2,784	2022	1,949	2020	1,989	2019
208	Burkina Faso *	Africa			2,663	2022	2,279	2020	2,178	2019
209	Gambia	Africa			2,646	2022	2,278	2020	2,223	2019
210	Togo *	Africa			2,599	2022	2,224	2020	1,597	2019
211	Mali *	Africa			2,575	2022	2,339	2020	2,322	2019
212	Zimbabwe *	Africa			2,523	2022	2,895	2020	2,836	2019
213	Afghanistan *	Asia			2,456	2020	2,088	2020	2,065	2019
214	Solomon Islands *	Oceania			2,385	2022	2,619	2020	2,663	2019
215	Kiribati *	Oceania			2,148	2022	2,418	2020	2,272	2019
216	Eritrea *	Africa			2,101	2022	1,626	2011	1,600	2019
217	Yemen *	Asia			2,078	2022	3,689	2013	2,500	2017
218	Sierra Leone *	Africa			1,958	2022	1,739	2020	1,718	2019
219	Liberia *	Africa			1,779	2022	1,428	2020	1,428	2019
220	Madagascar *	Africa			1,778	2022	1,593	2020	1,647	2019
221	Chad *	Africa			1,705	2022	1,603	2020	1,580	2019
222	North Korea *	Asia			–		–		1,700	2015
223	Malawi *	Africa			1,603	2022	1,568	2020	1,060	2019
224	Mozambique *	Africa			1,439	2022	1,297	2020	1,281	2019
225	Niger *	Africa			1,435	2022	1,263	2020	1,225	2019
226	Somalia *	Africa			1,322	2022	875.2	2020	800	2020
227	DR Congo *	Africa			1,316	2022	1,131	2020	1,098	2019
228	Central African Republic *	Africa			1,102	2022	979.6	2020	945	2019
229	South Sudan *	Africa			928	2022	1,235	2015	1,600	2017
230	Burundi *	Africa			856	2022	771.2	2020	700	2020

Table of GDP(PPP) per capita by country: from identified sources

https://en.wikipedia.org/wiki/List_of_countries_by_GDP_(PPP)_per_capita

The International Monetary Fund (IMF) is a major financial agency of the United Nations, and an international financial institution funded by 190 member countries, with headquarters in Washington, D.C. It is regarded as the global lender of last resort to national governments, and a leading supporter of exchange-rate stability. Its stated mission is "working to foster global monetary cooperation, secure financial stability, facilitate international trade, promote high employment and sustainable economic growth, and reduce poverty around the world. "Established on December 27, 1945 at the Bretton Woods Conference, primarily according to the ideas of Harry Dexter White and John Maynard Keynes, it started with 29 member countries and the goal of reconstructing the international monetary system after World War II. It now plays a central role in the management of balance of payments difficulties and international financial crises. Through a quota system, countries contribute funds to a pool from which countries can borrow if they experience balance of payments problems. As of 2016, the fund had SDR 477 billion (about US$667 billion).

The IMF works to stabilize and foster the economies of its member countries by its use of the fund, as well as other activities such as gathering and analyzing economic statistics and surveillance of its members' economies. IMF funds come from two major sources: quotas and loans. Quotas, which are pooled funds from member nations, generate most IMF funds. The size of members' quotas increase according to their economic and financial importance in the world. The quotas are increased periodically as a means of boosting the IMF's resources in the form of special drawing rights.
https://en.wikipedia.org/wiki/International_Monetary_Fund

World GDP per capita (US$ PPP) Tables

GDP per capita (PPP) is the monetary exchange rate adjusted individual purchasing power in each country. As one might suspect there is magic and scientific guesswork involved in coming up with the final numbers so the rankings are not precise but more relative. They also may not exactly match the way people feel about their prosperity in each country but then again they have nothing with which to compare personally. But they do represent an attempt to understand the world's economic situation. For this reason, they are useful. Green signifies a Western World nation, Gold shows those other countries whose economic policies have been heavily influenced by the West or anomalies.

The United States is the recognized leader in economic prosperity when size and wealth sources are considered. The other obvious finding is the consistently high standing of countries from the Western or Christian-dominant world, highlighted in green. Countries highlighted in gold are ones heavily influenced by the Western World, stories to be told. All these estimates are the results of educated efforts to evaluate the economic situation around the world. The tables have three different estimates from three different sources, the IMF, the World Bank, and the CIA, yes the US Central Intelligence Agency. For example, Switzerland, estimates of GDP (PPP) per capita are as follows:

Estimates of Swiss GDP PPP
>   IMF ⋯⋯⋯⋯⋯⋯ $84,658 in 2022
>   World Bank ⋯⋯⋯ $71,352 in 2020
>   CIA ⋯⋯⋯⋯⋯⋯ $68,400 in 2020

Also, note that most of the countries ranked higher than the United States have certain conditions that slant the rankings, they have very small populations as shown compared to the US, they may be a tax haven that attracts large deposits of money in banks, and they may incentivize their tax laws to attract corporate operations. Thirdly some get their capital primarily from oil and gas reserves rather than any citizen productive activity. When these factors are taken into account the United States (population estimates 2022: 332,403,650) is basically at the top of the list.

Also, consider that economic prosperity is just a starting point. It indicates the relative ease by which anyone can pursue their dreams or talents. It is an indicator of the options reasonably available. One way to look at GDP is that it indicates the number of goods and services produced and sold in a given period. That means that the higher the GDP the more options individuals have to earn and spend money, all to upgrade their lives or provide those special treats that enrich one's life.

The GDP PPP of the United States is $78,000+ while the GDP PPP of Guatemala, number 153 on the charts is $9,900+. That is the difference in goods and services available per person between the two countries. The result is that it's hard to buy many things in Guatemala that we have flowing off our grocery or Walmart shelves. That's why there is much

Western Hemisphere Rank	World Rank	Country	Location	Source	Pop	IMF Estimate	Year	World Bank Estimate	Year	CIA Estimate	Year
		GDP per capita (US$ PPP) Western Hemisphere				IMF		World Bank		CIA	
1	10	Bermuda*	Caribbean	Tax Haven		–		80,830	2020	81,800	2019
2	13	United States*	North America			76,027	2022	63,544	2020	60,200	2020
3	15	Cayman Islands*	Caribbean	Tax Haven		–		71,594	2020	73,600	2019
4	16	Falkland Islands*	South America		3,398	–		–		70,800	2015
5	31	Canada*	North America			57,812	2022	48,073	2020	45,900	2020
6	51	Saint Pierre and Miquelon*	Caribbean			–		–		46,200	2006
7	53	Puerto Rico*	Caribbean			42,759	2022	35,279	2020	33,400	2020
8	54	Greenland*	Caribbean			–		–		41,800	2015
9	58	Bahamas*	Caribbean			40,274	2022	32,454	2020	30,800	2020
10	60	Aruba*	Caribbean			39,508	2022	38,897	2017	37,500	2017
11	62	Guyana*	South America			38,258	2022	19,706	2020	13,082	2019
12	65	U.S. Virgin Islands*	Caribbean			–		–		37,000	2016
13	68	Panama*	Central America			36,085	2022	26,776	2020	31,459	2019
14	69	Sint Maarten*	Caribbean			–		35,977	2018	35,300	2018
15	74	British Virgin Islands*	Caribbean			–		–		34,200	2017
16	75	Montserrat*	Caribbean			–		–		34,000	2011
17	80	Trinidad and Tobago*	Caribbean			29,884	2022	25,031	2020	23,700	2020
18	83	Chile*	South America			28,526	2022	25,068	2020	24,226	2019
19	84	Saint Kitts and Nevis*	Caribbean			27,608	2022	24,537	2020	23,300	2020
20	85	Uruguay*	South America			26,663	2022	22,795	2020	21,561	2019
21	86	Argentina*	South America			25,822	2022	20,768	2020	22,064	2019
22	90	Costa Rica*	Central America			24,490	2022	21,032	2020	19,700	2020
23	91	Dominican Republic*	Caribbean			23,983	2022	17,937	2020	17,000	2020
24	93	Turks and Caicos Islands	Caribbean			–		22,286	2020	21,100	2020
25	94	Mexico*	North America			22,216	2022	18,833	2020	19,796	2019
26	95	Antigua and Barbuda*	Caribbean			21,890	2022	18,942	2020	18,000	2020
27	97	Curaçao*	Caribbean			–		21,423	2020	24,500	2019
28	101	Saint Martin*	Caribbean			–		–		19,300	2005
29	108	Grenada*	Caribbean			18,293	2022	15,893	2020	15,100	2020
30	109	Colombia*	South America			18,225	2022	14,565	2020	14,722	2019
31	112	Barbados*	Caribbean			17,408	2022	13,577	2020	12,900	2020
32	114	Suriname*	South America			17,300	2022	17,016	2020	16,525	2019
33	115	Brazil*	South America			17,208	2022	14,836	2020	14,652	2019
34	121	Saint Lucia*	Caribbean			16,509	2022	12,944	2020	12,300	2020
35	123	Saint Vincent and the Grenadines*	Caribbean			15,505	2022	12,770	2020	12,100	2020
36	126	Peru*	South America			15,035	2022	11,879	2020	12,848	2019
37	129	Dominica*	Caribbean			14,491	2022	10,435	2020	9,900	2020
38	130	Paraguay*	South America			14,430	2022	13,013	2020	12,685	2019
39	139	Ecuador*	South America			12,664	2022	10,896	2020	11,375	2019
40	141	Cuba*	Caribbean			–		–		12,300	2016
41	143	Anguilla*	Caribbean			–		–		12,200	2008
42	146	Jamaica*	Caribbean			11,802	2022	9,222	2020	8,700	2020
43	149	El Salvador*	Central America			10,581	2022	8,499	2020	8,100	2020
44	153	Guatemala*	Central America			9,911	2022	8,854	2020	8,400	2020
45	154	Bolivia*	South America			9,856	2022	8,367	2020	8,724	2019
46	162	Belize*	Central America			7,147	2022	6,456	2020	6,100	2020
47	163	Nicaragua*	Central America			7,071	2022	5,570	2020	5,300	2020
48	167	Honduras*	Central America			6,740	2022	5,421	2020	5,100	2020
49	176	Venezuela*	South America			5,949	2022	17,528	2011	7,704	2018
50	201	Haiti*	Caribbean			3,189	2022	2,925	2020	2,800	2020

Table of GDP(PPP) per capita (Western Hemisphere) by country: from identified sources
https://en.wikipedia.org/wiki/List of countries by GDP (PPP) per capita

interest in immigrating to the US. The downside is that the immigrants must earn their share of the wealth, they don't get $76,000+ in goods and services just from being here, no one does. In any event, the Western World certainly tops the Economic Prosperity charts as an indicator of high personal prosperity.

Economic Ratings of Western Hemisphere Countries

The United States began with excellent input data. England and Europe evolved into similar situations. Other countries, such as those in Central and South America, have begun development with a mix of good and bad ideas, and some with just pure evil ideas. Argentina, Mexico, Brazil, and Venezuela are highlighted in the following table. Note that Venezuela has fallen pretty hard under the socialist practices which are controlling the country.

This should be a dire warning for any country, that when principles of prosperity are violated that country's economy, even one with some heritage of Christianity, can be devastated. Socialism, Communism, and dictatorships win by deception. They first sell the population on the need to punish free enterprise, the wealthy who create jobs, and economic freedom, pitting one class against another and then take control of the engines of prosperity, driving the economy and prosperity into a dumpster fire. Beware of cries for equality and equity and blaming the wealthy for every problem in society. Those are the tactics of Nazi Germany and Communist Russia. They are alive and well in the Western World and are seeking your vote.

What separates the rest of the Western Hemisphere from the United States and Canada are their cultural and governmental roots that created a sufficiently different view of life. That view of life in turn changed the character of government sufficiently to create the current difference in GDP shown in the table below. Each country has its own story. The situation in Venezuela is the result of a dictator plus socialism. The story in Brazil is much more complex with a wide range of bad decisions that we will address in detail in the next chapter.

Median Disposable Household Income

A further refinement of GDP is to assess disposable income PPP per the Organization for Economic Co-operation and Development (OECD) evaluation. This further balances the equation and moves the United States to the top of the rankings, but this organization is made up of the wealthiest nations only and does not rank or evaluate every country.

OECD Household Disposable Income per capita (including social transfers in kind)					
Rank	Country	PPP adjusted 2021	Rank	Country	PPP adjusted 2021
	European Union	35,400	18	Japan	32,600 (2020)
1	United States	62,300	19	New Zealand	32,600 (2019)
2	Luxembourg	51,400	20	Slovenia	30,900
3	Australia	45,000	21	Lithuania	30,900
4	Germany	44,400	22	Czechia	30,800
5	Switzerland	44,400	23	Spain	29,500
6	Norway	44,300	24	South Korea	29,000
7	Austria	41,800	25	Portugal	28,100
8	Netherlands	41,400	26	Estonia	26,900
9	Belgium	40,800	27	Poland	26,200
10	France	39,800	28	Latvia	25,700
11	Canada	38,900	29	Hungary	25,000
12	Finland	37,400	30	Greece	23,800
13	Denmark	37,100	31	Slovak Republic	23,400
14	United Kingdom	36,900	32	Russia	20,600 (2019)
15	Sweden	36,800	33	Chile	20,400 (2020)
16	Italy	34,300	34	Mexico	16,400 (2020)
17	Ireland	33,000	35	Costa Rica	16,300 (2020)

These alternate rankings don't change the global results, the Western Christian-based world dominates the listings, but a link is provided here if you're interested in looking at different ways of tabulating data.

https://en.wikipedia.org/wiki/Disposable_household_and_per_capita_income

The rankings by OECD and especially the value of disposable income are after social transfers, which are tax dollars that fund certain expenses. We in the US are indeed rich by these metrics compared to most all other countries on a per capita basis.

The Organization for Economic Co-operation and Development (OECD); French: Organisation de coopération et de développement économiques, OCDE) is an intergovernmental organization with 38 member countries, founded in 1961 to stimulate economic progress and world trade. It is a forum whose member countries describe themselves as committed to democracy and the market economy, providing a platform to compare policy experiences, seek answers to common problems, identify good practices, and coordinate the domestic and international policies of its members.

The majority of OECD members are high-income economies with a very high Human Development Index (HDI) and are regarded as developed countries. Their collective population is 1.38 billion. As of 2017, the OECD member countries collectively comprised 62.2% of global nominal GDP (US$49.6 trillion) and 42.8% of global GDP (Int$54.2 trillion) at purchasing power parity. The OECD is an official United Nations observer.https://en.wikipedia.org/wiki/OECD

OECD's "median disposable income per person" metric, *which does all forms of income as well as taxes and transfers in kind from governments for benefits such as healthcare and education and is equivalised by dividing by the square root of household size. This metric, in addition to using a median rather than a mean, use "data calculated according to the new OECD terms of reference"; compared to previous terms of reference, these "include a more detailed breakdown of current transfers received and paid by households as well as a revised definition of household income, including the value of goods produced for own consumption as an element of self-employed income." https://en.wikipedia.org/wiki/Disposable_household_and_per_capita_income#Disposable_income_per_capita_(OECD)*

When the economic evaluation includes disposable incomes (actual spendable dollars), the United States leads the rest of the Western World. This could just be that many social services including education, drugs, and medicines are paid for through taxes in other places rather than as needed in the US. That is the Government takes your money and spends it for you.   What should be clear is that the Christian Philosophy of Life motivates individuals to be productive, not just in earning money but in all sorts of creative ways that enrich lives.   The other observation is that Government policies can significantly affect economic prosperity, not only directly but by the influence of those policies on the habits and actions of the population.

Washington Crossing the Delaware, 1851 by Emanuel Leutze

The Metropolitan Museum of Art, Public Domain,
https://commons.wikimedia.org/w/index.php?curid=9520770

5. Western Influence Around the World

Third World Countries are those with impoverished citizenship and who seem beyond any help to get themselves out of a life of economic poverty. Second World Countries are those economically developing countries that have appeared to break free of the grasp of poverty to begin creating wealth and opportunity for their citizens. The primary basis for this newly created wealth, measured in terms of GDP is the industrialization of the nation. That is the emergence of a manufacturer of goods and services. As an example, Mexico has a well-established manufacturing base for vehicles and appliances but none of that is found in

Guatemala. These industries pay for skilled workers, raising income levels and the GDP.

Middle East

The Arab / Middle Eastern world is somewhat prosperous solely due to the treasure of oil found on their land and developed by the capitalist Western world. They have some different ideas about economics however that come from Islam, so their governments and motivations for prosperity are quite different. They live in a country, generally of either strong-armed secular dictators or an Islamic religious dictatorship, both of which grant the population some limited measure of independence. The apparent wealth and prosperity of those Middle Eastern Arab / Muslim nations and especially those with some appearance of capitalism however is an aberration created by the oil revenues that flood the country and are usually not available to the general population. And it is indeed a limited form of Western capitalism that is the engine of the physical appearance of prosperity. But the prosperity is not created by the industriousness of the citizens, but by the spending of an inheritance gained from the oil.

Two special cases of prosperity in the Middle East are Israel and Lebanon. Lebanon was an oasis of prosperity for many years until their religious civil war broke out. That prosperity had been the result of years of Christian influence that created a capitalist environment.

Lebanon

Despite its small size, the country has developed a well-known culture and has been highly influential in the Arab world. Before the Lebanese Civil War (1975–1990), the country experienced a period of relative calm and renowned prosperity, driven by tourism, agriculture, commerce, and banking. Because of its financial power and diversity in its heyday, Lebanon was referred to as the "Switzerland of the East" during the 1960s, and its capital, Beirut, attracted so many tourists that it was known as "the Paris of the Middle East". At the end of the war, there were extensive efforts to revive the economy and rebuild the national infrastructure. Despite these troubles, Lebanon has the highest Human Development Index and GDP per capita in the Arab world, to the exclusion of the oil-rich economies of the Persian Gulf.

Lebanon is the most religiously diverse country in the Middle East. As of 2014 the CIA World Factbook estimates the following: Muslim 54% (27% Shia Islam, 27% Sunni Islam), Christian 40.5%.

The Lebanese legal system is based on the French system, and is a civil law country, with the exception for matters related to personal status (succession, marriage, divorce, adoption, etc.), which are governed by a separate set of laws designed for each sectarian community. For instance, the Islamic personal status laws are inspired by the Sharia law.
   https://en.wikipedia.org/wiki/Lebanon

Israel

In its Basic Laws, Israel defines itself as a Jewish and democratic state. Israel is a representative democracy with a parliamentary system, proportional representation, and universal suffrage. The prime minister is the head of government and the Knesset is the legislature. Israel is a developed country and an OECD member, with the 34th-largest economy in the world by nominal gross domestic product as of 2016. The country benefits from a highly skilled workforce and is among the most educated countries in the world with one of the highest percentages of its citizens holding a tertiary education degree. Israel has the highest standard of living in the Middle East and has one of the highest life expectancies in the world.
   https://en.wikipedia.org/wiki/Israel

What sets Lebanon and Israel apart is their philosophy of life values that promote free enterprise and capitalism. Lebanon itself has been up to 40% Christian and has been aided by European interests and capitalism which influences its thinking. Israel has a philosophy of life derived from the Bible's Old Testament which also formed a prototype foundation for the Christian philosophy. Israel has taken that prototype philosophy, Jewish philosophy to them, and used it for their nation's economic benefits. And like the United States and much of the Western World, its Jewish philosophy is strongly embedded in the lives of its citizens. The threats of war from their Arab neighbors have not hurt the building of a strong national team as well.

When we look elsewhere what we can see is that where Christianity may be theoretically the dominant influential force in a society, that influence does no good if it's not well communicated and inculcated into the thinking of the population.

What happened in Germany to cause World War II is most interesting given its historical Christian base. Unfortunately, that's a research project all on its own, notably driven by the harsh terms that ended World War I. The other obvious factor is that many good people kept out of politics and allowed the lawless Nazi party to intimidate society for so long that it could not be undone.   The other observation to make here is how quickly Germany recovered and became a sane democratic partner to the West, and how quickly West Germany was able to bring East Germany into its Western sphere of thinking after the collapse of the Soviet Union and the end of the Cold War.   They were very resilient people who responded well to the Christian treatment by the West at the end of WW II.

A different example is found in the Central and South American countries which, while somewhat Christian, have a version of Christianity that has been infiltrated by local tribal religious influences and robs local Christianity of its Biblical philosophy and power.   Here there is a smattering of hit-and-miss economic prosperity.

Examining the GDP (PPP) per capita of North and South American countries (see the table in the last chapter) we can see the relative ranking of each country v.s. the world, and their ranking in the Western Hemisphere.

Venezuela is the loser here with a socialist government with questionable voting legalities, run by a dictator who seems intent on running this once flourishing country, into the ground.   Its GDP is only higher than the GDP of Haiti.   Mexico, Argentina, and Brazil are large nations with little to show for their size and wealth, as shown by smaller nations around them.

While these nations are nominally Christian they all suffer from various cultural abnormalities that have hindered their economic development.   Each country has a different story, historical culture, and economic outcome and we have to consider that the GDP per capita does not fully describe economic prosperity but is valuable for purposes of comparison.

Brazil

Brazil is considered an emerging economic giant, but comes with some difficult problems.   Even though it is a Christian nation with>80% popular preference, it suffers from major philosophical problems at both the governmental and collective individual levels.

From Brazil's beginnings, its government was run by military dictatorships. The press and elections were controlled by the government This lasted until the 1950s when the military installed a democratic system with elections. That didn't last and in 1964 a coup put the military back in direct power. Again in the 1980s democracy returned and civilians took over the power of the government. The corruption, bribery, hyperinflation, and ineffective public policies had taken their toll on popular support, however. So while there have been some elections and transfers of power between political parties, the government is still a shaky proposition. Wikipedia expands on this story below. It's a little long but it validates the conclusion that prosperity requires good thinking on the part of the population, and on the part of the government leadership. And it shows how even minor perturbations in that thinking can make a big difference in outcomes.

>   ***Brazil*** *The "early republican government was little more than a*
>   *military dictatorship, with the army dominating affairs both at Rio de*
>   *Janeiro and in the states. Freedom of the press disappeared and elections*
>   *were controlled by those in power". In 1894, following the unfoldings of two*
>   *severe crises, an economic along with a military one, the republican civilians*
>   *rose to power.*
>
>   *If in relation to its foreign policy, the country in this first republican*
>   *period maintained a relative balance characterized by success in resolving*
>   *border disputes with neighboring countries, only broken by the Acre War*
>   *(1899–1902) and its involvement in World War I (1914–1918), followed by a*
>   *failed attempt to exert a prominent role in the League of Nations; Internally,*
>   *from the crisis of Encilhamento and the Armada Revolts, a prolonged cycle of*
>   *financial, political and social instability began. Until the 1920s, keeping the*
>   *country besieged by various rebellions, both civilian and military.*
>
>   *Little by little, a cycle of general instability sparked by these crises*
>   *undermined the regime to such an extent, that in the wake of the murder of*
>   *his running mate, the defeated opposition presidential candidate Getúlio*
>   *Vargas supported by most of the military, successfully led the October 1930's*
>   *Coup. Vargas and the military were supposed to assume power temporarily,*
>   *but instead closed the Congress, extinguished the Constitution, ruled with*

emergency powers, and replaced the states' governors with their own supporters.

In half of the first 100 years of the republic, the Army exercised power directly or through figures like Getúlio Vargas. In the 1930s, three failed attempts to remove Vargas and his supporters from power occurred. The first was the Constitutionalist Revolt in 1932 led by the Paulista oligarchy, the second was a Communist uprising in November 1935, and the last one a Putsch attempt by the local fascists in May 1938. The 1935 uprising created a security crisis in which Congress transferred more power to the executive. The 1937 coup d'état resulted in the cancellation of the 1938 election, installed Vargas as a dictator, and began the Estado Novo era, noted for government brutality and censorship of the press.

The foreign policy during Vargas's years was marked by the antecedents and occurrence of World War II. Brazil remained neutral until August 1942, when the country entered on the Allied side, after suffering retaliations undertaken by Nazi Germany and Fascist Italy, in the context of the strategic dispute over the South Atlantic. In addition to its participation in the battle of the Atlantic, Brazil also sent an expeditionary force to fight in the Italian campaign.

With the Allied victory in 1945 and the end of the Nazi-fascist regimes in Europe, Vargas's position became unsustainable and he was swiftly overthrown in another military coup, with Democracy being "reinstated" by the same army that had discontinued it 15 years earlier. Vargas committed suicide in August 1954 amid a political crisis, after having returned to power by election in 1950.[122][123]

Contemporary era: Brazilian military government and History of Brazil since 1985

Several brief interim governments followed Vargas's suicide. Juscelino Kubitschek became president in 1956 and assumed a conciliatory posture towards the political opposition that allowed him to govern without major crises. The economy and industrial sector grew remarkably, but his greatest achievement was the construction of the new capital city of Brasília, inaugurated in 1960. His successor, Jânio Quadros, resigned in 1961 less than a year after taking office. His vice-president, João Goulart, assumed the presidency, but aroused strong political opposition and was deposed in April 1964 by a coup that resulted in a military regime.

The new regime was intended to be transitory but gradually closed in on itself and became a full dictatorship with the promulgation of the Fifth Institutional Act in 1968. Oppression was not limited to those who resorted to guerrilla tactics to fight the regime, but also reached institutional opponents, artists, journalists, and other members of civil society, inside and outside the country through the infamous "Operation Condor". Despite its brutality, like other totalitarian regimes, due to an economic boom, known as an "economic miracle", the regime reached a peak in popularity in the early 1970s.

Slowly however, the wear and tear of years of dictatorial power that had not slowed the repression, even after the defeat of the leftist guerrillas, plus the inability to deal with the economic crises of the period and popular pressure, made an opening policy inevitable, which from the regime side was led by Generals Geisel and Golbery. With the enactment of the Amnesty Law in 1979, Brazil began its slow return to democracy, which was completed during the 1980s.

Civilians returned to power in 1985 when José Sarney assumed the presidency, becoming unpopular during his tenure through failure to control the economic crisis and hyperinflation inherited from the military regime. Sarney's unsuccessful government led to the election in 1989 of the almost-unknown Fernando Collor, subsequently impeached by the National Congress in 1992.

Collor was succeeded by his vice-president, Itamar Franco, who appointed Fernando Henrique Cardoso as Minister of Finance. In 1994, Cardoso produced a highly successful Plano Real, that, after decades of failed economic plans made by previous governments attempting to curb hyperinflation, finally granted stability to the Brazilian economy, leading Cardoso to be elected that year, and again in 1998.

The peaceful transition of power from Cardoso to his main opposition leader, Luiz Inácio Lula da Silva (elected in 2002 and re-elected in 2006), was seen as proof that Brazil had finally succeeded in achieving long-sought political stability. However, sparked by indignation and frustrations accumulated over decades from corruption, police brutality, and inefficiencies of the political establishment and public service, numerous peaceful protests erupted in Brazil from the middle of the first term of Dilma Rousseff, who succeeded Lula in 2010.

Enhanced by political and economic crises with evidence of involvement by politicians from all the primary political parties in several bribery and tax evasion schemes, with large street protests for and against her, Rousseff was impeached by the Brazilian Congress in 2016. In 2017, the Supreme Court has asked for the investigation of 71 Brazilian lawmakers and nine ministers in President Michel Temer's cabinet allegedly linked to the Petrobras corruption scandal. President Temer is himself accused of corruption.

https://en.wikipedia.org/wiki/Brazil

This describes Brazil's history of corruption, dictatorships, and military rule over more than a hundred years, including the instability of its current 2000-era government. The bottom line is that there is neither a firm commitment to a democratic or principled-based government by those in leadership positions. Because of its size, its economy is large, but it suffers not only from unstable governments but also contorted and confusing legal and court systems and extensive poverty and illiteracy brought about by a lack of vision on education and values.

The following additional views of Brazil come from the same reference as above and provide some insight into the culture within Brazil that has contributed to the chaos.

Brazilian Cultural Influences
https://en.wikipedia.org/wiki/Brazil
The rule of law: easily changed by current academic thinking
Most of the Brazilian law is codified, although non-codified statutes also represent a substantial part, playing a complementary role. Court decisions set out interpretive guidelines; however, they are seldom binding on other specific cases. Doctrinal works and the works of academic jurists have a strong influence on law creation and law cases.

> NOTE: This is the same source of corruption of the rule of law, by academia, as in the USA. It comes from uneducated thinking, blind to the lessons of history, and being willing to retry communism and socialism. And they feel justified in undermining and changing current US constitutional law without due process. They also lack understanding of the values inherent in the Constitution and are willing to change laws by presidential edict, deceit, lies, and collusion. When this happens no one can know the law and chaos results. We see this in the lack of clarity with crime in the USA, and maybe elsewhere, and we'll see a similar problem in the Middle East with Islamic Rule in Chapter 17.

Corruption
Corruption costs Brazil almost $41 billion a year alone, with 69.9% of the country's firms identifying the issue as a major constraint in successfully penetrating the global market. Local government corruption is so prevalent that voters perceive it as a problem only if it surpasses certain levels, and only if a local media e.g. a radio station is present to divulge the findings of

corruption charges. Initiatives, like this exposure, strengthen awareness which is indicated by Transparency International's Corruption Perceptions Index; ranking Brazil 69th out of 178 countries in 2012. The purchasing power in Brazil is eroded by the so-called Brazil cost.

Poverty

Among the challenges is the still high number of poor Brazilians living in urban slums (Favela) and in rural areas without access to piped water or sanitation; water scarcity in the Northeast of Brazil; water pollution, especially in the South-East of the country; the low share of collected wastewater that is being treated (35% in 2000); and long-standing tensions between the federal, state and municipal governments about their respective roles in the sector.

Education and illiteracy

The Federal Constitution and the Law of Guidelines and Bases of National Education determine that the Federal Government, States, Federal Districts, and municipalities must manage and organize their respective education systems. Each of these public educational systems is responsible for its own maintenance, which manages funds as well as the mechanisms and funding sources. The constitution reserves 25% of the state budget and 18% of federal taxes and municipal taxes for education.

According to the IBGE, in 2011, the literacy rate of the population was 90.4%, meaning that 13 million (9.6% of the population) people are still illiterate in the country; functional illiteracy has reached 21.6% of the population. Illiteracy is highest in the Northeast, where 19.9% of the population is illiterate.

Religion

Religion in Brazil was formed from the meeting of the Catholic Church with the religious traditions of enslaved African peoples and indigenous peoples. This confluence of faiths during the Portuguese colonization of Brazil led to the development of a diverse array of syncretistic practices within the overarching umbrella of the Brazilian Catholic Church, characterized by traditional Portuguese festivities, and in some instances, Allan Kardec's Spiritism (a religion which incorporates elements of spiritualism and Christianity). Religious pluralism increased during the 20th century, and the Protestant community has grown to include over 22% of the population. The most common Protestant denominations are Pentecostal and Evangelical ones. Other Protestant branches with a notable presence in the country include the Baptists, Seventh-day Adventists, Lutherans, and the Reformed tradition.

https://en.wikipedia.org/wiki/Brazil

Brazil's mediocre performance in many areas indicates a lack of consensus on Christian values inculcated into the psyche of its population and this is indicated by the acceptance of non-Christian religious values and traditions into the Christian church in Brazil. While done probably to gain approval and acceptance by the local population, it also handicaps the Church's teachings of the tenets of Christianity where they conflict with native religious traditions. It not only weakens the teachings of the philosophy of life but also weakens spiritual principles that provide additional motivations for individuals to succeed. The instabilities of the government, the frequent violent changes in government, and the high levels of corruption are telling evidence of the lack of the moral imperatives of the two commandments that deal with private property and ownership.

The bottom line is that merely the predominance of Christianity as an official preference in a nation is not enough to create prosperity. Its fundamental principles must be rigorously taught, and accepted by the population. When its message is watered down and when the morality of the principles is not valued, the principles that promote prosperity are not as strong.

This problem is symptomatic of many South American and Central American countries. Christianity is watered down, diluted, and robbed of its essential values that produce prosperity. The results are varied because the levels of dilution and loss of values differ with each government. Argentina is the perfect example where Christianity has maintained its pure heritage from Spain and Italy and the result is that Argentina has about a 30 percent higher GDP than Brazil. Argentina has had its political instabilities so it's not perfect, having dabbled with socialism and uncontrolled spending, but it's better. The prosperity of a nation is not the result of the values or overt approach to government, but the result of the values of the population of that nation. And the values that make a difference, those embodied in the United States founding documents are fundamental principles of Christianity and its philosophy of life.

We have another example of this influence of Christian values on two nations, both Christian in historic culture and both of whose populations went through some trying times. Yet one emerged from those trials with a prosperity that is about as good as it gets and the other is still slow to gain any momentum. The change came from the collapse of the Soviet Union, the end of communism there as a failed economic policy, and the freedom of all the Eastern Block European nations from occupation by the Soviet Union. All these Soviet-run countries returned to a democratic form of government and a capitalist economic system immediately. Most surprising was the immediate reunification of East and West Germany.

Russia and East Germany

The two nations with the most significant changes are Russia and Germany, mainly East Germany. To be fair, the Russian people were much more severely repressed under communism than were the East Germans due to an extended generation under an atheistic dictatorship. But the difference is there. Russia has yet to fully escape from its past so the tendency is a totalitarian form of government, with elections but still having an authoritarian nature. The result is that its economic progress has been slow compared to the recoveries of the Eastern European nations formerly under Soviet control.

https://en.wikipedia.org/wiki/East_Germany#/media/File:Soviet_Sector_Germany.png
PUBLIC DOMAIN

Russia, to its credit, did something miraculous at the end of the Soviet empire and communism, at the end of the cold war. It restored the private property confiscated by the communist government some 50 or so years earlier, to its rightful owners from the time when communism took over. They also turned the economy into a quasi-free enterprise economy where the citizens now had to get a job and earn a living. This has been a traumatic experience for the Russian people who had been living under the communist welfare state, even to the present time, and even for young people who were children when communism collapsed. The spirit of independence and self-reliance had been quenched under Russian communism and revival has been slow.

When the "Cold War" ended East Germany's recovery was so rapid that the signs of poverty and the gray hapless life of communist control is gone, in part thanks to West Germany's help but also due to the spirit of the East German people who rejoiced when the Berlin wall came down. Now some 25-plus years later the only difference between East and West Berlin is that East Berlin is newer and more modern, having replaced the drab remnants of the Soviet occupation. They even have a museum in Berlin dedicated to the spartan life in East Berlin under communism to remind them of how far they've come.

There is one big area that differentiates the old territories of East and West Germany, the view of religion. On the map of German local government areas, the shades of blue represent pluralities of Protestant Christian association percentages, the green shades, pluralities of Catholic Christian percentages, and the red shades represent pluralities of no religious affiliation.

For each group, the lighter shades represent a majority of 50 to 75% and the darker shades represent a majority of over 75%. While the East had its religious traditions suppressed by communism under Soviet occupation, those values and traditions were held throughout the occupation and worked to restore the East after unification. This map represents the sentiment in 2011 or some 20 years later. There is a whole generation now who grew up under an authoritarian communist regime and without a Christian upbringing.

East Germany is predominantly religiously unaffiliated, with large areas where they have a majority of over 75%. Given the lighter shade of red is a majority as small as 50% majority, there is still a large presence of Christians in the old East German sector. But most have lost their Christian identity and therefore possibly some of the values and philosophy that create Western prosperity. The rest of Germany remains much more associated with its Christian roots.

The point here is that the further down the wrong path a nation or culture goes, the longer and harder the recovery. But it's not impossible, and dramatic change is not impossible either. We have such an example of a significant cultural turnaround driven by a charismatic leader.

Turkey

Modern-day Turkey is a country that lives and somewhat thrives as an oil-poor Muslim country because of the efforts of a single individual. Turkey experienced perhaps the most dramatic turnaround in history under the leadership of Mustafa Kemal Pasha (Atatürk) after WWI.

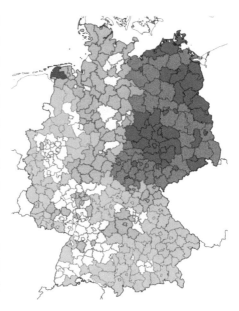

Under the Ottoman Empire, Turkey had entered WWI on the German side and suffered, as the loser, with occupation in some areas by the Greeks, French, Italians, and British. This prompted a National Movement to arise in Turkey that led to a revolt against both the Ottoman Government and the occupation forces. The Turkish War of Independence ended in 1923 with the occupying forces pushed out and the Sultanate abolished which ended 623 years of Ottoman Empire rule. Interestingly, very similar to the evolution of Germany with Hitler's rise after WW I where Hitler campaigned against the peace treaty and the German government that had gotten them into the war in the first place.

The Turkish War of Independence (19 May 1919 – 24 July 1923)
was a series of military campaigns waged by the Turkish National
Movement after parts of the Ottoman Empire were occupied and partitioned
following its defeat in World War I. These campaigns were directed against

In 1924, during Atatürk speech in Bursa
https://en.wikipedia.org/wiki/Mustafa_Kemal_Atatürk   Public Domain

Greece in the west, Armenia in the east, France in the south, loyalists and separatists in various cities, and British and Ottoman troops around Constantinople (İstanbul).

The ethnic demographics of the modern Turkish Republic were significantly impacted by the earlier Armenian genocide and the deportations of Greek-speaking, Orthodox Christian Rum people. The Turkish nationalist movement carried out massacres and deportations to eliminate native Christian populations—a continuation of the Armenian genocide and other ethnic cleansing operations during World War I. Following these campaigns of ethnic cleansing the historic Christian presence in Anatolia was destroyed, in large part, and the Muslim demographic

Kamâl Atatürk; 1881 – Nov 1938)
https://commons.wikimedia.org/wiki/
Public domain, via Wikimedia Commons

had increased from 80% to 98%.

While World War I ended for the Ottoman Empire with the Armistice of Mudros, the Allied Powers continued occupying and seizing land. Ottoman military commanders, therefore, refused orders from both the Allies and the Ottoman government to surrender and disband their forces. This crisis reached a head when sultan Mehmed VI dispatched Mustafa Kemal Pasha (Atatürk), a well-respected and high-ranking general, to Anatolia to restore order; however, Mustafa Kemal became an enabler and eventually leader of Turkish nationalist resistance against the Ottoman government, Allied powers, and Christian minorities.

https://en.wikipedia.org/wiki/Turkish_War_of_Independence

Mustafa Kemal Pasha (Atatürk) led the Nationalist movement in revolt against both the Ottoman government and the Allied occupation, and he succeeded in ousting both the Ottoman rulers and the occupying forces. The Republic of Turkey emerged from this in 1923 and Mustafa Kemal Pasha was elected as the first President. He then proceeded to completely redefine modern Turkey, not by restoring the previous version of Turkey, but by completely changing its culture into a Western European country, something that it had never been. As the Turkish leader, he made a number of progressive changes to the country. He introduced a Latin-based Turkish alphabet to replace the Ottoman Empire version, instituted free and compulsory primary education, and opened thousands of schools across the country. He also introduced women's rights to vote and made the Turkish language mandatory in public but at the same time allowed minority populations to use their own languages in private, he also required everyone to get a Turkish surname, even minorities.

Mustafa Kemal Atatürk,[a] or Mustafa Kemal Pasha[b] until 1921, and Ghazi Mustafa Kemal[c] from 1921 until 1934 *(c. 1881[d] – 10 November 1938) was a Turkish field marshal, revolutionary statesman, author, and the founding father of the Republic of Turkey, serving as its first president from 1923 until his death in 1938. He undertook sweeping progressive reforms, which modernized Turkey into a secular, industrializing nation. Ideologically a secularist and nationalist, his policies and socio-political theories became known as Kemalism. Due to his military and political accomplishments,* ***Atatürk is regarded as one of the most important political leaders of the 20th century.***

Atatürk with his Panama hat just after the Kastamonu speech in 1925
https://en.wikipedia.org/wiki/Mustafa_Kemal_Atatürk   Public Domain

Atatürk came to prominence for his role in securing the Ottoman-Turkish victory at the Battle of Gallipoli (1915) during World War I. Following the defeat and dissolution of the Ottoman Empire, he led the Turkish National Movement, which resisted mainland Turkey's partition among the victorious Allied powers. Establishing a provisional government in the present-day Turkish capital Ankara (known in English at the time as Angora), he defeated the forces sent by the Allies, thus emerging victorious from what was later referred to as the Turkish War of Independence. He subsequently proceeded to abolish the decrepit Ottoman Empire and proclaimed the foundation of the Turkish Republic in its place.

As the president of the newly formed Turkish Republic, Atatürk initiated a rigorous program of political, economic, and cultural reforms with the ultimate aim of building a modern, progressive, and secular nation-state. He made primary education free and compulsory, opening thousands of new schools all over the country. He also introduced the Latin-based Turkish alphabet, replacing the old Ottoman Turkish alphabet. Turkish women received equal civil and political rights during Atatürk's presidency. In particular, women were given voting rights in local elections by Act no. 1580 on 3 April 1930 and a few years later, in 1934, full universal suffrage.

Atatürk (right) with Reza Shah Pahlavi (left) of Iran, during the Shah's visit to Turkey https://en.wikipedia.org/wiki/Mustafa_Kemal_Atatürk   Public Domain

His government carried out a policy of Turkification, trying to create a homogeneous, unified, and above all secular nation under the Turkish banner. Under Atatürk, the few surviving indigenous minorities were asked to speak Turkish in public, but also were allowed to maintain their own languages at the same time; non-Turkish toponyms and minorities were ordered to get a Turkish surname as per Turkish renditions. The Turkish Parliament granted him the surname Atatürk in 1934, which means "Father of the Turks", in recognition of the role he played in building the modern Turkish Republic. He died on 10 November 1938 at Dolmabahçe Palace in Istanbul, at the age of 57; he was succeeded as president by his long-time prime minister İsmet İnönü and was honored with a state funeral. https://en.wikipedia.org/wiki/Mustafa_Kemal_Atatürk

A part of Turkish history worth noting came in the period before WWI that saw a major genocide campaign against the Armenians in eastern Turkey and Christians in Anatolia, western and central Turkey.   Ethnic cleansing eliminated most of the Christian and Armenian minorities.   In 1915 and 1916 a million Armenians were sent on death marches to the Syrian desert where they were robbed and massacred.   Other large groups were sent to the same fate later by the same Ottoman government.   This

Armenian civilians being deported during the Armenian genocide Picture
By anonymous German traveler - Published by the American red cross,
it was first published in the United States prior to January 1, 1923. [Aus: Politisches
Archiv des deutschen Auswärtigen Amtes. Bestand: Konstantinopel 169.], Public Domain,
https://commons.wikimedia.org/w/index.php?curid=2902685

A LONG LINE THAT SWIFTLY GREW SHORTER One of the most striking
photographs of the deportations that have come out of Armenia. Here is shown a
column of Christians on the path across the great plains of the Mamuret-ul-Aziz. The
zaptieths are shown walking along at one side.
https://commons.wikimedia.org/wiki/ Public domain, via Wikimedia Commons

history is what has led to a very high Muslim majority country. (Perhaps
this is where Hitler got his ideas for the persecution of the Jews.) Many
Armenians ended up in what is now Israel and Jerusalem has a large sector
of Armenian Christians.   The question not so easily answered is the
involvement of Atatürk in these genocide campaigns.   While he had been

associated with the nationalist movement that created the genocide, he had left the organization before WWI and was serving as a Lieutenant Colonel in western Turkey, far from the Armenian areas.   He later criticized the genocide/resettlement program of the Ottomans and it appears his objective was to unite all the minorities under a secular banner.

> Atatürk's relation to the late Ottoman genocides committed by the Young Turk movement and the dying Ottoman Empire, which to this day are denied by the Turkish government, has been the subject of his most major controversy. Atatürk had been a member of the Young Turk movement in 1908, but so had many Arabs, Albanians, Jews, and initially, Armenians and Greeks, as it was then simply an anti-Abdul Hamid movement. As for the actual occurrences of the genocides, Atatürk had since divested from the movement and was serving as a relatively junior Lieutenant Colonel fighting in Gallipoli and Western Thrace during the Armenian genocide. Historical evidence proves decisively that he was not involved with the killings, and that he later went on to condemn them. One such explicit condemnation was in September 1919, when Atatürk met with the United States Army General James Harbord, the leader of the Harbord Commission into the genocides, in Sivas. Harbord would later recall that Atatürk told him of his disapproval of the Armenian genocide and that he had allegedly stated that "the massacre and deportation of Armenians was the work of a small committee who had seized power", rather than by the government in actuality. In 1920, before the Turkish Parliament, Atatürk called the genocides a "shameful act" and made no effort to publicly deny them at that time.
>
> Atatürk's relations with Enver Pasha, a key perpetrator of the genocides, have also been controversial but poorly understood. While the two men may have been close at times, Atatürk held a personal dislike of Enver Pasha; he once said to a confidant that Enver Pasha was a dangerous figure who might lead the country to ruin.
>
> The primary concern towards Atatürk was the Turkish government's involvement with and reaction to the burning of Smyrna in 1923, which saw Muslim Turkish mobs and paramilitaries openly engaged in the mass murder of Greeks and Armenians and destroy the city's Greek and Armenian quarters, killing an estimated 100,000 people. Whether these atrocities, including the fire, were part of the genocides of Asia Minor's Christian minorities that the Turkish army and government carried out during WWI is unclear, the responsibility remains a contentious debate and it is unclear if the Turks entered the city these intentions. Many Turkish apologists argue

that the regular Turkish Army did not play a role in these events. At the time, Atatürk was commander of the Turkish armed forces and sent a telegram to Minister of Foreign Affairs Yusuf Kemal that described the official version of events in the city. In the telegram, he alleged the Greek and Armenian

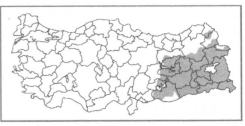

Turkey's Kurdish majority-inhabited area
by CIA (1992).jpg, By Çalak talkCC BY-SA 3.0, https://commons.wikimedia.org/w/index.php?curid=37073927

minorities had "pre-arranged plans" to "destroy İzmir". There are allegations Atatürk chose to do little about the Greek and Armenian victims of the fires caused by Muslim rioters in order to rebuild the city as Turkish-dominated İzmir.   https://en.wikipedia.org/wiki/ Mustafa_Kemal_Atatürk#Ottoman_genocides_(1913–1924)_and_Atatürk

Atatürk miraculously and completely changed the character of Turkey. Turkey's GDP places it right below Lebanon and its lifestyle still exhibits that of a European nation, especially in urban areas. The major limitation comes from political instability probably rooted in ethnic minorities wanting too much independence and a hardline authoritarian government as a balance. The balance between these two conflicting forces developed by Atatürk had created a national identity, but that has slowly been eroded. From the 1960s to 1984 the government had been subjected to several military coups and a continued internal conflict with the Kurdistan Workers' Party or PKK a Kurdish ethnic minority in eastern Turkey and Northern Iraq who are seeking a level of autonomy and freedom within Turkey. The liberalism of the economy, with less control, in the 1980s has kept it in relatively good shape.

But the current government is dramatically Islamist and eager to carry it back toward its feudal religious dictatorship past of the Ottoman Empire. This is a reversal of Atatürk's secular government approach. In any event, the westernization of Turkey by Atatürk has had a marked influence on prosperity up to the current time. A better approach to the Kurds, who occupy portions of northern Iraq, and Syria, and a small slice of Iran would be helpful.

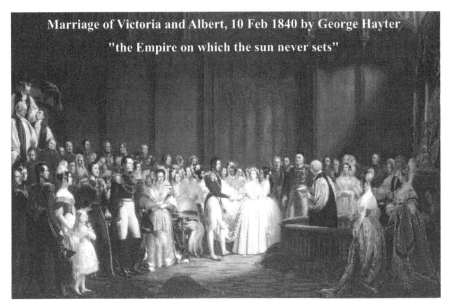

Marriage of Victoria and Albert, 10 Feb 1840 by George Hayter
"the Empire on which the sun never sets"

By George Hayter - Royal Collection RCIN 407165 http://www.royalcollection.org.uk/egallery/
object.asp?object=407165, Public Domain, https://commons.wikimedia.org/w/index.php?curid=3840797

6. The Far East: War in the Pacific

The Far East from China to Australia to India was dominated by the British into World War II. Their colonies were an active and unified part of the Allied forces in the Pacific, but it was the British influence on the governments that would later become independent that made the difference. Especially the spreading of English Common Law traditions.

Three city nation-states show a high level of financial prosperity and are worth noting. They are predominantly Asian city-states but their history has been as a city-state established and managed under European principles and law under the British and Portuguese colonial empires. They are the semi-independent Chinese cities of Hong Kong and Macau and the independent nation of Singapore.

Colonial City States

Hong Kong (British) and Macau (Portuguese) grew into thriving democratic and capitalist city-states under the guidance and direction of their colonial founders. Both were leased by the Chinese to the colonial powers for 100 years and when the lease ran out some 30 years ago they reverted to Chinese control. China at that time was emerging from the slavery of communism and turning to capitalism as a means to modernize their country, perhaps seeing the power of capitalism to create prosperity in those city-states. When China took over they did something extraordinary, similar to Russia returning property to pre-communist owners. China left the local governments, laws, and capitalist environment to continue with little interference, only demanding their acceptance as part of China. The result was that these city-states are some of the most prosperous mini nations in the world, all thanks to their founding principles and Western European laws, the justice system, and Christian-influenced way of life.

Singapore, like Hong Kong, is a former British colony and follows the British common law and Westminster form of government. The government is more autocratic and controlling than others with some controls over the press and some harsh punishments for convicted criminals, especially political corruption and drug and gun law violations. English is the official language of government and education, and Christianity is the religion of about 18% of its people with Buddhism the most popular with about 33%.

> Singapore has a highly developed market economy, based historically on extended entrepôt trade. Along with Hong Kong, South Korea, and Taiwan, Singapore is one of the original Four Asian Tigers but has surpassed its peers in terms of GDP per capita. Between 1965 and 1995, growth rates averaged around 6 percent per annum, transforming the living standards of the population. The Singaporean economy is known as one of the freest, most innovative, most competitive, most dynamic, and most business-friendly. The 2015 Index of Economic Freedom ranks Singapore as the second freest economy in the world and the Ease of Doing Business Index has also ranked Singapore as the easiest place to do business for the past decade. According to the Corruption Perceptions Index, Singapore is consistently perceived as

one of the least corrupt countries in the world, along with New Zealand and the Scandinavian countries.   https://en.wikipedia.org/wiki/Singapore

Japan

Modern Japan is as much the creation of General Douglas MacArthur as anything else. His management of the Allied Occupation at the end of WWII guided Japan toward a future they could never have imagined. A brief review of MacArthur's life is necessary to set the stage.

Douglas MacArthur *(26 January 1880 – 5 April 1964) was an American military leader who served as General of the Army for the United States, as well as a field marshal to the Philippine Army. He was Chief of Staff of the United States Army during the 1930s, and he played a prominent role in the Pacific theater during World War II. MacArthur received the Medal of Honor for his service in the Philippines campaign. This made him along with his father Arthur MacArthur Jr. the first father and son to be awarded the medal. He was one of only five to rise to the rank of General of the Army in the U.S. Army, and the only one conferred the rank of field marshal in the Philippine Army.*

General of the Army Douglas MacArthur smoking his corncob pipe, probably at Manila, Philippine Islands, Public Domain Army Signal Corps, 2 August 1945   https://en.wikipedia.org/wiki/ Douglas_MacArthur

Raised in a military family in the American Old West, MacArthur was valedictorian at the West Texas Military Academy where he finished high school, and First Captain at the United States Military Academy at West Point, where he graduated top of the class of 1903. During the 1914 United States occupation of Veracruz, he conducted a reconnaissance mission, for which he was nominated for the Medal of Honor. In 1917, he was promoted from major to colonel and became chief of staff of the 42nd (Rainbow) Division. In the fighting on the Western

Front during World War I, he rose to the rank of brigadier general, was again nominated for a Medal of Honor, and was awarded the Distinguished Service Cross twice and the Silver Star seven times.

From 1919 to 1922, MacArthur served as Superintendent of the U.S. Military Academy at West Point, where he attempted a series of reforms. His next assignment was in the Philippines, wherein 1924 he was instrumental in quelling the Philippine Scout Mutiny. In 1925, he became the Army's youngest major general. He served on the court-martial of Brigadier General Billy Mitchell and was president of the American Olympic Committee during the 1928 Summer Olympics in Amsterdam. In 1930, he became Chief of Staff of the United States Army. As such, he was involved in the expulsion of the Bonus Army protesters from Washington, D.C., in 1932, and the establishment and organization of the Civilian Conservation Corps. In 1935 he became a Military Advisor to the Commonwealth Government of the Philippines. He retired from the U.S. Army in 1937 and continued being the chief military advisor to the Philippines.

MacArthur was recalled to active duty in 1941 as commander of the United States Army Forces in the Far East. A series of disasters followed, starting with the destruction of his air forces on 8 December 1941 and the Japanese invasion of the Philippines. MacArthur's forces were soon compelled to withdraw to Bataan, where they held out until May 1942. In March 1942, MacArthur, his family, and his staff left nearby Corregidor Island in PT boats and escaped to Australia, where MacArthur became supreme commander of the Southwest Pacific Area. Upon his arrival, MacArthur gave a speech in which he promised "I shall return" to the Philippines. After more than two years of fighting, he fulfilled that promise. For his defense of the Philippines, MacArthur was awarded the Medal of Honor. He officially accepted the surrender of Japan on 2 September 1945 aboard the USS Missouri, which was anchored in Tokyo Bay, and he oversaw the occupation of Japan from 1945 to 1951. As the effective ruler of Japan, he oversaw sweeping economic, political, and social changes.

He led the United Nations Command in the Korean War with initial success; however, the invasion of North Korea provoked the Chinese, causing a series of major defeats. MacArthur was contentiously removed from command by President Harry S. Truman on 11 April 1951. He later became chairman of the board of Remington Rand. He died in Washington, D.C. on 5 April 1964 at the age of 84.

https://en.wikipedia.org/wiki/Douglas_MacArthur

General Pershing decorates Brigadier General MacArthur with the Distinguished Service Cross. 1 Jan 2018 US Army, Public domain, via Wikimedia Commons   https://commons.wikimedia.org/wiki/

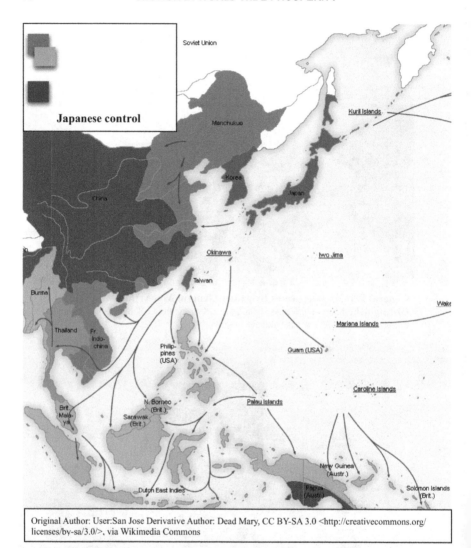

The War in the Pacific

The day after Pearl Harbor, on 8 Dec 1941 Japan launched a major offensive to capture the Philippines which had a large American force under General Douglas MacArthur.   MacArthur chose to defend his position from the Bataan Peninsula and the Island of Corregidor, which was situated west of Manila Bay and the city of Manila, to prevent the Japanese access and use of Manila Bay. When supplies and ammo ran low

MacArthur (center) with his Chief of Staff, Major General Richard K. Sutherland, in the Headquarters tunnel on Corregidor, Philippines, on 1 March 1942
https://commons.wikimedia.org/wiki Ç Public domain, via Wikimedia Commons

Roosevelt ordered MacArthur to leave for Australia.

Lieutenant General Jonathan M. Wainwright assumed command in the Philippines. The Japanese had taken Manila and Bataan fell on 9 April, with the 76,000 American and Filipino prisoners of war captured and forced to endure a 66-mile forced evacuation, known as the Bataan Death March. The remaining forces on the island of Corregidor surrendered on 6 May. Wainwright received the Congressional Medal of Honor for his service and stood behind MacArthur at the Japanese surrender ceremony.

Corregidor
Manila Bay
and Bataan

By Hellerick - Own work, CC BY-SA 3.0, https://commons.wikimedia.org/w/index.php curid=26702961

MacArthur had been appointed Supreme Allied Commander for the South West Pacific but had to work with Admiral Chester Nimitz, who had responsibility for the rest of the Pacific Ocean. This dual command of American forces required major negotiations on strategies and tactics as the plan emerged to gradually retake islands held by the Japanese and move toward the Philippines and then toward Japan. The island-hopping approach required

Wainwright ordering the surrender of the Philippines while being monitored by a Japanese censor https://commons.wikimedia.org/wiki File:Jonathan_Wainwright_under_Imperial_Japanese_ army.jpg
比島派遣軍報道部, a sort of Imperial army's news agency, Public domain, via Wikimedia Commons

major support from the Navy and Nimitz. Many key naval battles took place as this plan proceeded, to culminate with the Battle of the Philippine Sea and then the Battle of Leyte Gulf. These two sea battles ended

Conference in Hawaii, July 1944. Left to right:
General MacArthur, President Roosevelt,
Admiral Leahy, Admiral Nimitz.
https://commons.wikimedia.org/wiki/

"I have returned" 20 Oct 1944– General MacArthur returns to the Philippines with
Philippine President Sergio Osmeña to his right, Philippine Foreign Affairs Secretary Carlos P.
Romulo at his rear, and Lieutenant General Richard K. Sutherland on his left.
File:MacArthur_and_Sutherland_s265357.jpg U.S. Army Signal Corps, Public domain, via Wikimedia Commons

Japanese domination of the seas and opened the door to MacArthur's
return to the Philippines and further island hopping toward Japan which
the Japanese were unable to withstand.

Significant and brutal battles for the islands of Iwo Jima and Okinawa
resulted in the occupation of key airstrips for the bombardment of Japan
and a launching point for an invasion of Japan.

Ending the War

Hard-fought battles on the Japanese islands of Iwo Jima, Okinawa, and
others resulted in horrific casualties on both sides but finally produced a
Japanese defeat. Of the 117,000 Okinawan and Japanese troops defending
Okinawa, 94 percent died. Faced with the loss of most of their experienced
pilots, the Japanese increased their use of kamikaze tactics in an attempt to
create unacceptably high casualties for the Allies. The US Navy proposed to
force a Japanese surrender through a total naval blockade and air raids.
Many military historians believe that the Okinawa campaign led directly to

the atomic bombings of Hiroshima and Nagasaki, as a means of avoiding the planned ground invasion of the Japanese mainland.
https://en.wikipedia.org/wiki/Pacific_War

Raising the Flag on Iwo Jima, by Joe Rosenthal https://www.apncws.com/Public Domain, https://commons.wikimedia.org/w/index.phpcurid=77823832

The view that the decision making to use the atomic bomb was a result of the fierce battles for Iwo Jima and Okinawa is explained by Victor Davis Hanson:

"Because the Japanese on Okinawa... were so fierce in their defense (even when cut off, and without supplies), and because casualties were so appalling, many American strategists looked for an alternative means to subdue mainland Japan, other than a direct invasion. This means presented itself, with the advent of atomic bombs, which worked admirably in convincing the Japanese to sue for peace [unconditionally], without American casualties."

(Hanson, Victor Davis (2004). Ripples of Battle: How Wars of the Past Still Determine How We Fight, How We Live, and How We Think (illustrated, reprint ed.). Anchor Books. ISBN 978-0-38572194-3.)

MacArthur signs the Japanese Instrument of Surrender aboard the USS Missouri. American General Jonathan Wainwright and British General Arthur Percival stand behind him.https://commons.wikimedia.org/wiki United States Navy, Public domain, via Wikimedia Commons

Some Additional resource information can be found here.

1. *The Untold Story of Douglas Mac Arthur by Frazier Hunt, The Devin-Adair Company New York 1954*
2. *War in the Pacific by Jerome T. Hagen © 2006, Volumes I, II, III ISBN Vol I, 0-9762669-3-8*
3. *Pacific War, Wikipedia https://en.wikipedia.org/wiki/Pacific_War*

Rebuilding Japan

As Supreme Commander for the Allied Powers (SCAP) in Japan, MacArthur and his staff helped Japan rebuild itself, eradicate militarism and ultra-nationalism, promote political civil liberties, institute democratic government, and chart a new course that ultimately made Japan one of the world's leading industrial powers. The U.S. was firmly in control of Japan to oversee its reconstruction, and MacArthur was effectively the interim leader of Japan from 1945 until 1948. In 1946, MacArthur's staff drafted a new constitution that renounced war and stripped the Emperor of his military authority. The constitution—which became effective on 3 May

1947—instituted a parliamentary system of government, under which the Emperor acted only on the advice of his ministers. It included the famous Article 9, which outlawed belligerency as an instrument of state policy and the maintenance of a standing army. The constitution also enfranchised women, guaranteed fundamental human rights, outlawed racial discrimination, strengthened the powers of Parliament and the Cabinet, and decentralized the police and local government.

> A major land reform was also conducted, led by Wolf Ladejinsky of MacArthur's SCAP staff. Between 1947 and 1949, approximately 4,700,000 acres (1,900,000 ha), or 38% of Japan's cultivated land, were purchased from the landlords under the government's reform program, and 4,600,000 acres (1,860,000 ha) were resold to the farmers who worked them. By 1950, 89% of all agricultural land was owner-operated and only 11% was tenant-operated. MacArthur's efforts to encourage trade union membership met with phenomenal success, and by 1947, 48% of the non-agricultural workforce was unionized. Some of MacArthur's reforms were rescinded in 1948 when his unilateral control of Japan was ended by the increased involvement of the State Department. During the Occupation, SCAP successfully, if not entirely, abolished many of the financial coalitions known as the Zaibatsu, which had previously monopolized industry. Eventually, looser industrial groupings known as Keiretsu evolved. The reforms alarmed many in the U.S. Departments of Defense and State, who believed they conflicted with the prospect of Japan and its industrial capacity as a bulwark against the spread of communism in Asia.
> _https://en.wikipedia.org/wiki/Douglas_MacArthur#Occupation_of_Japan_

Another document that sheds further light on MacArthur's role in creating a new government and culture in Japan is a University of New Orleans thesis on MacArthur's relationship with the Japanese people and why they were attracted to him.

> An Honors Thesis Presented to the Dept of International Studies of the University of New Orleans
> Title: American Shogun: Reasons Why the Japanese were Fascinated with General MacArthur by Tommy Louk, May 2012
> https://scholarworks.uno.edu/honors_theses/15/

Abstract *This paper will provide insight into why the Japanese liked General MacArthur during the American occupation of Japan after World War II. By using letters that the Japanese sent to MacArthur I will show that the Japanese saw him as a liberator. The Japanese people were tired of the brutal rule by the military and were pleased with free speech and the right to assembly that MacArthur bestowed upon them. The Japanese people did not trust their leaders but trusted MacArthur to fix their country. The Japanese people thought that MacArthur was liberating them from war, poverty, and despair.*

The most interesting way the Japanese people expressed themselves to MacArthur was through fan mail. MacArthur received almost 500,000 letters from the Japanese people. Some of them thanked him and America for their generosity or policies; others asked him for favors or gave suggestions. Few were criticisms of the occupation

It is clear in the letters written to MacArthur that the Japanese people thought he was a liberator. The letters provide many explanations and examples of the Japanese treating MacArthur as a liberator and their motivations for doing so. General MacArthur liberated the Japanese people from the war, hunger, the Japanese politicians, the emperor, and from despair. Most of the Japanese truly enjoyed MacArthur's actions and rule as Supreme Commander. The Japanese liked MacArthur because they believed his actions and policies were more beneficial compared to the old ways and old government. **MacArthur was seen as a liberator to the Japanese people during the occupation of Japan.**

The author points out however that it was more than MacArthur himself that caught the attention of the Japanese people. During the occupation, more than 350,000 US personnel were stationed throughout Japan. The local population had heard the horror stories of their own troops' occupation of China and elsewhere so were expecting the worst. They warned people to flee the cities if they could and for women to not come out of their houses unless absolutely necessary.

What happened was totally unexpected by the Japanese. The anticipated atrocities never occurred. Further, the occupying forces were kind to the Japanese, especially the children, and helped with disasters, provided food where needed, and even gave up their seats on crowded trains and buses to the Japanese women, something the women had never seen before. None of this was forced upon the occupying personnel, it was something that came from their inner being as to how to treat people who were suffering.

The transformation of Japan can actually be credited to two people, President Harry Truman and Douglas MacArthur. Truman appointed MacArthur, as the Supreme Commander of Allied Powers, SCAP, to supervise the occupation of Japan. Initially, it was expected that occupation would be jointly performed by each major member of the Allied Powers, which included Russia, in a similar manner to the occupation of Germany. Between Truman and MacArthur, they took over the entire job. This probably came from Truman's distrust of Stalin and the Russians after he met with them at Yalta. In any event, it prevented Japan from being split up and forming a communist Japanese nation, similar to North Korea.

Harry S. Truman (May 8, 1884 – December 26, 1972) was the 33rd president of the United States, serving from 1945 to 1953. A leader of the Democratic Party, he previously served as the 34th vice president from January to April 1945 under Franklin Roosevelt and as a United States senator from Missouri from 1935 to January 1945. Assuming the presidency after Roosevelt's death, Truman implemented the Marshall Plan to rebuild the economy of Western Europe and established both the Truman Doctrine and NATO to contain the expansion of Soviet communism. He proposed numerous liberal domestic reforms, but few were enacted by the conservative coalition that dominated the Congress.

President Harry S. Truman
National Archives and Records Administration. Office of Presidential Libraries. Harry S. Truman Library. -, Public Domain, https:// commons.wikimedia.org/w/ index.php?curid=79198241

Truman grew up in Independence, Missouri, and during World War I fought in France as a captain in the Field Artillery. Returning home, he opened a haberdashery in Kansas City, Missouri, and was elected as a judge of Jackson County in 1922. Truman was elected to the United States Senate from Missouri in 1934. In 1940–1944 he gained national prominence as

chairman of the Truman Committee, which was aimed at reducing waste and inefficiency in wartime contracts. Truman was elected vice president in 1944 and assumed the presidency following the death of Roosevelt.
https://en.wikipedia.org/wiki/Harry_S._Truman

Truman knew MacArthur was a "take charge" leader, and that was exactly what MacArthur did when he took the job. MacArthur was also the master of the image. One of the most famous pictures in Japanese history is the picture of MacArthur with the Emperor of Japan, Hirohito. The emperor is dressed in his formal attire with a tie while MacArthur chose to wear his military work uniform rather than his dress uniform, thus demonstrating that this was indeed an occupation. At the same time, MacArthur resisted urgings and attempts by the Japanese relatives of Hirohito to force him to abdicate

MacArthur and the Emperor of Japan, Hirohito, at their first meeting, September 1945 Public Domain U.S. Army photographer Lt. Gaetano Faillace - United States Army photograph https://en.wikipedia.org/wiki/Douglas_MacArthur

and kept Hirohito as the symbolic Japanese leader during the occupation.

Truman established the mission of the occupation in a document titled, "US Initial Post-Surrender Policy for Japan". This document was put in place on 6 Sept, 4 days after the official Japanese surrender on 2 Sept 1945. It became MacArthur's marching orders. The document had two main objectives for the occupation and MacArthur was the ideal leader to make that happen.

Occupation of Japan: Two Objectives

1. Eliminating Japan's war potential
2. Turning Japan into a Western-style nation with a pro-American orientation.

The initial image of MacArthur as the man in charge of the Occupation probably could not have been worse for the Japanese people. Here was a man who had been driven from the Philippines, chased all over the South Pacific, seen hundreds of thousands of American lives lost in battle, and yet had been tenacious enough to persevere to a successful conclusion of the war despite all Japan could muster. The Japanese people were expecting exactly what their own leaders had done to the Chinese and Koreans earlier. And certainly, if anyone would have felt righteous indignation toward a nation, you would think it would be MacArthur. But he brought a different mindset to the occupation.

His first two edicts were that no Occupation forces were to assault Japanese citizens or eat any local Japanese foods. Food supplies and starvation were an immediate crisis, solved by multiple approaches from the charitable groups and the US government. MacArthur was on top of all the details, and flexible enough to reverse or change any policy that was not effective. Policies were initiated, operated for a while, and then seemingly abandoned in favor of something new.

The reversal of Japan's fortunes took place because of the fierce determination of MacArthur, who was on top of the politics and the details and had a grand vision guiding him. It didn't hurt to have an equally hardheaded and pragmatic president behind him. His experience with setbacks and defeats during WWII perhaps also aided his resiliency to quickly adapt to changing circumstances. They supported labor unions against the wishes of the industrial powers and broke up the large farming conglomerates that had owned most of the farmland, returning most of it to local farmers who occupied the land and farmed it. For additional details look here.

https://en.wikibooks.org/wiki/Japanese_History/The_American_Occupation_of_Japan

Japan Recovers The current government of Japan is now a constitutional monarchy similar to Great Britain but with two houses of elected representatives that select the Prime Minister who is the head of government. The judicial system which had been based on Chinese law was changed in the late 1800s to a European style of civil law largely modeled on the German judicial system. Christianity itself has had little following in Japan (about 2.3%) with Folk Shinto the predominant religion with flavors of Buddhism often mixed into Shinto.   But Japan is a homogeneous nation ethnically with only a few percent born outside Japan and most of those to Japanese nationals of foreign descent.   Tradition reigns, but the influence of MacArther and the 350,000 Christian soldiers, at least in terms of philosophy, have had a distinct impact on Japan's resulting prosperity in terms of how it conducts its government and businesses around the world. Japan's economic ranking on the GDP PPP charts is 45th, in the lower Western World-dominated area but even higher in a broader assessment to be discussed later.

South Korea

South Korea is one of the "Four Tigers of Asia" along with Singapore, Taiwan, and Hong Kong. It has two distinct differences from its cousins, a lack of ties to one of the old Colonial empires and an extremely large Christian base, unique in that part of the world. But it also shares a factor with Japan, a connection with Douglas MacArthur.

The Korean War: Following the end of WWII Korea, which had been under the control of Japan, was split between North and South by an agreement between the US and the Soviet Union.   This was perhaps a concession with the Soviet Union after President Truman kept Japan from being divided. After both North and South had determined their political leaders, the Soviet Union, supported by China, declared the leader of North Korea to be the head of all of Korea.   North Korean troops, reinforced by the Soviet Union invaded the South on 25 June 1950. At this time the Soviet Union had boycotted the United Nations so it forfeited its voting rights, and veto power allowing the UN to intervene in the civil war when the North's victory seemed to be certain.

Thus a fluke of luck over a procedural issue at the UN came to the rescue of South Korea and would bring Douglas MacArthur back to the battlefield. MacArthur had spent 5 years acting as the surrogate leader of Occupied Japan and dealing with all manner of political and administrative policies. He returned to the battlefield when the war was seemingly lost, and as he had done in the War in the Pacific, launched a masterpiece strategic and tactical battle plan that completely reversed the fortunes of the Korean War.   US forces had been driven down to the southern end of the Korean Peninsula, losing the city of Soul to the North Korean Army.

Seeking a way to reverse the fortunes of the war, MacArthur developed a bold plan of attack but was met with resistance from other US and UN commanders.   MacArthur was determined to make it happen, however. He had had the same command problems during WWII, having to negotiate with the Navy for support on the island-hopping strategy. After many hours and days of arm-twisting and lobbying, he finally received the concurrence of the other field commanders to proceed with his plan. The plan was a tactical encirclement and landing at lightly defended Inchon on the west central coast of Korea. They would then go on to encircle, cut off, and capture large numbers of North Korean troops to the south.

At the beginning of Sept 1950, UN and US forces had been driven down into a small segment of southeastern South Korea.   MacArthur's attack on Inchon began on the 15th of Sept and by the end of the month had retaken most of South Korea from the North Korean troops. Soul was liberated and the North Korean Army was pushed all the way north to the Chinese border.   By Dec 1950, UN forces had occupied most of North Korea when the Chinese communist army entered the war on North Korea's side.

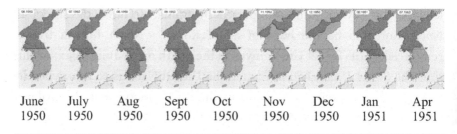

| June 1950 | July 1950 | Aug 1950 | Sept 1950 | Oct 1950 | Nov 1950 | Dec 1950 | Jan 1951 | Apr 1951 |

Rapid Swing of Korean War June 1950 - Apr 1951
Pink area occupied by North Korean forces, Green area occupied by UN
Individual gif files taken from https://commons.wikimedia.org/wiki/File:Korean_war_1950-1953.gif

The Battle of Incheon (Korean: 인천상륙작전*; Hanja:* 仁川上陸作戰*;*
RR: Incheon Sangnyuk Jakjeon), also spelled Battle of Inchon, was an
amphibious invasion and a battle of the Korean War that resulted in a

decisive victory and strategic reversal in favor of the United Nations
Command (UN). The operation involved some 75,000 troops and 261 naval
vessels and led to the recapture of the South Korean capital of Seoul two
weeks later.[4] The code name for the operation was Operation Chromite.

The battle began on 15 September 1950 and ended on 19 September.
Through a surprise amphibious assault far from the Pusan Perimeter that
UN and Republic of Korea Army (ROK) forces were desperately defending,
the largely undefended city of Incheon was secured after being bombed by
UN forces. The battle ended a string of victories by the North Korean People's
Army (KPA). The subsequent UN recapture of Seoul partially severed the
KPA's supply lines in South Korea.

The UN and ROK forces were commanded by General of the Army
Douglas MacArthur of the United States Army. MacArthur was the driving
force behind the operation, overcoming the strong misgivings of more
cautious generals to a risky assault over extremely unfavorable terrain. The
battle was followed by a rapid collapse of the KPA; within a month of the
Incheon landing, the Americans had taken 135,000 KPA troops and
prisoners.

https://en.wikipedia.org/wiki/Battle_of_Inchon.

MacArthur observes the naval shelling of Inchon from USS Mount McKinley, 15
September 1950 with Brigadier General Courtney Whitney (left) and Major General
Edward M. Almond (right)..
https://commons.wikimedia.org/wiki/File:IncheonLandingMcArthur.jpg
Nutter (Army), Public domain, via Wikimedia Commons

MacArthur developed several alternatives to deal with the Chinese army but lost his arguments with President Truman and was relieved of his command for taking the negotiations with Truman public.   With MacArthur gone the resulting battle strategy allowed the Chinese to retake the North Korean territories and the battle ended in a stalemate about the 38th parallel where it had begun.

A euphoric ticker-tape parade for MacArthur in Chicago on 26 April 1951. The general is in the second car, a bright red Cadillac convertible about to turn off the Michigan Avenue Bridge

Relieved of his command, MacArthur returned to the US for the first time in 14 years to a rousing welcome from Americans who had followed the results of both wars and the occupation of Japan. He received a ticker-tape parade in Chicago and spoke before 50,000 people at Soldier Field, his goodbye to a life serving in the Military. Later speeches to Congress and West Point are also memorable and can be found in audio format on the internet.

South Korea emerges from War

The war was devastating to both North and South Korea, virtually all of their major cities were destroyed and over 3 million civilians were killed, a higher percentage than in both WWII and the Vietnam War. Korea had only an autocratic ruler history and tradition so South Korea began with somewhat that same mindset after the war. Political instability eventually drove the first president, Syngman Rhee out of office in 1960 and after 13 months of instability, a coup led by General Park Chung Hee took over.

Chung Hee was considered a ruthless dictator but at the same time, he presided over rapid economic growth based on exports, and South Korea also took an active role in the Vietnam War. Chung Hee was assassinated in 1979 after 17 years in office, during which time the government developed a nationwide expressway system and the Seoul subway system.

Park Chung-hee 5-9th president of South Korea, public domain

The political battle that followed Chung Hee's assassination brought General Chun Doo-hwan to power and he ruled as president until 1987. Doo-hwan's rule ended when a Seoul University student was tortured to death and the Catholic Priests Association for Justice revealed the incident. Protests across the country caused Doo-hwan's political party leader, Roh Tae-woo to announce the June 29 Declaration that included the direct election of the president. Roh narrowly won the election and the following year, 1987 South Korea hosted the Olympic Games, a big boost to their world image and economy. Presidential politics has remained rocky up to the Covid pandemic with the first woman president being kicked out of office for corruption and put in jail. This political turmoil has been somewhat the result of North Korea's continued belligerence and military attacks on South Korean land and their military. Despite the political turmoil, the economy of South Korea has continued to excel.

The economy of South Korea *The economy is a technologically advanced developed country driven by a highly educated and skilled workforce, having the world's eighth-highest median household income, the highest in Asia. Globally, it ranks highly in personal safety, job security, ease of doing business, and healthcare quality, with the world's third highest health-adjusted life expectancy and the fourth most efficient healthcare system. It is the world's largest spender on R&D per GDP, leading the OECD in graduates in science and engineering and ranking third in the Youth Wellbeing Index. Home of Samsung, LG, and Hyundai-Kia, South Korea was named the world's most innovative country for 4 consecutive years since 2014 in the Bloomberg Innovation Index, ranking first in business R&D intensity, manufacturing value-added, patents filed per GDP, second in higher education efficiency and fourth in high-tech density and researcher concentration. In 2005, it became the world's first country to fully transition to high-speed Internet and today it has the world's fastest Internet speed and highest smartphone ownership, ranking first in ICT Development, e-Government, and 4G LTE coverage.* **South Korea currently provides the world's second-largest number of Christian missionaries, surpassed only by the United States.**

Although South Korea experienced a series of military dictatorships from the 1960s up until the 1980s, it has since developed into a successful liberal democracy. Today, the CIA World Factbook describes South Korea's democracy as a "fully functioning modern democracy".
https://en.wikipedia.org/wiki/South_Korea

Did you notice that last statement about Christian Missionaries from South Korea? With some 56% of the population claiming no religious affiliation, Christianity, at about 27% is by far the largest with Buddhism at about 15%. (Wikipedia gives some conflicting numbers for this statistic. Regardless the number of missionaries certainly speaks of Christianity's influence.) Christianity is also not a recent phenomenon but began back in the 18th century and took hold due to the weaknesses of the Korean Sindo religion (an animistic folk religion) which predominated at that time.

South Korea's prosperity, then, is a product of its large Christian population and its capitalist and democratic society. Uniquely it has become prosperous all on its own, without the help of former colonial powers creating and managing the government and creating the society first.

People's Republic of China (PRC):
Administrative Divisions & Territorial Disputes

China

We can't conclude this discussion without addressing China as it is a world economic power. That power has come however from a partial abandonment of the communist centrally planned economy.

> NOTE: The flavor of the Wikipedia article below on Shanghai China has changed significantly during the course of research on China. The new text de-emphasizes the capitalist leanings and accomplishments in line with China's renewed emphasis on communism. The older article included here shows the early emphasis by China on economic competition with the West. China is now feeling the pinch of competition with other SE Asia countries so their move to re-adjust is maybe only a response to that competition by exerting more control over the economy. Time will tell. The old article below is, at least, a historical look at China's thinking about its economy before 2020.

> ***SHANGHAI China:*** *From its founding in 1949 until late 1978, the People's Republic of China was a Soviet-style centrally planned economy. Following Mao's death in 1976 and the consequent end of the Cultural*

Revolution, Deng Xiaoping and the new Chinese leadership began to reform the economy and move towards a more market-oriented mixed economy under one-party rule. Agricultural collectivization was dismantled and farmlands privatized, while foreign trade became a major new focus, leading to the creation of Special Economic Zones (SEZs). Inefficient state-owned enterprises (SOEs) were restructured and unprofitable ones were closed outright, resulting in massive job losses. Modern-day China is mainly characterized as having a market economy based on private property ownership and is one of the leading examples of state capitalism. The state still dominates in strategic "pillar" sectors such as energy production and heavy industries, but private enterprise has expanded enormously, with around 30 million private businesses recorded in 2008."

Since economic liberalization began in 1978, China has been among the world's fastest-growing economies, relying largely on investment- and export-led growth. According to the IMF, China's annual average GDP growth between 2001 and 2010 was 10.5%. Between 2007 and 2011, China's economic growth rate was equivalent to all of the G7 countries' growth combined. According to the Global Growth Generators index announced by Citigroup in February 2011, China has a very high 3G growth rating. Its high productivity, low labor costs and relatively good infrastructure have made it a global leader in manufacturing. However, the Chinese economy is highly energy-intensive and inefficient; China became the world's largest energy consumer in 2010, relies on coal to supply over 70% of its energy needs, and surpassed the US to become the world's largest oil importer in September 2013. In the early 2010s, China's economic growth rate began to slow amid domestic credit troubles, weakening international demand for Chinese exports and fragility in the global economy.(From a no longer available text in Wikipedia)

While we are missing a hard reference now, the true reality is that, like Russia, China has abandoned communism and recognized that private property and to some extent, free enterprise is the road to prosperity. How far they will go depends on the top managers. At any time they can get cold feet or become afraid of the changes and modify them. They still control some large industries that are under state management, a form of socialism called state capitalism. Those in the one-party government who manage these enterprises are still answerable to the national government leadership for failures, especially economic failures. Thus the government has the added burden of making the same business decisions that are made by competition in a truly capitalist economy, all the while being careful to make the correct political decisions that keep those government decision-makers out of jail.

China does have a very large economy, but with approximately 1.4 billion people and a workforce approaching 800 million the wealth is spread around. This has produced a rising middle class, with many now living in large high rises in the great cities of eastern China. Its political nature continues to be its own worst enemy so the future of prosperity as we are discussing it is uncertain. The heavy-handed suppression of alternative thinking is never a formula for success.

Shanghai, Macau, Hong Kong, a nod to the West

It's too early to tell whether China will gradually become more democratic and turn over all industries to a competitive capitalist approach or not. Certainly, they have role models to emulate in Hong Kong and Macau. Hong Kong and Macau were British and Portuguese-run Asian trading regions that became prosperous under capitalism but were returned to Chinese control in the late 1990s. China has let them continue with their capitalist

CC BY-SA 3.0, https://commons.wikimedia.org/w/index.php?curid=1466594

economies and apparently seeing the light, they made Shanghai a special case of a more open free enterprise and competition-based economy, a set aside as a pilot program by the Chinese government. Indeed Shanghai is allowed a measure of autonomy from China's totalitarian government management and has competitive shipbuilding and auto manufacturing enterprises. It is also China's financial and commercial center. As such it is China's role model for its economic future and is responsible for most of China's high scores in world GDP economic analysis. China's heavy-handed COVID policies, especially those that shut down all outdoor activities for many days, actually locking people in their apartments had led to large-scale criticisms by the public and in response, autocratic crackdowns on speech. China is quick to try and gain an advantage against the US wherever it senses a weakness so we don't know where these current policies are headed. For a while, it seemed as if China had learned its free enterprise lessons, but the totalitarian political power, (in 2023) controlled by its leadership seem to be growing more rigid and unyielding. Threats against Taiwan and attempts to control world open seas regions in SE Asia that are unfriendly to their SE Asia neighbors, including Viet Nam make China indeed a work in progress.

Taiwan

Taiwan is one of the four tigers of Asia along with Hong Kong, South Korea, and Singapore, known for its rapid industrialization in the latter part of the 20th century often called the Taiwan miracle.   Taiwan is considered a developed country with a large technological and industrial base and has a very high level of education, perhaps the best in the world.

Political support from the US after WWII is probably a heavy influencer although there was no occupation by the US as was the case with Japan.   For 30 years after the end of WWII Taiwan was supported and defended by the US militarily from being taken over by the Chinese Communists on the mainland. US support came because of the Cold War and support for a wartime ally. With that support came a light version of the occupation of Japan, a friendly persuasion version that is probably a big contributing factor to Taiwan's economic success today.

Taiwan was the last stronghold of the anti-communist Chinese leader **Chiang Kai-shek** who was also the Allied Commander in Chief in China during WWII. This defense of Taiwan by the US was an enduring effort that included US Navy ships intervening in the sea between China and Taiwan and the deployment of US air defense weapons on Taiwan. During this time Taiwan was run by Chiang Kai-shek as a dictatorship with few freedoms for the population.   Chiang Kai-shek had been the Supreme Commander of Allied forces in China while Eisenhower was the Supreme Allied Commander in Europe. They had even met in 1943 at the Cairo Conference where the picture of Chiang Kai-shek with Roosevelt and Churchill was taken. Mainland China and Mao were brutal cold war

Franklin_D._Roosevelt,_Chiang,Kai_Shek,_and_Churchill_in_Cairo
,_Egypt 1943 **(Eisenhower was also an attendee at this meeting.)**
https://commons.wikimedia.org/wiki File: xxx NARA_-_196609.jpg
National Archives and Records Administration, Public domain, via Wikimedia

enemies and Taiwan became part of the West's territory to protect against the scourge of Communism.

The government was a dictatorship and Taiwan was under martial law until 1987, some 12 years after the death of Chiang Kai-shek in 1975. The first president took office in 1988 and the first elected president came in 1996.

Up until this point Taiwan claimed to be the legitimate government of mainland China.

American cultural influence has also been a big factor in establishing the character of the country. The top sports attractions in Taiwan are American baseball first followed by basketball. This hints at the American influence which also extended similarly to Japan with baseball.

Perhaps the picture of President Eisenhower visiting Taiwan is a clue to that friendly persuasion. China had been bombarding an island that was considered part of Taiwan and Eisenhower was visiting as a show of support for Taiwan.

With President Chiang Kai-shek of the Republic of China, the U.S. President Dwight D. Eisenhower waved hands to Taiwanese people during his visit to Taipei, Taiwan in June 1960.
https://commons.wikimedia.org/wiki/File:U.S._President_Eisenhower_visited_TAIWAN **Public Domain**

The other major American influence has been the spirit of freedom and independence. There are two major political parties one leaning toward becoming rejoined with mainland China and the other leaning toward full independence. In a poll taken every year from 1992 by a University, the personally assumed identity of the population is measured. The expanding independent leanings of the population are shown in the following chart. Results from an identity survey conducted each year from 1992 to 2020 by

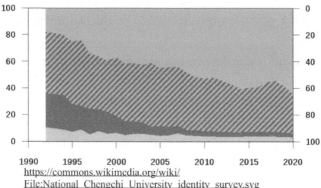

https://commons.wikimedia.org/wiki/
File:National_Chengchi_University_identity_survey.svg
Kanguole, CC BY-SA 4.0 <https://creativecommons.org/licenses/
by-sa/4.0>. via Wikimedia Commons

the Election Study Center, National Chengchi University.   Identity Responses are; Taiwanese (green), Chinese (red), Both Taiwanese and Chinese (hatched), and No response is shown as grey.

In 2020 over 60% in the survey identified as Taiwanese with only about 3% identifying as Chinese and about 32% identifying as both. Citizens are identifying increasingly as Taiwanese rather than Chinese as their economy booms.

Taiwan also has a strong religious freedom identity and hosts a number of religions with Buddhism, Taoism, Yiguandao, Roman Catholicism, and Protestantism, as the main ones. Christianity has about a 5.8% share.   Taiwan also has a tradition of freedom of speech and expression.   These openness traditions and especially the religious traditions represent an extreme contrast to the brutal life under communism that emerged in mainland China after WWII.   Taiwan's freedom of speech also strongly contrasts with the anti-free speech policies of Mainland China, demonstrated by the suppression of free speech advocates in Hong Kong and the Chinese hostility to Christianity in China.

Reference:https://en.wikipedia.org/wiki/History_of_Taiwan_(1945–present)

The Taiwan capital city of Taipei - Taipei 101, the tall tower, was the tallest building in the world until 2009.
https://commons.wikimedia.org/wiki/File:Taipei_Skyline_2022.06.29.jpg
毛貓大少爺, CC BY-SA 2.0 <https://creativecommons.org/licenses/by-sa/2.0>, via Wikimedia Commons

Christianity in China

Christianity in mainland China is seen as a threat to the authoritative rule by the Communist Party. While Christianity has been officially sanctioned by the Chinese government, it does, periodically, try to control speech, even in theological matters, so there have been waves of measures to suppress Christianity, especially the independent Christian Churches. The Catholic Patriotic Church and the Protestant Three-Self Patriotic Movement are the official government-sanctioned Christian institutions that are supposed to regulate all local Christian activities. But independent Catholic (called underground churches) and Protestant groups, (called house churches) exist to stay away from government control. There is also another large group of Christians in Chinese Independent Churches. All totaled the estimates for Christians in China run from 30 million to 100 million Christians in Mainland China today. A large number but a small percentage of the total population of about 1.4 billion people. Contrastingly Taiwan has a population of about 24 million.

Christianity in China has been present since at least the 3rd century, and it has gained a significant amount of influence during the last 200 years.

While Christianity may have existed in China before the 3rd century, evidence of its existence begins to surmount with the attestation of the Syriac ethnographer Bardesanes at the end of the 2nd century. However, authentic evidence of Christianity's existence in China only dates back to the 7th century. The lack of evidence of Christianity's existence in China between the 3rd century and the 7th century can probably be attributed to the barriers which were placed in Persia by the Sassanids and the closure of the trade route in Turkestan. Both events prevented Christians from staying in contact with their mother church, the Syriac Antiochian Church, thereby halting the spread of Christianity until the reign of emperor T'sai-tsung, or Taizong (627-649). Taizong, who had studied the Christian Scriptures that were given to him by the missionary Alopen, realized "their propriety and truth and specifically ordered their preaching and transmission."

In the early 2000s, there were approximately 38 million Protestants and 10-12 million Catholics, with a smaller number of Evangelical and Orthodox Christians. The number of Chinese Christians had increased significantly since the easing of restrictions on religious activities during the economic reforms of the late 1970s. In 2018, the Chinese government declared that

there are over 44 million Christians in China. On the other hand, some
international Christian organizations estimate that there are tens of millions
more, who choose not to publicly identify as such.
https://en.wikipedia.org/wiki/Christianity_in_China

When you're living right in the middle of dynamic world events it is hard to see the full implications or predict the future.   Secondly, the conflicts encountered are much closer to home with the potential to threaten your life in numerous ways. What we have seen is that even amid political turmoil and threats of war there can be an underlying economic stability based on free enterprise and personal freedom. South Korea has had a rocky democratic electoral process yet their economic engine has been free to preserve a much more prosperous outcome than North Korea, which is one of the world's biggest societal dumpster fires. Even Vietnam is somewhat recovering from the war and has become a major alternative to China as a provider of high-tech and low-tech products to the world.

While we've discussed other factors concerning prosperity, we've only quantified the economy at a national level.   The question is how do countries rank when intangibles such as personal welfare and life satisfaction are taken into account. We'll examine some intangible aspects of prosperity next.

Sagrada Familia, Barcelona Spain, July 2022 By Maksim Sokolov (maxergon.com) - Own work, CC BY-SA 4.0. https://commons.wikimedia.org/w/index.php?curid=121206268 cropped

7. The Pillars of Prosperity

The Sagrada Família, is a church under construction in the Eixample district of Barcelona, Catalonia, Spain. It is the largest unfinished Catholic church in the world. Designed by architect Antoni Gaudí (1852–1926), his work on Sagrada Família is part of a UNESCO World Heritage Site. On 7 November 2010, Pope Benedict XVI consecrated the church and proclaimed it a minor basilica.

Construction of the Sagrada Família began on 19 March 1882 under architect Francisco de Paula del Villar. In 1883, when Villar resigned, Gaudí took over as chief architect, transforming the project with his architectural and engineering style, combining Gothic and curvilinear Art Nouveau forms. Gaudí devoted the remainder of his life to the project, and he is buried in the church's crypt. At the time of his death in 1926, less than a quarter of the project was complete.

Construction resumed to intermittent progress in the 1950s. Advancements in technologies such as computer-aided design and computerized numerical control (CNC) have since enabled faster progress and construction passed the midpoint in 2010. However, some of the project's greatest challenges remained, including the construction of ten more spires, each symbolizing an important Biblical figure in the New Testament. It was anticipated that the building would be completed by 2026, the centenary of Gaudí's death, but this has now been delayed due to the COVID-19 pandemic.

Describing the Sagrada Família, art critic Rainer Zerbst said "it is probably impossible to find a church building anything like it in the entire history of art", and Paul Goldberger describes it as "the most extraordinary personal interpretation of Gothic architecture since the Middle Ages".
https://en.wikipedia.org/wiki/Sagrada_Família

So far the prosperity we've shown around the world is economic or material prosperity that gives everyone more opportunities to succeed and enjoy their lives. Christian principles aren't rules for operating a prosperous economy. They are principles for how we deal with others, and with our circumstances. It is through those principles that a character of society emerges that promotes not only economic prosperity but a contagious environment of optimism and feelings of well-being and satisfaction with life that permeates the population.

The Sagrada Família is just one example where Christian principles have motivated great people to do great things and create many avenues of prosperity for the world. This is a creation of beauty, a little bit of prosperity, and a symbol of Christianity shared with us. But we also have to follow those same principles if we're to appropriate that prosperity for ourselves and our families. The principles of Christianity do not create economic prosperity, they lay out a philosophy of life that, when followed by society, will result in economic prosperity.

And don't forget that Christian prosperity is much more than having the most toys or possessions when you die. Christian prosperity is getting the maximum enjoyment of life no matter how much money or property you have accumulated. The person who can ease his way through automobile traffic jams in his 10-year-old car without cursing the drivers who cut in front of him has way more prosperity than the elite Italian sports car owner who becomes enraged every day on his way to or from work. It's not what you have but what you think that matters.

This then begs the question that maybe measuring the economic/ monetary well-being of people is not the best or even an accurate picture of this prosperity that transcends material possessions. Perhaps we need another, more meaningful measure of prosperity.

The first thought might be to take a sample survey from around the world. But you couldn't phrase the questions well enough to get a true answer because the question itself challenges the respondent to reveal his true identity and level of satisfaction and comfort with everyday life events, something that may be hard to do. How do you get a straight answer to, "How happy are you?", or more accurately, "How satisfied are you with life?".

So while there may be surveys that try to answer this question, they will hardly be believable or convincing. But we're not stuck with just an evaluation of prosperity based on general monetary evaluations.

The Legatum Institute, (http://www.prosperity.com/) is a registered charity based in Great Britain that has as its mission the analysis and categorization of prosperity around the world. Each year they reassess the levels of prosperity in 167 countries. (Some countries are left out because of political situations that preclude the collection of data necessary to make a meaningful assessment.) This assessment is based on their premise that prosperity is based on two major intertwined factors, economic and social well-being. Effectively they have come up with a way of evaluating happiness from a number of life or social factors that while not happiness per se, are aspects of life beyond monetary prosperity that we could logically link to being primary causes of happiness.

They have identified twelve factors (called pillars) as the significant elements that create overall prosperity. Each of the 167 countries is evaluated on each of these twelve factors and ranked in each factor relative to every other country. Each factor has equal weight in determining the country's overall ranking on the list. The twelve factors are:

The Four Foundational Pillars of Prosperity

1. **Safety and Security** - national and personal
2. **Personal Freedom** - legal rights, individual freedoms, social tolerance
3. **Governance** - effectiveness, democracy, rule of law
4. **Social Capital** - the degree of interpersonal friendly and neighborly values and social interactions

The Supporting Pillars of Prosperity

5. **Investment Environment** - investments are adequately protected and are readily accessible
6. **Enterprise Conditions** - the degree to which regulations enable businesses
7. **Economic Quality** - economic indicators, openness, opportunities, growth potential
8. **Infrastructure and Market Access** - favorable infrastructure, support, barriers
9. **Living Conditions** - Quality of Life
10. **Education** - access, quality, human involvement
11. **Health** - levels of health, infrastructure, preventive care
12. **Natural Environment** - quality, robustness, preservation

The Legatum Institute identifies the first four factors as the "institutional foundations of prosperity". These foundational factors are considered critical to the development and improvement of the quality of life in the other factors.

The Legatum Prosperity Index for 2021

The following tables have the tabulated results for the 2021 Legatum Prosperity Index. The full report of 102 pages can be found here and downloaded. https://www.prosperity.com/download_file/view_inline/4429

Three pages of tables show the overall ranking of each country, as well as their rankings for each category. Rankings are color-coded from green for the higher rankings to yellow to red for the lowest ranking. The numbers in each block give the actual ranking for that category.

The Legatum Prosperity Index™ **Rank 1-56**

2011 rank	2020 rank	2021 rank	Country	Safety and Security	Personal Freedom	Governance	Social Capital	Investment Environment	Enterprise Conditions	Infrastructure and Market Access	Economic Quality	Living Conditions	Health	Education	Natural Environment
3	1	1	Denmark	7	2	2	1	4	5	9	8	3	18	3	8
2	2	2	Norway	1	1	3	2	5	9	19	11	7	4	10	10
1	5	3	Sweden	10	3	6	5	8	16	6	7	5	10	14	1
4	4	4	Finland	18	4	1	3	3	11	10	19	9	14	4	2
5	3	5	Switzerland	2	10	7	9	13	2	13	1	6	13	8	7
7	6	6	Netherlands	9	5	4	7	10	7	2	6	1	9	7	35
8	7	7	Luxembourg	3	7	8	19	22	6	11	2	8	12	34	11
6	8	8	New Zealand	26	11	5	4	6	14	23	17	30	24	12	4
9	9	9	Germany	21	12	9	16	16	13	5	10	2	16	23	14
14	10	10	Iceland	6	9	11	6	23	26	18	20	12	8	15	17
12	11	11	Austria	11	14	13	12	11	18	16	22	17	25	25	6
17	12	12	Ireland	13	6	15	18	25	19	24	4	19	26	13	13
13	13	13	United Kingdom	17	17	14	20	7	12	8	18	10	31	16	22
16	15	14	Singapore	8	101	27	10	1	3	1	5	4	2	1	86
11	14	15	Canada	19	8	12	11	21	17	21	40	16	34	5	19
10	16	16	Australia	27	15	10	8	12	24	33	23	13	22	9	24
23	19	17	Estonia	24	23	17	25	18	15	26	15	21	41	19	5
15	17	18	Hong Kong	16	62	22	87	2	1	3	3	26	15	6	34
19	18	19	Japan	5	34	18	143	9	8	7	25	11	1	11	16
18	20	20	United States	69	22	23	13	15	4	4	16	27	68	20	23
22	22	21	Taiwan, China	4	27	21	38	14	10	29	13	32	5	17	81
20	21	22	France	38	25	19	55	20	22	14	29	23	20	27	12
21	23	23	Belgium	30	19	16	60	24	25	15	34	15	19	18	39
26	24	24	Spain	28	18	25	31	26	31	12	54	20	21	24	37
25	25	25	Malta	22	20	26	22	38	27	36	14	14	11	37	102
24	26	26	Slovenia	14	32	36	35	35	33	27	36	25	23	21	3
29	29	27	Czechia	12	24	31	57	28	44	28	12	28	30	31	26
28	27	28	Portugal	29	13	24	63	31	28	20	46	18	38	39	36
27	28	29	South Korea	37	43	30	147	19	46	17	9	24	3	2	56
36	32	30	Latvia	35	31	35	84	34	34	42	26	42	72	26	9
31	31	31	Italy	23	26	39	74	39	30	25	55	29	17	33	40
35	30	32	Israel	111	56	20	49	17	23	37	21	22	6	29	104
40	33	33	Lithuania	36	37	32	112	32	32	38	35	39	67	28	15
30	34	34	Cyprus	44	29	33	110	47	35	30	42	33	28	36	38
33	35	35	Slovakia	32	30	41	53	30	53	44	38	35	43	49	20
32	36	36	Poland	20	47	40	56	46	40	40	39	31	56	32	44
38	39	37	Uruguay	47	16	28	30	43	62	63	57	43	35	51	46
34	37	38	Chile	92	33	29	90	33	39	32	43	44	53	43	48
39	38	39	Costa Rica	50	21	34	75	57	50	51	59	56	33	46	18
42	43	40	Croatia	25	39	47	125	49	75	31	51	38	52	44	27
44	40	41	United Arab Emirates	49	145	43	29	29	21	22	32	48	36	45	118
46	41	42	Malaysia	73	114	49	24	27	29	41	27	66	44	42	47
41	42	43	Greece	31	44	42	131	91	49	34	96	34	46	38	28
37	46	44	Hungary	34	81	82	48	42	78	43	33	37	51	41	33
43	44	45	Mauritius	42	42	37	37	37	43	49	61	61	83	62	107
45	45	46	Qatar	15	146	63	26	45	20	39	28	46	39	58	122
50	47	47	Romania	33	40	57	117	40	60	47	41	55	62	64	41
51	48	48	Bulgaria	53	58	58	83	52	55	55	30	50	63	47	70
53	51	49	Montenegro	41	48	56	40	55	54	61	77	49	95	50	105
49	50	50	Seychelles	57	70	46	41	67	52	64	71	70	37	65	50
47	49	51	Panama	52	49	65	65	54	88	52	50	78	48	92	31
64	53	52	Serbia	43	75	81	82	69	91	62	58	45	75	48	127
61	55	53	Georgia	81	60	50	59	44	56	59	81	84	93	55	124
63	52	54	China	86	199	86	36	48	36	46	24	52	7	57	136
74	54	55	Armenia	66	77	62	93	58	48	72	79	69	65	59	99
48	58	56	Bahrain	100	158	110	17	36	37	35	72	40	54	61	140

*Hong Kong is a Special Administrative Region of China

The Legatum Prosperity Index™ Rank 57-112

2011 rank	2020 rank	2021 rank	Country	Safety and Security	Personal Freedom	Governance	Social Capital	Investment Environment	Enterprise Conditions	Infrastructure and Market Access	Economic Quality	Living Conditions	Health	Education	Natural Environment
58	57	57	Argentina	74	28	54	97	79	117	90	146	58	42	52	55
52	60	58	Kuwait ★	51	119	91	52	73	64	57	52	36	45	74	137
54	59	59	Trinidad and Tobago	75	41	53	107	85	120	65	73	51	66	69	96
59	63	60	North Macedonia	54	68	73	103	56	77	73	67	53	69	89	98
60	56	61	Peru	95	53	68	149	65	63	77	60	99	49	66	30
72	61	62	Indonesia	85	102	64	15	68	58	67	56	108	80	88	83
56	62	63	Thailand	120	115	107	28	53	70	48	31	81	27	77	114
77	64	64	Kazakhstan	87	135	103	46	59	74	79	44	54	71	35	119
65	67	65	Jamaica	119	35	52	104	66	61	80	101	64	60	90	128
69	65	66	Belarus	61	142	111	122	89	90	70	47	41	55	30	68
57	66	67	Oman ★	39	149	87	33	51	47	53	87	67	57	76	151
55	68	68	Brazil	117	50	66	121	74	114	89	85	60	86	91	21
68	70	69	Albania	67	79	79	139	83	65	66	110	85	70	53	58
79	73	70	Russia	138	130	109	62	77	79	58	37	62	89	22	71
62	69	71	Mexico	148	72	84	126	60	68	50	45	82	79	72	63
90	76	72	Moldova	76	84	89	45	82	94	81	93	65	84	60	132
83	74	73	Dominican Republic	114	45	95	77	81	89	68	66	86	85	95	54
89	72	74	Vietnam	90	133	97	21	117	83	60	49	90	47	67	103
84	71	75	Saudi Arabia ★	108	163	96	43	61	38	45	63	71	64	63	145
76	77	76	Bosnia and Herzegovina	48	76	115	92	86	144	83	84	47	98	70	131
73	75	77	Colombia	155	67	71	106	71	98	69	82	88	32	73	29
91	88	78	Ukraine	134	73	77	102	123	72	74	75	76	104	40	106
82	79	79	Paraguay	70	69	98	61	84	134	95	68	77	91	106	32
75	78	80	Cabo Verde	40	38	44	67	115	100	122	139	102	87	99	85
70	81	81	Jordan ★	77	121	78	123	50	45	75	119	59	77	96	149
80	85	82	Botswana	71	57	38	111	72	82	105	53	114	131	101	141
97	83	83	Ecuador	89	59	99	124	94	123	82	123	96	78	82	45
88	82	84	Philippines	147	78	90	34	78	85	76	48	110	101	86	76
78	90	85	South Africa	137	36	48	39	70	59	86	69	106	140	108	144
101	80	86	Azerbaijan	104	147	130	94	63	42	71	90	63	74	79	152
94	87	87	Mongolia	62	61	67	54	107	102	116	94	107	107	54	147
98	86	88	Sri Lanka	130	93	76	51	100	84	91	111	101	40	71	59
71	84	89	Suriname	56	51	83	69	143	129	92	104	79	119	102	25
104	89	90	Kyrgyzstan	68	100	106	76	95	104	109	100	80	73	83	80
99	93	91	Morocco ★	60	116	85	160	64	73	56	99	92	88	110	126
81	91	92	Namibia	63	54	45	95	80	69	97	121	120	126	114	82
66	92	93	Turkey ★	146	154	127	140	62	57	54	62	57	58	78	91
95	94	94	Guyana	91	66	74	85	106	116	113	74	87	121	93	57
87	95	95	Belize	80	55	93	134	125	122	94	144	89	82	98	51
67	99	96	Tunisia ★	125	91	60	155	96	86	88	112	73	92	92	139
85	96	97	El Salvador	126	65	75	113	87	92	84	107	95	99	111	138
100	97	98	São Tomé and Príncipe	45	46	69	98	130	112	121	83	119	96	115	78
93	101	99	Ghana	82	52	59	96	111	66	110	137	115	117	116	111
107	98	100	Uzbekistan	55	151	141	27	93	105	99	78	103	50	80	163
112	103	101	India	139	106	51	68	75	51	78	91	122	111	118	160
92	100	102	Cuba	99	152	132	32	99	159	102	115	83	29	56	84
96	102	103	Guatemala	118	87	126	78	90	103	87	70	113	105	124	90
109	105	104	Rwanda	127	118	55	71	41	41	106	76	150	114	131	110
111	107	105	Senegal	83	63	61	50	102	87	119	125	125	120	144	79
103	106	106	Bolivia	101	82	119	130	105	148	108	118	104	112	97	42
106	108	107	Algeria ★	58	136	114	127	134	132	98	134	74	81	84	150
105	109	108	Turkmenistan	72	162	157	14	109	145	118	65	68	59	81	157
86	104	109	Lebanon ★	132	108	128	165	98	81	93	160	72	100	68	115
115	111	110	Tajikistan	78	150	143	23	120	96	127	105	98	90	87	142
108	110	111	Honduras	129	98	136	73	92	115	96	103	111	103	121	65
124	112	112	Kenya	145	95	92	79	76	67	101	97	131	115	109	133

The Legatum Prosperity Index™Rank 113-167

LEGATUM
INSTITUTE

2011 rank	2020 rank	2021 rank	Country	Safety and Security	Personal Freedom	Governance	Social Capital	Investment Environment	Enterprise Conditions	Infrastructure and Market Access	Economic Quality	Living Conditions	Health	Education	Natural Environment
102	113	113	Nicaragua	113	109	147	101	110	137	107	117	105	76	119	53
131	114	114	Nepal	94	74	88	116	122	124	141	95	128	118	117	143
117	115	115	Laos	64	156	134	105	141	110	103	88	118	116	105	62
121	116	116	The Gambia	79	99	72	42	104	93	136	149	124	141	136	73
122	117	117	Tanzania	109	112	94	64	116	106	124	92	132	124	134	66
120	118	118	Cambodia	96	139	156	72	124	138	100	64	126	94	126	88
129	123	119	Benin	65	80	70	151	132	80	130	126	143	139	138	125
144	119	120	Côte d'Ivoire	128	96	101	136	118	101	117	89	130	149	137	93
113	120	121	Egypt	149	161	142	141	97	71	85	131	91	109	104	153
119	122	122	Djibouti	84	140	121	132	101	99	112	86	121	122	140	154
125	121	123	Iran	131	165	145	89	126	152	104	138	75	61	75	156
114	125	124	Zambia	97	110	104	88	103	95	134	161	144	127	133	49
116	124	125	Gabon	103	113	129	152	153	146	135	114	109	138	100	72
130	126	126	Bangladesh	140	122	137	86	136	109	114	102	116	102	125	155
133	129	127	Uganda	133	117	120	120	88	97	125	113	140	133	135	117
118	127	128	Papua New Guinea	112	71	113	81	119	113	140	124	160	147	145	67
123	131	129	Malawi	107	85	80	157	108	108	139	135	154	125	152	69
126	128	130	Comoros	59	92	148	119	150	125	131	143	133	129	139	75
139	132	131	Eswatini	88	148	135	145	113	131	120	109	123	160	112	134
127	130	132	Equatorial Guinea	93	153	152	58	144	153	126	80	112	155	122	43
149	133	133	Myanmar	156	120	125	44	164	143	129	98	129	106	113	64
138	134	134	Burkina Faso	142	64	100	91	128	128	155	116	153	132	154	87
135	135	135	Lesotho	102	83	102	135	133	139	133	128	139	164	123	165
141	136	136	Madagascar	121	89	122	99	127	130	150	130	162	142	147	74
156	139	137	Togo	105	104	133	161	129	121	145	142	145	143	132	130
151	140	138	Pakistan	150	125	124	133	112	111	115	136	117	130	143	167
134	138	139	Liberia	110	97	105	70	138	118	160	145	148	159	162	60
158	141	140	Guinea	122	111	123	114	121	76	149	157	152	156	160	77
142	137	141	Iraq	164	141	138	142	137	126	111	132	93	113	120	166
150	142	142	Zimbabwe	115	137	146	137	140	150	137	147	136	145	103	129
143	144	143	Nigeria	153	105	131	108	114	119	143	151	138	158	142	123
145	146	144	Sierra Leone	106	86	108	66	151	142	164	153	155	162	150	100
152	147	145	Ethiopia	144	126	117	80	148	140	148	108	149	128	151	113
137	143	146	Mozambique	124	94	118	109	135	147	142	163	157	150	159	52
110	145	147	Venezuela	151	128	167	144	160	167	123	164	97	97	85	61
147	149	148	Niger	143	88	116	47	131	127	163	129	159	148	164	112
140	151	149	Cameroon	157	132	149	118	145	135	138	106	137	154	127	108
157	150	150	Guinea-Bissau	46	103	140	115	158	151	156	152	161	152	163	92
132	148	151	Mali	158	90	112	150	142	133	151	127	142	146	161	109
146	153	152	Congo	135	123	154	153	152	156	147	159	135	144	128	89
148	154	153	Mauritania	98	138	151	100	156	154	158	140	127	134	156	164
128	152	154	Libya	162	129	159	128	167	165	128	133	94	108	107	159
154	155	155	Haiti	123	107	155	158	159	166	157	141	147	151	130	146
153	156	156	Angola	116	131	139	146	166	160	144	158	146	157	157	120
159	157	157	Burundi	152	155	150	138	146	107	154	162	164	135	146	97
136	158	158	Syria	165	166	164	166	147	164	132	120	100	110	129	158
155	159	159	Sudan	161	157	160	148	139	141	146	167	134	123	148	161
162	161	160	Dem. Rep. of Congo	160	124	158	156	165	157	161	154	158	161	149	101
166	160	161	Somalia	159	144	162	129	149	161	152	166	156	163	141	135
164	162	162	Eritrea	136	167	163	162	155	158	162	156	163	136	155	116
163	163	163	Afghanistan	166	127	144	167	157	136	159	150	151	153	158	162
167	165	164	Chad	141	134	161	159	161	163	166	148	165	165	165	95
160	164	165	Yemen	163	164	166	154	162	155	153	165	141	137	153	148
165	166	166	Central African Republic	154	143	153	163	163	162	167	122	167	167	166	94
161	167	167	South Sudan	167	160	165	164	154	149	165	155	166	166	167	121

*From 2011 Sudan excludes South Sudan.

What should be obvious is that the nations at the top of the list, i.e., the most prosperous taking into account the additional factors developed by the Legatum Institute are for the most part those same Western World Christian Nations that also head the list based on GDP PPP. We won't try to explain anomalies here but do note that sometimes aspects that might be considered big factors seem to have little effect on the overall assessment.

Look at the top 50 countries (of 167) in terms of overall prosperity, shown in the tables as predominately dark green, and two factors are obvious. Christian nations dominate the top 50 and the smaller more homogeneous Christian nations are at the top of the list. This simply says that any group with a very large majority of shared values will operate in accord with those values and that the quality of those values will determine the levels of prosperity that result.

Given that countries are evaluated over 11 different categories so that no one aspect can dominate, it is quite interesting that the same Western World countries dominate the list just as they do in the GDP evaluations. These categories are also rather subjective which adds another variable to the evaluation. An evaluation of the complete report would be necessary to clear up obvious questions that pop up from the color coding.

There are two obvious conclusions one could make from the rankings and the prosperity factors.

- **Quality of Life drives material prosperity, not the other way around.**
- **Inherited and high material prosperity (oil, gold, diamonds, etc) does not compensate for Quality of Life factors that come from the philosophy of the citizens.**

Note that Taiwan, despite its almost 40-year dictatorship history, emerged from that authoritarian rule and after 25 years or so was ranked Twenty-second in the world in 2011. The 2021 rating is Twenty-first, and is due to an across-the-board high rating in all of the areas evaluated as contributing to prosperity including a fourth place in the world in Safety and Security. Taiwan is a small country population-wise so its citizens are perhaps highly homogeneous. A second observation is how Turkey has fallen from sixty-sixth in 2011 to ninety-third in 2023. We discussed the reasons for this change previously.

Also note that as you go down the list and the categories change from green to yellow and then to red the relative rankings have not materially changed from 2011 to 2021, and the countries that are predominately red or yellow are obviously a less desirable place to live.

The Conclusions of The Legatum Institute

The Forward statement to the 2017 report sums up the basic conclusions for the 2021 year and states the observed conclusions on world prosperity.

The Legatum Prosperity Index 2017, Forward

Reflecting the deeper foundations of success, this year's report focuses on the institutional elements of prosperity. We look at the role of Governance, Personal Freedom, Social Capital, and Safety and Security in underpinning both wealth and well-being. The strengthening of these pillars enables the development of other aspects of prosperity. When they are undermined, we see a corresponding decline across other pillars.
Ref, http://www.prosperity.com/

What they are saying is that the overall prosperity of a nation is dependent on getting these four pillars or factors right. When the values and culture of a nation or people have these four factors as key principles to live by, these factors enable the development of the remaining factors. And conversely when these four foundational factors are poorly held as cultural and valuable principles, then the other prosperity factors are going to be adversely affected. This gives a much broader assessment of prosperity than just economics so it provides some valuable insight into these other factors.

Foundational Principles of the United States

Declaration of Independence

We hold these truths to be self-evident, that all men are created equal, that they are endowed by their Creator with certain unalienable Rights, that among these are Life, Liberty, and the pursuit of Happiness. That to secure these rights, Governments are instituted among Men, deriving their just powers from the consent of the governed. That whenever any Form of Government becomes destructive of these ends, it is the Right of the People to alter or to abolish it, and to institute new Government, laying its foundation on such principles and organizing its powers in such form, as to them shall seem most likely to effect their Safety and Happiness.

Preamble to the U.S. Constitution

*We the People of the United States, in Order to form a more perfect Union, **establish Justice, insure domestic Tranquility, provide for the common defence, promote the general Welfare, and secure the Blessings of Liberty** to ourselves and our Posterity, do ordain and establish this Constitution for the United States of America.*

These documents embrace the foundational pillars of Governance, Personal Freedom, Safety, and Security. The fourth foundational pillar of prosperity, **Social Capital** - the degree of interpersonal friendly and neighborly values and social interactions, is the embodiment of Christianity's foundational principle, "Love your neighbor as yourself" which was an imbedded ideal in the culture of America as its people were approximately 90% to 95% of Christian heritage and beliefs.

The results of the Legatum Institute's evaluation of national prosperity closely mirror our initial economic income and GDP-based assessment and their evaluation is that the driving function of economic prosperity is the same foundational value pillars documented by the founding documents of the United States.

- **Governance** - effectiveness, democracy, rule of law
- **Personal Freedom** - legal rights, individual freedoms, social tolerance
- **Social Capital** - the degree of interpersonal friendly and neighborly values and social interactions
- **Safety and Security** - national and personal

The question is, why do some countries possess high levels of the four foundational pillars plus the other pillars of prosperity? And secondly, why do the other countries not do the same thing? From what we can see in the surveys the observed answer is Christianity. There is something about the Theology and the Philosophy of Life that changes the thinking of the citizens and creates the conditions for the prosperity observed.

This leaves two questions to be pursued, what is that original thinking of mankind that gets him off the prosperity track, and what is the Christian thinking that leads to prosperity?

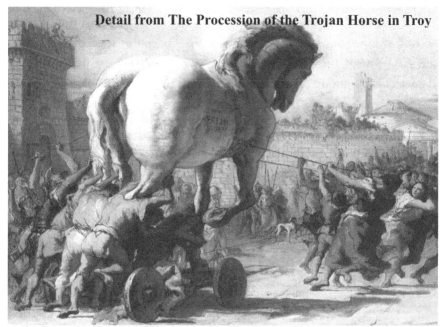

Detail from The Procession of the Trojan Horse in Troy

by Domenico Tiepolo (1773), inspired by Virgil's Aeneid
Unknown source, Public Domain, https://commons.wikimedia.org/w/index.php?curid=173986

8. Thinking Determines Your Prosperity

We have first evaluated prosperity from the standpoint of Economics or personal wealth. From the Legatum Institute, we have identified four primary factors and eight supplemental factors that influence prosperity from an environmental standpoint. These factors are all intertwined in life, each supporting the other.

The Legatum Institute Primary Pillars of Prosperity
- **Governance** - effectiveness, democracy, rule of law
- **Personal Freedom** - legal rights, individual freedoms, social tolerance
- **Social Capital** - the degree of interpersonal friendly and neighborly values and social interactions
- **Safety and Security** - national and personal

In a society that responds to the thinking of the citizens, these pillars come from the consensus Philosophy of Life. In more totalitarian societies the government ultimately decides, usually to weaken or deny many of them as detrimental to those in power. When these primary factors and the eight secondary factors are well crafted in a society individuals have the maximum opportunity for shalom prosperity.

> **Happiness=Shalom:** שָׁלוֹם šālôm 237x peace, safety, prosperity, well-being; intactness, wholeness; peace can have a focus of security, safety which can bring feelings of satisfaction, well-being, and contentment.
> (Enhanced Strong's Dictionary © 2011 Olive Tree Bible Software, Inc. All rights reserved)

These factors or elements of a prosperous society are enablers only, however. There is another factor that is responsible for real personal prosperity, your systematic responses to your thinking or your own personal Philosophy of Life. Thinking is the filter through which we each evaluate our lives but the actual prosperity is the result of our natural automatic responses to life based on our own, personal Philosophy. That personal philosophy involves not only our environment but how we view our life and how we respond to life. Prosperity results from what one thinks about life, based on our philosophy of life. Right thinking can provide the Pillars of Prosperity for a nation and Shalom Happiness for you. Conversely, wrong thinking can give you a Dumpster Fire Life, nationally and personally. Accepting the Trojan Horse was a bad idea, it did not turn out well.

When the Pillars or elements of prosperity are in place they provide the framework for individuals to maximize prosperity in their own lives. We still must have a personal Philosophy of Life that guides us through life to maximize that personal shalom prosperity.

You can live in some very red countries in the Legatum Institute tables and still have that shalom prosperity, that happiness factor in your life if your Philosophy of Life has you thinking and doing the right things. It may matter little what the economics or the Four Main Pillars of Prosperity may be like, it's what the person thinks and how they respond to life, that can bring shalom life prosperity in the middle of a chaotic environment. Or the reverse can also be true, poor thinking during great life opportunities can become a dumpster fire life.

We see this all the time with wealthy people, especially entertainers, people who may be more sensitive to life and therefore react more, care more, or search more for that perfect happiness. They can be very wealthy and miserable at the same time because they have trouble managing life to their satisfaction. This is the same issue in prosperous nations where prosperity comes from mimicking the lives and actions of people in the Western World. They may live in all the right environmental factors of economics, governance, personal freedom, and social capital, but also may lack key elements of the Christian Philosophy of Life related to their personal lives to mentally put life in perspective, and enjoy it.

We've picked on entertainers because they are successful prosperous people whose lives are open to the public. But they are not alone in their struggles with life. We all struggle with weaknesses and poor judgments. What we've seen from these surveys is that there is a major influencer of good judgments and good decisions that can improve prosperity significantly.

You can find this same situation in every Christian nation with exceptional prosperity as well. The difference that a Christian nation provides is a robust Christian heritage and an active Philosophy of Life classroom that reinforces that Philosophy in the minds of Christians. The robustness of this heritage in turn depends on the ability of the Christian Church organizations to continually renew and reinforce that philosophy.

The local Church is the center for learning and applying both the spiritual and the Philosophical values to life and achieving maximum happiness. It is also the source of inspiration and motivation to examine one's life and thinking and to make corrections where necessary. Non-Christian nations lack this self-correcting and life-improving factor.

What should also be evident is that prosperity in non-Christian nations can also be lost at the whim of government leaders alone, whereas, in Christian nations, the Christian Church stands as a bulwark against government tyranny. Only when the Christian Church fails to uphold its responsibilities, and the citizens become passive, can prosperity be lost in a Christian nation. Germany and Russia come to mind.

We've given numerous examples from recent history of Christian influence on prosperity around the world. An extraordinary testimony to the important role Christianity plays comes from a famous British and Christian-raised atheist Richard Dawkins. Dawkins considers religion, and by experience Christianity, to be not just a valuable part of society, but an essential part because of the value of the Christian Philosophy of Life in shaping society. He was quoted in a London Times article as saying,

> **Richard Dawkins,**
> **"People may feel free to do bad things because they feel God is no longer watching them"**

A key to this belief was an experiment performed by one of his former students. The experiment involved a university coffee shop that had set up an "honor pay box". Over the honor pay box, the shop displayed the price incorporated into two alternate pictures, one, a picture of flowers, the other a picture of two staring eyes. What they found was that the honor pay box collected about three times the amount when the "staring eyes" picture was in place.

Thus Dawkins concluded that the idea of God observing people's behavior caused people to behave in a better fashion than they might otherwise behave. His unhappy conclusion was that belief in God and religion are, or can be very beneficial to mankind and societies. This of course presented him with a dilemma. His campaign against the existence of God was therefore a campaign against the very thing that he had concluded was of great benefit to civilization.

https://www.thetimes.co.uk/article/ending-religion-is-a-bad-idea-says-richard-dawkins-sqqdbmcpq
https://premierchristian.news/en/news/article/richard-dawkins-admits-a-world-with-no-god-would-be-immoral

What Dawkins overlooked, because he doesn't understand Christianity, was the idea that the "eyes of God", just as likely reminded people to be honest and follow the Philosophy of Christianity. This philosophy can even penetrate the thinking of people in non-Christian nations so that they can adopt Christian values in a non-Christian world. What Dawkins is also pointing out is most significant. It's not just following the rules or violating them for some perceived benefit. It's that people also plot and calculate risks and rewards. Mankind is basically a conniving malevolent actor, always calculating and plotting to get an advantage in life.

Unfortunately, this human nature we all possess has a Philosophy of Life that is often opposed to both the 12 elements or pillars of prosperity and to a shalom-producing Philosophy of life. This is easy to see in the red countries in the Legatum Institute tables. There is a battle for the souls of people between two opposing forces, two opposing views of life. One view leads to a malevolent and destitute society and life, and the other view leads to a prosperous society and a shalom prosperous life. What our surveys on prosperity have said so far is that Christianity has been a major influence on prosperity from both the principles of society, the 12 pillars, and from a personal Philosophy of Life or thinking standpoint. Not everyone in Christian societies sees or has a high level of prosperity because the malevolent philosophy of human nature is alive and well in everyone. Prosperity comes only when we can overcome our human natures and follow a better philosophy.

This is the exact struggle going on in China today. They are suffering from a deficiency in honesty and fairness toward others which is leading them down the path that Russia has followed, Crony Capitalism with a large criminal element in the mix. China is overrun with corruption and a criminal element that the government doesn't know how to control, probably because it spends all its energy trying to maintain political power. China's obvious solution is to promote Christianity.

Now what Dawkins also fails to see is that not only does Christianity promote the thinking that creates a better society but it influences non-Christians as well who can see the value of a Christian-influenced society, a society that mimics Christian thinking and behavior. This is a story we've already documented, how the most prosperous non-Western cultures have been influenced by and adopted Western and Christian-created standards of operation for societies, and how individuals in those societies have adopted Christian values for living.   Dawkins believes that mankind invented morality as a necessity to make societies work.   He should look at the world's prosperity situation and the factors that affect prosperity around the world.

So we can see how everyone who adopts the actions of Christian principles makes life better and more prosperous for themselves and all around them, not just on the material level, but on a social level as well. In fact, some of those principles rub off on them when they observe the Christian whose attitude and response to circumstances seem to give him or her joy and peace in a world of turmoil and friction. So an atheist can follow the Christian philosophy of life when it is endemic in his culture, even while rejecting the Theology.   This is the subtle influence of Christianity on society.

Only one caveat to add, however. Where prosperity has developed due to the influence of Christianity but where Christianity itself, that is the Theology, has not taken root there is no independent training ground for the next and future generations to use as they seek revisions to the management approaches and rules of their elders. This is the situation with some of those prosperous non-Christian nations.

Without local Christian Churches with a cadre of teachers of both the Theology and Philosophy, the fundamental principles of prosperity are only a generation away from becoming lost to the nation. There is no residual source of influence to maintain the Philosophy of Prosperity within the thinking of the citizens. It's at that point that prosperity is lost and no longer recoverable.

Prosperity depends on the rigor of generational training and operational management. A number of the moderately prosperous countries we've discussed have lost much of their Christian training base, however. Russia lost its training base, the church, during the communist revolution and it was gone (devalued and left to die) for 70 or so years, three generations if a generation is counted as twenty years. So when Russia restored private property ownership, its population emerged somewhat bewildered as to what to do with the newborn freedoms as well concerned as about who would take care of them. Germany's Christian base survived the Nazi era and Soviet control but suffers from the same morass as much of the West.   A loss of respect for the efficacy and Theology of Christianity and the value of its Philosophy.

Another example is Turkey, a nation that went through a fantastic makeover and because the turmoil at the time was great enough, people completely bought into it.   But they lack the Christian training base for private property and free enterprise so each succeeding generation becomes more and more likely to revert back to the religious state and religious power politics that is quick to control what people can do, especially on a large scale.   This is indeed the fear of the Turkish people who have made a prosperous life for themselves but see their leaders moving back to a controlled life environment.

Even in Western Europe where Christianity has been devalued and somewhat forgotten, the loss of principles and values in younger people are sprouting weeds of forced adherence to whatever the government decides is right in areas that were formerly private matters of consciousness.   This includes restrictions on what to do with their own private property.   There is a move in the Netherlands to remove farmers from their farms and have the government take over farm production to reduce their carbon footprint coming from agriculture.   But the Netherlands is a major producer of agricultural exports.   To quote Forrest Gump, "Stupid is as stupid does".

The Dutch Government Proposes Restrictions on Food production to reduce the carbon footprint of fertilizer manufacturing and methane gas production from large bovine farm animals (cows).

The Dutch agricultural sector is highly mechanized and has a strong focus on international exports. It employs about 4% of the Dutch labour force but produces large surpluses in the food-processing industry and accounts for 21% of the Dutch total export value. The Dutch rank first in the European Union and second worldwide in value of agricultural exports, behind only the United States, with agricultural exports earning €80.7 billion in 2014, up from €75.4 billion in 2012. In 2019 agricultural exports were worth €94.5 billion. In an effort to reduce agricultural pollution, the Dutch government is imposing strict limits on the productivity of the farming sector, triggering Dutch farmers' protests, who fear for their livelihoods.

One-third of the world's exports of chilis, tomatoes, and cucumbers go through the country. The Netherlands also exports one-fifteenth of the world's apples.

A significant portion of Dutch agricultural exports consists of fresh-cut plants, flowers, and flower bulbs, with the Netherlands exporting two-thirds of the world's total

https://en.wikipedia.org/wiki/Netherlands#Agriculture_and_natural_resources

It should be obvious now that Christian principles of living heavily promote prosperity, and that nations can make use of those principles in many ways. But unless those principles are actively being taught to each new generation, that prosperity, especially economic prosperity, can degrade and eventually die out. National prosperity, both material and cerebral, what you have and what you think, is derived from the quality of the economic and social well-being of citizens. Let me repeat that. Prosperity is more than economics or material goods. Prosperity within a nation is dependent on both the homogeneity and quality of core values held by its citizens. What you think and how you act directly affects not only material prosperity but also inner peace and happiness, social well-being, and satisfaction with your own life. A "satisfied life" comes from having a good role model, and having the right philosophy of life.

There is a second major factor at work here. Let's call it trickle-down prosperity. When the government and/or leadership in a country exhibits and promotes the core principles of prosperity, those values flow down to the entire population of the country. When leaders promote the negative aspects of the four primary ingredients of prosperity the country can descend into chaos quickly. We have 5 examples of this in the last hundred years or so. Germany, Russia, China, Cuba, and Venezuela. (North Korea is straight out of "1984", the book, and is a very special case of a malevolent dystopian society.) There have been other countries that have had periods of decline but none so severe or obvious as these. In all five cases, it began with a weakness in the primary prosperity factors that promoted some level of dissatisfaction with the government. In all five cases, the government was taken over by an authoritarian dictatorship that instituted policies that disrupted effective governance, democracy, and the rule of law. Like dominos, in quick succession, the remaining three key factors in prosperity disappeared and chaos was the result. Germany was slightly different in that it was in economic recovery from WWI and the more draconian government measures were directed at a single segment of society. This allowed those who were not part of that persecuted segment to bury their head in the sand and ignore what was happening. The story of German scientists during the Nazi reign probably helps to clarify this difference (Ref. Vol II). People were aware of the Jewish persecution but not necessarily the severity of it. They tried to influence the circumstances of those around them but had little ability as individuals to combat the government, especially when confronted with extreme violence and power if they protested too much.

So first the quality of Governance is affected. Then personal freedom is attacked, always with a rationale to make it appear necessary. In parallel Social Capital is destroyed by pitting one group against another, always under the guise of social justice. To justify new government controls and further loss of freedom, the safety and security of life are threatened by violence and intimidation. This is the scenario that played out in Germany, Russia, China, Cuba, and Venezuela. In Germany, the targeted group was the Jewish communities. In Russia, China, Cuba, and Venezuela it was the land owners and independent business people who provided food, goods, and services. All of this persecution was in the name of equality and equity, a key Communist area of attack to provide cover for the confiscation of property and elimination of the offending owner. The Russian and Chinese revolutions were equally ignorant and brutal in their purges of ownership and oppression of anyone who would get in their way. Cuba and Venezuela were perhaps a little more relaxed in their approach because these revolutions were more personal power and riches-motivated than ideologically driven.

Take note, when totalitarian power promotes any ideology, that is a clue that the success of the ideology will become most devastating to societies and individuals. In Russia especially, they took over the farms of people who knew how to farm and placed the farms in the hands of people who didn't have a clue as to how to produce crops. Then they killed many knowledgeable farmers ensuring that Russia would not be able to feed itself; the law of unintended consequences. The European Union and the Netherlands' attacks on farmers under the guise of necessary climate change response is a certain clue as to a possible future catastrophe.

Similar draconian government policies on economic and personal freedom can also be seen in Australia, New Zealand, and Canada, all under the label of necessity for Global Warming or the Covid pandemic. Europe and especially Germany are in for a rude awakening concerning energy policies that have been draconian responses to climate change, revamping energy sources without concern for the consequences.

Even the United States and Great Britain are not immune from government attacks on the fundamental markers of prosperity. All four of the keys to prosperity are under attack with government leaders at all levels proposing or supporting actions that directly break down these key factors.

The Four Foundational Pillars of Prosperity

1. **Governance** - effectiveness, democracy, rule of law
2. **Personal Freedom** - legal rights, individual freedoms, social tolerance
3. **Social Capital** - the degree of interpersonal friendly and neighborly values and social interactions
4. **Safety and Security** - national and personal

The path to political power is the breakdown (real or imagined) of society to the extent that the population welcomes totalitarian policies to control the chaos that results. A primary aspect supporting this is blind political party loyalty which seems to cause people to support destructive principles of their own party, even as it destroys their own well-being. The point of attack is to upset the **Social Capital** first by pitting different elements of society against each other. Once people are split into opposing groups then the rest of the factors of prosperity can be weakened and totalitarian political power is easily justified to fix the problem, but instead used to institutionalize that political power.

The bottom line is that prosperity can be lost on a national level, brought about by a concerted effort of politics and we can see those actions at work in the world today. But prosperity can be lost on a personal level just as easily when individuals abandon or never understand the principles that come from Christianity and permeate Christian countries.

A Harvard Case Study

This conclusion or assessment of the intertwining of material and lifestyle prosperity was brought out similarly by a 75-year-long Harvard study on physical and emotional well-being. Harvard's Grant and Glueck Study Objectives from the Harvard website state:

> *The Study of Adult Development is a longitudinal study that has been following two groups of men over the last 75 years to identify the psychosocial predictors of healthy aging. We have two groups of participants: The Grant Study which is composed of 268 Harvard graduates from the classes of 1939-1944 and the Glueck Study group that is made up of 456 men who grew up in the inner-city neighborhoods of Boston. We are particularly interested in what psychosocial variables and biological processes from earlier in life predict health and well-being in late life (the 80s and 90's), what aspects of childhood and adult experience predict the quality of intimate relationships in late life, and how late-life marriage is linked with health and well-being. We are now beginning to study the children of our original participants in our G2 (Second Generation) study.*
> *http://www.adultdevelopmentstudy.org/grantandglueckstudy*

The conclusion from the study made by Robert Waldinger, director of the Harvard Study of Adult Development was one thing surpasses all the rest in terms of importance.

> *"The clearest message that we get from this 75-year study is this: Good relationships keep us happier and healthier. Period."*
>
> *"It's not just the number of friends you have, and it's not whether or not you're in a committed relationship," says Waldinger. "It's the quality of your close relationships that matters." Robert Waldinger*

The study was reviewed by inc. magazine on their website by Melanie Curtin with the title,

"This 75-Year Harvard Study Found the 1 Secret to Leading a Fulfilling Life"
https://www.inc.com/melanie-curtin/want-a-life-of-fulfillment-a-75-year-harvard-study-says-to-prioritize-this-one-t.html

Again, this assessment of having a fulfilling life & peace/happiness goes back to the Legatum Institute's similar assessment that Social Capital, the degree of interpersonal friendly and neighborly values and social interactions, is a direct indicator of overall prosperity.   But Ms. Curtin's assessment of the study goes further. Her own conclusion from the study confirms a significant negative result of the study.

> *"the data is clear that, in the end, you could have all the money you've ever wanted, a successful career, and be in good physical health, but without loving relationships, you won't be happy" Melanie Curtin*

As a reminder happiness is not that "ha, ha" party happiness but more along the lines of satisfaction with life, a sense of well-being encompassed by "Shalom". This shalom life, (peace, economic prosperity, happiness/satisfaction) is at the heart of Christian Philosophy which encompasses learning how to embrace relationships no matter how "messy and complicated" they may be. The significance is that the alternative to this philosophy doesn't work.   If you withdraw from relationships and emotional involvement with other people, as one of those other religions promotes (story to come), you'll miss out on "Happiness" no matter how great all your other circumstances may be. We'll have a bit more to say on this subject when we discuss the alternatives to Christianity, as well as when we address some of those Christian principles that promote prosperity.

There is another example to support the importance of social capital on prosperity and happiness. An investigative report on a large number of both planned and random or bystander murders in Milwaukee, WI., and the decline and blight in the neighborhood quality of life and conditions had some interesting observations by people living in the blighted communities.

The observations by both residents and police trying to deal with the crime and murder were good but no one, including the city had any solutions.

> NOTE: This was reported on a local news website but the source has been lost within a multitude of similar stories.

Neighborhood and Police Observations

1. People didn't care for one another anymore, they weren't helping each other,"
2. The values of the residents had deteriorated significantly.
3. The lack of father figures in the homes of children, especially male children,
4. The lack of jobs
5. Drug dealing became a primary source of income.

Secondly, this community/city situation didn't occur all at once and the decline is certainly indicative of the state of those pillars of prosperity and their claimed effect on driving the other factors in the Legatum Institute evaluation of national prosperity.

Pillars of Prosperity

- **Governance** - effectiveness, democracy, rule of law
- **Personal Freedom** - legal rights, individual freedoms, social tolerance
- **Social Capital** - the degree of interpersonal friendly and neighborly values and social interactions
- **Safety and Security** - national and personal

The loss of a measure of prosperity in local areas may be the result of just bad luck but it could also be the beginning of a spreading blight that could affect the entire country. While Milwaukee citizens recognized some of the root causes, their response did not touch on any solutions. There were no signs of Christian missions in the area nor any signs of revitalizing the city through the re-establishment of the values and Social Capital or the other pillars of prosperity.

The impact of Social Capital is also very similar to the dynamics of a winning sports team, the embodiment of teamwork, and the positive motivation it provides. This again reminds us of another aspect of the Christian philosophy of life that is essential to prosperity. It's not just enough to state principles or rules. Christianity has developed a great delivery system, a superior coaching, training, and learning experience that incorporates motivation and teamwork and at the same time builds Social Capital, the degree of interpersonal friendly and neighborly values and social interactions. The very idea of teamwork and being part of a team as one of the secrets to the success of winning teams is the essence of building social capital within the team.

Christianity has a significant influence on what people think
- The level of Christian involvement is a factor in the level of prosperity
- Christian influence on non-Christian societies does improve prosperity
- Maximum prosperity comes from a mix of good government and good personal values.
- Christian Theology and Philosophy, both, contribute to good values
- Prosperity suffers when Christian values are diluted, distorted, or abandoned for another set of values that appears to be innate in human nature.

The Big Prosperity Picture
- **Thinking(Philosophy+Action) —> The Pillars of Prosperity**
- **Thinking(Philosophy+Action) —> Shalom Happiness**

Prosperity is then the story of a conflict between two world views of life. One worldview is basic Human Nature. It has a conniving malevolent nature, always calculating and plotting to get an advantage in life. This mindset leans toward a totalitarian form of government that opposes the elements of a prosperous society and is prevalent around the world. It is in opposition to the Christian Theology and Philosophy of Life that maximizes the potential for prosperity, which will be addressed more fully in a later chapter.

Human nature is who we are when we act out our basic instincts. This comes from two sources from mankind's prehistoric past, his genetic characteristics and his response to becoming a conscious human being. These two influences produced that conniving malevolent human nature that we have to live with every day. A third influence was human religion, adopted to try and overcome those forces of human nature but with mixed results. These we will examine next, the three big influences on thinking.

These are the big three of basic human thinking and they are the source of all the human-induced misery in the world. Christianity charts Theological and Philosophical courses in a completely different direction to provide prosperity rather than misery. And on this subject everyone agrees, that mankind's deluded thinking can easily drive society's train off the tracks, often on purpose, to advance one's self personally. We've given enough examples of that already.

The Thinker and the Sitting Woman
(Hamangia (Chalcolithic) culture)

9. Genetics: The Foundation of Thinking

We've discussed a great deal about how the good life and prosperity are dependent on a society having a good set of norms and standards. From our evaluation, we have concluded that Christianity appears to have the best Theology and Philosophy of Life, a set of principles, rules, and standards to achieve maximum prosperity.

We have also seen that even some atheists and Humanists, who generally believe that mankind has or can create their own morality through human thinking, also recognize that Christianity, and maybe some other religions as well, are necessary to control the harmful actions of humans. This is a recognition that there is a fundamentally "bad seed" philosophy within mankind that produces an evil, self-serving, and malevolent individual. And some external philosophy of good, such as Christianity, is required to control those malevolent tendencies.

We have also shown that these rules and standards must be in the hearts of the citizens, they must be ubiquitous within the thinking of society.

Prosperity comes from thinking, right? That means when we think and act the right way about life events the outcomes will be better and when we think and act the wrong way the outcome will be worse.

Thinking is much more than decision-making about choices great and small, from what kind of car to buy or what job to take to how to deal with a bad neighbor or whether I should visit my mother this weekend, or how much of a tip I should leave for that overcooked steak. Thinking includes how I view the world around me and my circumstances and opportunities. It includes how I view other people and circumstances and then respond to them in good moments and bad.

We live life by a process that takes us from thinking to believing to actions. Sometimes those thinking and believing steps are quite short, the result of "snap" decisions, the type of response needed while driving a car, and the reason elderly people sometimes should not be doing so.

Thinking: how we perceive and evaluate the world
Believing: weighing the alternatives and picking one
Action: implementing the selected choice

Thinking is the precursor to action but it needs something to think about, a set of rules or standards, a Philosophy, to serve as the basis for evaluating alternatives

Thinking or Thought: In their most common sense, the terms thought and thinking refer to conscious cognitive processes that can happen independently of sensory stimulation. Their most paradigmatic forms are judging, reasoning, concept formation, problem-solving, and deliberation. But other mental processes, like considering an idea, memory, or

imagination, are also often included. These processes can happen internally independent of the sensory organs, unlike perception. But when understood in the widest sense, any mental event may be understood as a form of thinking, including perception and unconscious mental processes. In a slightly different sense, the term thought refers not to the mental processes themselves but to mental states or systems of ideas brought about by these processes.
https://en.wikipedia.org/wiki/Thought

The trick to life is knowing which way to think, and what rules or standards to follow, the bad news is that some rules and standards, some philosophies, can be disastrous and lead to a dumpster fire life. What is even more important is that often we don't have time to think about an event, we have to respond, or do respond, without a deliberation in our brain as to what to do.

The even worse news is that the core of our thinking is built into our genes. And then we have other outside bad influences on our thinking that may even make matters worse. All of the bad influences have to be overcome on a day-by-day basis and substituted with good influences to prevent that dumpster fire life and to achieve that "shalom" life.

This is the challenge of life and we see it playing out in people's lives every day. For the most part, we win some and lose some. We make some good choices and some horrible choices. When we look at the world we see a long history of good and bad choices. The survey of prosperity around the world testifies to that. But those surveys also show that Christianity and the Christian Philosophy of Life have certainly had a positive effect on improving good outcomes.

The conclusion is that there are forces in our thinking and thought that can cause us to make bad decisions, decisions that can significantly reduce the chances of "shalom" prosperity as well. There is within us a battle of ideas and philosophy competing for our attention and driving our actions. Civilization is the result of a collective attempt to bring a little peace and sanity to life through rules that limit chaos. But we are still stuck with some basic behavioral instincts that drive how we think as well. And of course, the quality of your little piece of civilization may not be that perfect as well. And if you thought this couldn't get even worse, all those built-in behavioral instincts never cause one to hesitate or even consider another choice, those instincts just jump up and holler, DO IT.

The problem with thinking is that we don't think much about it.

Survival challenges are typical subjects of stories, books, TV, and movies. If you've been a fan of these stories, they all have some things in common. The very first action the heroes or heroines have to take is to discover the nature of their environment. What is it like and what resources do they have to survive? This is also a good approach to life in general. We're dumped into life, just like those survival stories, so knowing our environment and the resources we have gives us an advantage in surviving the challenge and making a success of life.

Our basic behaviors come from our genes. Science also knows that our environment influences our actions as well. Both of these historical influences drive our basic thinking. Even your hobbies can come from genetic influences passed down from previous generations. We know that our biological digestive systems are tuned to a diet that was established in the distant prehistoric past and for many people not only influences their diet but controls it.

The Egyptian beliefs of preserving bodies after death have given us a grand view of the harm of changing eating habits from a meat-based to a grain-based diet. These well-preserved bodies showed numerous illnesses and short lives that resulted from this change in diet. That was six thousand years ago and we now have only partially recovered from such a change, many of our current health problems come from the impact of grains on our body's food chemistry. The point of this is that genes are not forever but they don't change easily. For a diet change our bodies have to redesign themselves and six thousand years is not enough time for that to happen.

But there's more to genes than diet, they direct life for survival, and survival of mankind in the prehistoric stage required brain power so our thinking has been genetically programmed to think and act in a way that promotes survival. Before consciousness, this thinking was all instinctual, and it has been built into our genetic thinking over the many years mankind spent living in prehistoric societies and circumstances. From a Christian Biblical perspective that could be considered the length of time mankind spent living in the Garden of Eden. That is the unspecified time between the creation of the world and the "fall of man" and his expulsion from the Garden. The expulsion from the Garden of Eden was a thinking game changer all on its own.

Genetic influences called "Behavioral Genetics" is the study of the influence of genetics on behavior. It is part of a separate field of psychology called "Differential Psychology". The impact of genes on behavior is an active field of analysis of the behavior of humans.

> *Differential psychology* studies the ways in which individuals differ in their behavior and the processes that underlie it. This is a discipline that develops classifications (taxonomies) of psychological individual differences. This is distinguished from other aspects of psychology in that although psychology is ostensibly a study of individuals, modern psychologists often study groups, or attempt to discover general psychological processes that apply to all individuals.[1] This particular area of psychology was first named and still retains the name of "differential psychology" by William Stern in his book (1900).
>
> https://en.wikipedia.org/wiki/Differential_psychology
>
> *Behavioural genetics,* also referred to as behaviour genetics, is a field of scientific research that uses genetic methods to investigate the nature and origins of individual differences in behaviour. While the name "behavioural genetics" connotes a focus on genetic influences, the field broadly investigates the extent to which genetic and environmental factors influence individual differences and the development of research designs that can remove the confounding of genes and environment. Behavioural genetics was founded as a scientific discipline by Francis Galton in the late 19th century, only to be discredited through association with eugenics movements before and during World War II. In the latter half of the 20th century, the field saw renewed prominence with research on inheritance of behaviour and mental illness in humans (typically using twin and family studies), as well as research on genetically informative model organisms through selective breeding and crosses. In the late 20th and early 21st centuries, technological advances in molecular genetics made it possible to measure and modify the genome directly. This led to major advances in model organism research (e.g.,

knockout mice) and in human studies (e.g., genome-wide association studies), leading to new scientific discoveries.

Findings from behavioural genetic research have broadly impacted modern understanding of the role of genetic and environmental influences on behaviour. **These include evidence that nearly all researched behaviours are under a significant degree of genetic influence, and that influence tends to increase as individuals develop into adulthood.** *Further, most researched human behaviours are influenced by a very large number of genes and the individual effects of these genes are very small. Environmental influences also play a strong role, but they tend to make family members more different from one another, not more similar.*

https://en.wikipedia.org/wiki/Behavioural_genetics

The basic consensus of this field of study is that nearly all researched behaviors are significantly influenced by genetics. To this we might add that research has shown that even hobbies or interests in activities are inherited. Even such activities as stamp collecting or sports or interests in occupations. Like father, like son, is a pretty accurate assessment. That doesn't mean that grandparents can "wash their hands" of any responsibility for their grandkids, however.

Behavioral Genetics is an active field that takes studies over large samples and long timeframes to assess, so the research and conclusions are somewhat controversial. The basic findings have been summarized as follows.

*****Behavioral Genetics:*** *In response to general concerns about the replicability of psychological research, behavioural geneticists Robert Plomin, John C. DeFries, Valerie Knopik, and Jenae Neiderhiser published a review of the ten most well-replicated findings from behavioural genetics research. The ten findings were:*

1. *"All psychological traits show significant and substantial genetic influence."*
2. *"No behavioral traits are 100% heritable."*
3. *"Heritability is caused by many genes of small effect."*
4. *"Phenotypic correlations between psychological traits show significant and substantial genetic mediation."*
5. *"The heritability of intelligence increases throughout development."*
6. *"Age-to-age stability is mainly due to genetics."*
7. *"Most measures of the 'environment' show significant genetic influence."*

8. *"Most associations between environmental measures and psychological traits are significantly mediated genetically."*
9. *"Most environmental effects are not shared by children growing up in the same family."*
10. *"Abnormal is normal."*
https://en.wikipedia.org/wiki/Behavioural_genetics

Our genes are pretty much universally similar across all civilizations because of common life experiences in the prehistoric past. We also know that genetic traits, both good and bad, rise and fall through generations and that genetic dispositions, our personality, can be amplified by culture and passed down to future generations. The term "bad seed" isn't talking about a random chance condition but about the fact that our children can inherit both good and bad tendencies from several generations in the past. And "bad seeds" can envelop an entire society. (This answers the question as to "why the flood" and why was Israel told to wipe out an entire competing tribe by God.)

A key to the impact of genes on an individual is the culture and the philosophy of life into which he or she is born. Take for example the genetic disposition of innate musical talent. It may pop up anywhere and if a parent has the gene it is more likely to exist in the child. But whether that child develops that innate talent or not is directly a function of his or her environment. The child of a practicing musical talent will likely grow up in a music-rich environment that encourages the development of that talent. And quite often that talent is developed, maybe not on the scale of the parent's achievement, but it is there and can even be greater than the parents. There can also be environmental distractions that disrupt the development of that musical talent. Nothing is certain.

On the other hand children with musical genes who grow up in a non-musical environment likely will never develop their musical genetic disposition. It can happen of course through musical opportunities in school or even through friends who introduce them to music. The key of course is that genetics predispose talent while the environment may either help make it a reality or kill it completely.

How we behave and act in life and how we handle the problems and difficulties in life is no doubt a function of both our inherent genetic code and our philosophy of life. Our philosophy of life is of course learned from our surrounding environment and culture. It begins with our parents and then evolves through the influence of our peers, our education, our neighborhood, and our society as a whole. As we live life we have many opportunities to learn and if we live long enough and learn from our experiences we may even become that wise old man or woman who always wishes they knew when they were young what they know now.

Notice however that it is the cultural environment that dictated much of the successes or failures in both developing our genetic talents and suppressing our weaknesses, and in the same fashion developing good or bad coping mechanisms. We may have bad genes in terms of having a quick and violent temper but our environment and culture may help us overcome that genetic deficiency or use it more productively. For example, instead of getting even, we may learn to use that aggression to make ourselves better individuals.

There is also the sense that unless you use your innate talents and capabilities and align your life with good principles, at best, you will only experience pseudo-happiness, not true happiness. Pseudo means phony, fake, false, deceptive, or contrived. We all know people who live with pseudo-happiness. They seem to be enjoying life, but the circumstances of that life are a mess. Good examples are anyone who has a drug, alcohol, or food addiction problem. They lie to themselves every day that they are having "the good life" no matter how those addictions affect their lives. The life of drug addicts is one of waking up every day plotting how to beg, barter, or steal enough money to get their daily fix so that they can experience those fleeting few minutes of euphoria the drugs deliver. But every day is a step further away from a much more prosperous and happy life and from remembering the dreams of what could have been. You are what you think and what you think is, at a fundamental level, the sum total of your ancestral heritage and living experiences.

All of this is to make the point that two major factors influence how we, as individuals, respond to life; our genes and our environment. And this idea is nothing new, it's been a popular topic of discussion for as long as anyone can remember. But the one piece that may not be so obvious is that the environment is much more than rich or poor which is the simplistic and popular point of discussion. The environment includes the entire cultural philosophy of life to which an individual is exposed.

In your lifetime you may encounter 100,000 challenges to your life, each slightly different and having a unique tailored optimum response. Your response to each may be good or bad or some level in-between, all depending on your wisdom and knowledge about how to address each challenge. Your wisdom and knowledge come from the following broad sources or influences in your life. The problem is that each guiding influence may offer good or bad advice for those challenges, how do know which to use? Perhaps within Christianity lies the answer.

Significant Guiding Influences in Life
1. **Genes** - built-in but changeable design of physical, personality, and moral characteristics
2. **Experiences** - events we encounter in our lives, all those "ah hah" and "gosh shang-it *%#*" moments.
3. **Culture;** Norms and Standards; and values from three competing sources that are themselves intertwined
   a. **Society** - Norms and standards for living life imposed by parents, peers, stories, nature, and rulers/governments.
   b. **Religion** - an external source of norms and standards purported to have come from a superior spiritual source.
   c. **Human Philosophy** - norms and standards created from the thinking of human beings, including all the novels, comic books, self-help books, and YouTube video advice you can find.

Your challenges in life can be big and small, life-changing, or a blip in a daily event. But every challenge will require a response from you, good or bad. Now to be clear let's look at a single example that's not likely to offend anyone. Cannibals in the jungle ate their enemies, their competitors, because they believed that by eating them they would gain the "spirit" strength of their enemies. This was a philosophy of life that came from their religious beliefs, those ideas that have to do with the spiritual nature, the unseen nature of life. If one believes that mankind has an unseen spirit nature that gives each one some kind of extra power and that by eating your enemy, or your neighbor who offends you or competes with you for food, you can acquire his spirit power for yourself and become more powerful, then you too can become a cannibal. This of course does not bode well for merging societies to work together because there is also no way to prove that these religious/spiritual ideas are not true. We have no persuasive scientific logical factual argument to demonstrate that the cannibal is wrong.

The cannibal then has three influences on his life and decision-making. His genes, his own life experiences, and thirdly his culture which includes tribal values and traditions and his religious beliefs, his view of the unseen spiritual world. Three prime factors that determine how he lives, genes, culture, and experiences pretty much define the box that confines his life experiences and the results.

Cultural Norms and standards are the set of operational guidelines that are considered normal and acceptable rules for living in a society or culture with other individuals. Cultures are a creation of the major influencing factors identified above. This is not an exhaustive and finally certain, all-inclusive listing of influences by any means. The objective here is to give a broad overview of the factors that make us who we are because we're going to examine the results, and who we have become, and make some assessments as to the causes and effects.

Whenever we take a snapshot of human beings all over the world we see many different webs of cultures with many different outcomes and many different features, some of which may be abhorrent to other cultures. As with everything in life, there are risks and rewards and regrets, all because we humans are not robots, all designed and operating alike.

We are, of course, stuck with our genes and genes can be a real detriment to prosperity and happiness in life. Many of the human failings and weaknesses as well as strengths are a matter of our genetic disposition. What's more interesting is that some of these factors are inherited traits from our parents who got the same genes from their parents. Also, some of our genetic traits could have been bred into our parents and grandparents based on significant influences in their own lives. That is, life can influence genes. Life can supply rewards, disciplines, and other responses that all can cause chemical and biological changes within us and potentially affect and modify our genes and genetic behavior. Once the biological coding for these genes is modified they are then passed down to future generations. This is cutting-edge genetics in a relatively new field called epigenetics. The following information comes from the Psychology Today.com website.

Epigenetics

Epigenetics is the study of how the environment and other factors can change the way that genes are expressed. While epigenetic changes do not alter the sequence of a person's genetic code, they can play an important role in development. Scientists who work in epigenetics explore the mechanisms that affect the activity of genes.

Each person's DNA lays the groundwork for the development of physical and psychological characteristics—providing complex instructions for the creation of proteins and other molecules. But the manner in which these instructions are used can be modified by various factors. The chemical modifications that influence gene activity in this way are collectively called the epigenome.

These modifications occur naturally and help to steer development—for example, they enable cells in the brain and in other parts of the body to perform specialized roles based on the same underlying genetic code. But the epigenome is also susceptible to influence by exposure to toxins and other environmental factors.

https://www.psychologytoday.com/us/basics/epigenetics

Changes can be caused by diet, exercise, smoking, drug use, and early life stress. That is life can cause epigenetic changes in people and those changes can be for the better or for worse life outcomes. This can include vulnerability to various forms of mental illnesses and can be passed from one generation to the next. There are associations with depression, schizophrenia, and bipolar disorders. Stress disorders caused by trauma can even be passed on to children.

Simplistically, science is saying that there is more going on than just having 40,000 to 140,000 genes in the human DNA. There are also genetic switches that turn genes on or off and also amplifiers that

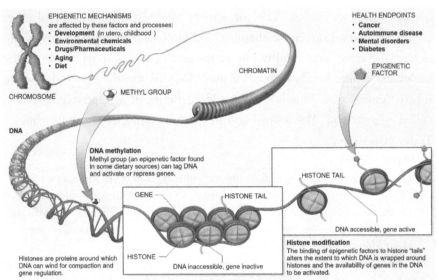

EPIGENETIC MECHANISMS
are affected by these factors and processes:
- **Development** (in utero, childhood)
- **Environmental chemicals**
- **Drugs/Pharmaceuticals**
- Aging
- Diet

CHROMATIN

CHROMOSOME   METHYL GROUP

DNA

DNA methylation
Methyl group (an epigenetic factor found in some dietary sources) can tag DNA and activate or repress genes.

GENE   HISTONE TAIL

Histones are proteins around which DNA can wind for compaction and gene regulation.

HISTONE —   DNA inaccessible, gene inactive

HEALTH ENDPOINTS
- Cancer
- Autoimmune disease
- Mental disorders
- Diabetes

EPIGENETIC FACTOR

HISTONE TAIL

DNA accessible, gene active

Histone modification
The binding of epigenetic factors to histone "tails" alters the extent to which DNA is wrapped around histones and the availability of genes in the DNA to be activated.

https://commonfund.nih.gov/epigenomics/figure

moderate the effect of the gene. This is another mechanism for genetic change.

In a recent book on this subject, it is asserted that 95% of disease-related gene mutations can be influenced by diet, behavior, and environmental factors.

Dr. Rudolph Tanzi is a professor of neurology at Harvard University Medical School. Among his many accomplishments, he co-discovered three genes that cause early-onset familial Alzheimer's disease. Along with Dr. Deepak Chopra, a global leader in the field of mind-body medicine, he co-authored this book:

> ### Super Genes: Unlock the Astonishing Power of Your DNA for Optimum Health and Well-Being. Nov 10 2015 Harmony
>
> *The authors of the New York Times bestseller Super Brain present a bold new understanding of our genes and how simple changes in lifestyle can boost genetic activity. The leap into "radical well-being" is a promise waiting to be fulfilled.*
>
> *"You are not simply the sum total of the genes you were born with," writes Deepak Chopra and Rudy Tanzi. "You are the user and controller of your genes, the author of your biological story. No prospect in self-care is more exciting."*

Learning how to shape your gene activity is at the heart of this exciting and eagerly-anticipated book from the bestselling duo behind Super Brain, which became a nationwide hit on public television.

For decades medical science has believed that genes determined our biological destiny. Now the new genetics has changed that assumption forever. ***You will always have the genes you were born with, but genes are dynamic, responding to everything we think, say, and do. Suddenly they've become our strongest allies for personal transformation. When you make lifestyle choices that optimize how your genes behave, you can reach for a state of health and fulfillment undreamed of even a decade ago.*** *The impact on prevention, immunity, diet, aging, and chronic disorders is unparalleled.*
https://www.amazon.com/Super-Genes-Astonishing-Optimum-Well-Being/dp/0804140154

Now the point of all this is that even though you may have the genes of a cannibal or a serial killer, you're not without hope, those bad genes can be overcome by choices and influences. Similarly, you may have the genes of a master musician but life choices may preclude their development.

There is a key area of your life where you have choices and those choices can influence your life either positively or negatively. One of those choices is your occupation, your career, or your life's work. These choices and capabilities are determined by desire, drive, innate talents, education, etc. Your challenge is to find out what you like to do, what interests you, what challenges you, what you feel comfortable doing, what you're capable of doing well, and what brings you satisfaction in a job well done.

Something is missing from this generalization of choosing a satisfying life occupation, however. Individuals are severely limited in choices by the culture in which they live. That culture may be severely influenced by environmental, religious, or local human philosophies which can and do severely limit career options. There are no remote primitive tribe job openings for computer scientists, nor are there any taxi driver openings for females in Saudi Arabia, yet. Or worse yet, you could be a female in Afghanistan. The point is that our local situation may be rich or poor in terms of opportunities and similarly influencing factors. Everyone does not have the same choices available to them and the result is that there are differences in possible or likely outcomes for individuals. This is certainly the case for those growing up in parts of inner city Milwaukee, a story we discussed earlier where the job choices were few and drug dealing was a high-paying job. The outlook for kids in that environment was not good, especially when the community social capital was low or missing entirely.

Similar logical and human responses to the other two major factors that influence your life can also occur. You can grow up in a great family environment and still be a rebel and become a serial killer by rejecting all the great and positive life influences. But that's not likely. What each of us can expect is that the three major influences in your life, Genes, Experiences, and Culture will play a big role in how your life turns out.

Now we have shown, or at least implied that your genes do not critically determine your outcome in life. We will also assert that your environment is a similar case, one where many people have demonstrated the ability to rise above their childhood environment and even an adult environment and become prosperous and happy people. It is your culture however, your philosophy of life, the totality of influences in life, that drives how you respond to and handle both your genes and environment.

We have now identified the major influences in shaping our thinking and thus affecting our ability to have a life of prosperity, peace, and happiness within our capabilities.

Life Influences
1. **Genes - our biological design & instincts**
2. **Experiences - life's events, food and drugs**
3. **Culture; Norms and Standards, Values**
   a. **Society: The Structure and fabric of life - the way our community works**
   b. **Religious Environment and Philosophies of Life**
   c. **Human Philosophy - formal and informal**

These are the broad categories of influences. Most all the specifics you could think of, or have maybe experienced, should fit into one of these categories. Remember however that these categories or influence factors don't directly affect our prospects for shalom. They affect and influence our thinking about life's choices. For example, one child in a poverty neighborhood turns into a drug addict and a drug dealer, and another turns into a brain surgeon. One used the negative factors he experienced to reject those influences and prosper. The other accepted them as the norm and way of life and lost his life's prosperity potential in favor of a dumpster fire life.

We've been emphasizing life choices, a big factor in the direction of your life, but equally influential are all those small daily choices about how you respond to those around you. These are equally important, and in fact, you can be on an important career path and destroy it with words or actions toward your boss or others in the field. Similarly, you might have the best mate in the world and destroy that relationship based on a poor choice of words or actions even minor seeming ones over years of poor choices.

Another way to look at prosperity and happiness is that it is based on who we are, what we experience, and what we learn.

- **Who we are: Our genes**
- **What we experience: Our environment**
- **What we learn from: Our Cultural influences**

Now we have talked a bit about the variability of genes and environment and the fact that we have choices as to our responses to our genes and environment. The big factor that helps us manage and control our genes and environment is our culture, the norms, and the standards that help us navigate through life. As we've also pointed out, these cultural norms and standards may be either a positive or a negative influence on our lives. That is they may show us how to mitigate our genetic or experientially induced weaknesses or they may make things worse. There are also many habits and idiosyncrasies that can undermine our success and prosperity as well, probably as important as any life decisions. These are factors that would cause us distress no matter what life we choose. For example, your life can become a dumpster fire by thousands of nasty comments directed toward people every day, or by heading down a singularly really bad path, such as drug addiction.

We have also broken down the cultural norms and standards into three sources of influence on our lives. They answer the question, "How does a Culture develop its norms and standards, its values?".

Sources of Cultural Norms and Standards, Values
a. **Tradition: The Structure and fabric of life - the way our community works**
b. **Religious Environment and Philosophy**
c. **Human Philosophy - formal and informal**

In most societies around the world, the dominant influencing factors in life are genes and religion. Genes provide instinctive survival instructions and guidance while religion provides, first of all, an orientation to life, and secondly, some principles, guidelines, and rules for living and succeeding in that life situation. Religion is such a powerful force that it inculcates its viewpoint and ideas into the very fabric of life to the extent that the two other contributors to culture; society and human philosophy; and then also, your life experiences, are colored or flavored by religion.

This influence of religion on human life may be hard to see if you're not religious. If you've had no religious upbringing or experiences or perhaps have had some exposure to religion and have rejected it, your view of religion is perhaps relegated to the observed periodic religious rituals alone. However, the influence of religion on almost every nation is evident in the culture and values of the inhabitants. Even those antagonists of popular religion, such as Thomas Jefferson, were more antagonistic toward certain aspects and beliefs of the formal religious organizations than the Christian philosophy of life contained in the Bible. This was exemplified of course by his study and revision of the Bible's New Testament which he reordered, combining and omitting passages, according to his own sensibilities. So while many hold Jefferson as the example of "non-Christians" forming the United States, he was certainly a philosophical Christian at heart. He just had a hard time believing every Christian theological idea presented to him.

Likewise, most of the philosophers of the last 500 years or so after the Western World's awakening were profoundly influenced by Christianity.

The cultures of societies in the Western world were likewise colored by the Christian flavor of those who lived and made the laws and established the norms and standards.

Without going into a historical account of similar events or evidence in the rest of the world it should be fair to say that the other primary religions of the world have had a similarly large impact on the cultures they dominate as well.

In some religions, this cultural influence may be very direct, imposing, and much more visible, such as Hinduism, Buddhism, and Islam.   In others such as Christianity, it may be more subtle, more friendly persuasion than authoritative.   What each religion does however is to present a worldview, an orientation to life, and a view of the god(s) of that world.   Secondly, religion will provide the follower with some specific directions and guidance on dealing with life according to that worldview and the god it presents.

We have thus somewhat modified our view of the factors which influence societies and the resultant shalom, prosperity, and happiness, by downgrading society and philosophy visually to emphasize the big role religion plays.   If you live in the Western World and don't participate in religion the point is that much of society's influence and philosophy's influence comes from a Christian worldview environment.

1. **Genes - our biological design & instincts**
2. **Experiences - life's events, food and drugs**
3. **Culture; Norms and Standards, Values**
    a. Society: The Structure and fabric of life - the way our community works
    b. **Religious Environment and Philosophy**
    c. Human Philosophy - formal and informal

That is, we have argued that religion is the primary influence on cultures around the world, including the Western World. Not the religion of ritual or worship attendance but the religion of life's traditions, values, order, and rules that come from the writings, doctrines, and religious teachers. These are the things that affect, direct, and transform the society in which you live whether or not you subscribe to the ritual and religious beliefs of that religion. If you have heard the term "love your neighbor" or "do unto others ...." Then your world has been colored by Christian philosophy.

One last observation is that we tend to think that everyone thinks as we do. Parents all over the world love their kids, we all believe lying, cheating, and stealing are wrong, and all faiths, and religions can work together for the good of our communities. But there's more to religion and philosophy of life than bumper sticker slogans. If we know anything about sports this is an obvious principle that we should all recognize. When teams have generally equal talent, the championships go to the teams with better coaches, better performance fundamentals, better game plans, better motivation, and better training regiments. Football quarterbacks and baseball pitchers are usually the linchpins to a good or great team and even the most talented of these players have much to learn even after reaching the professional ranks and usually throughout their careers. The best athletes are masters of their game, they never stop studying and learning new techniques and strategies to play the game.

The point is that there is another significant aspect to maximizing prosperity, peace, and happiness. To take advantage of any philosophy it has to become part of your life. So the quality of the training program is of significant importance. Christianity may have a superior philosophy or game plan for life but if the philosophy is not effectively taught or communicated to individuals it is not effective. Not because the philosophy is defective but because the individual fails to learn. And the failure of the individual to learn may be the fault of the teachers as well as the student.

In other words "You are what you think". You can live under the very best philosophy and still fail if you fail to inculcate and absorb that philosophy into your way of thinking. Several secular books address this very concept in different ways.

1. **Think and Grow Rich**
2. **The Power of Positive Thinking**
3. **The Seven Habits of Highly Successful People**

These are three that appeared in the mid to late Twentieth century with much popular success. The first one, "Think and Grow Rich" was so intent on the importance of taking its message to heart, making it real in the life of the reader, that it never articulated its key principle in writing, requiring the reader to surmise the message. These three books, as well as others, reinforce this idea of making the ideas and philosophy your own in different ways. The third, for example, put the keyword right in its title, "habits", what you do instinctively. So while the philosophy the religion espouses is important, the documentation and delivery of that philosophy to the followers are also important. But even more important is that the points, principles, and guidelines of the philosophy become second nature to the follower. You can't just know the rule by memory, you have to be able to use it when the situation arises without taking out your notebook and trying to find an answer.

Prosperity, Peace, and Happiness in Life Training Elements
1. **Motivation**
2. **Coaching**
3. **Performance fundamentals (philosophy)**
4. **Game Plan**
5. **Training**

We've alluded to these training factors previously when examining where prosperity in various Christian-dominated countries failed to inculcate Christians with the details of the philosophy, a training failure, and an adverse effect on the prosperity outcome resulted. The importance of training is, in fact, a significant part of Christian philosophy, as it is in some other religious traditions.

You are what you think based on the influencers in your life, genes, experiences, and culture. Religion is often bigger and more significant in projecting your thinking and prosperity than others because it often forms the basis for societies and human philosophy. There is a bigger overall influencer in life that can override, modify, or control, all of these however, consciousness. At one point in pre-history mankind lived without consciousness, but when it happened, everything changed. Consciousness began to dominate all the factors of thinking.

Expulsion from Paradise, painting by James Tissot (c.

(French)Google Art Projectでのアーティストの詳細 - igGZ-wF6_0XnlQ at Google Cultural Institute maximum zoom level, Public Domain, https://commons.wikimedia.org/w/index.php?curid=22493007

10. Consciousness: A New World View

There is another event in human history that dramatically changed the course of human thinking forever. An event that overwhelms and alters the nature of all the drivers of thinking we've discussed and caused the birth of religions. A long period of prehistory has altered our genes and created the self-serving, malevolent creature we know. That event is mankind's transition to consciousness. Before consciousness, mankind's thinking is primarily a blinded genetic response to life with experiences and tribal nomadic hunter-gatherer life adding some extended social contact to consider. Cultural Norms, Standards, and Values are all about the small close-knit tribe and how to deal with adjacent tribes when they are encountered.

Our thinking is programmed by our genes. Initially, in pre-history, our genes were simple survival techniques as mankind walked in an animal-like pre-conscious existence. But Consciousness changes everything it gives mankind a much bigger picture of life. Mankind now sees the world with different eyes, he now has the full influential sources of thinking available, plus he now sees there is an opportunity to exploit his neighbor for his benefit.

Mankind experienced two distinct periods of history that are confirmed in the Bible. We existed as human beings for an unknown period in the Biblically named Garden of Eden. This period is characterized by the Bible as a peaceful stress-free existence that included modern features such as language and animal and crop husbandry. Archeology portrays mankind in this first phase of existence as a hunter-gatherer with a sense of a God who ruled a spiritual world where one went after death. This leap of logic would come from early man's religious tendencies displayed at burial sites. It is this first period of existence of early man, the time in the Garden of Eden, where genes developed their baseline characteristics. The second period begins when mankind is expelled from the Garden of Eden. This expulsion presents mankind with a different set of living conditions. Gone is the easy life and now he must work diligently for food and shelter. The key descriptor of this change is that mankind now knows about Good and Evil.

What was missing during this first period of human history, life in the Garden, was a sense of consciousness. The consequence of consciousness was leaving that Garden. The Garden was the idyllic life, no stress, no worries, no knowledge of right and wrong, and no thoughts of doing good or evil. God expelled mankind from the Garden and prevented their return, but He did this through their own actions. Once consciousness makes you aware of good and evil there's no going back into that idyllic life.

This sense of consciousness would give mankind a much broader view of life and circumstances and the ability to manipulate life and others. It ultimately altered his original genetic thinking as significant new options were added to life. Consciousness would also lead to the formation of religions. These three factors then, new genes, consciousness, and religion became the three driving forces in mankind's second phase of history. The transition to consciousness is lost in prehistoric events but it is captured in the Biblical narrative that gives us a good picture of the impact on genetics and thinking. Consciousness and genetic changes from this new view of life explain much of the Biblical narrative concerning the evil, malevolent people that existed, especially in the accounts of Noah and the flood and life through the Exodus experience.

The change to being a conscious human being was perhaps very subtle personally, but the impact was significant and somewhat uniform in that everyone in this new world had a similar reaction. Each one was now aware of his or her responsibilities for their own life. A similar situation arose when the Soviet Union and communism collapsed and everyone was now on their own to get a job, earn money and pay their rent and utilities, buy their food at full price, i.e., value. This was a traumatic experience for all those who had only known life with everything given to them, over 70 plus years and several generations.

This change in consciousness, therefore, created a similar experience in everyone it touched. And what it did was twofold. First, it altered the perspective of everyone toward life. And secondly, it caused people to seek help from that superior force they had known about in their previous semiconscious state. That is, the advent of consciousness also caused the birth of religion as an attempt to return to that previous unconscious state and call upon that superior spiritual being they had known, for help in their brave new world.

This seismic shift in humanity was most likely not instantaneous where all mankind was headed in one direction culturally and some cosmic event such as a meteor strike, as postulated for the decline of the dinosaurs occurred, causing all mankind to head in a different direction. Rather it appears to have been a gradual change where individuals throughout the world were randomly waking up in a new world yet still surrounded by many old-world thinkers, so to speak. This change was so outwardly subtle on a community basis that the difference between the two was hardly noticed until one day the old-world humans were completely replaced by new-world humans. The seismic aspect of this was that the new-world humans had an entirely different view of life from their old-world cousins.

A well-documented example of such a subtle yet dramatic transformation was the Christian takeover of the Roman Empire and pagan Europe over 600 years or so without a single battle, confrontation, or demand for change. It began with Christians being ridiculed and persecuted and ended with Christians dominating the governments of the entire Roman countryside and Christians as rulers of the city-states that emerged as the central Roman government declined in influence.

The advent of human consciousness was also dramatic enough to be the primary cause for the formation of religions. The impact of the event on life established the religious thinking, direction, and view of life that shaped most all early religious thoughts. The question then is, what exactly is this transformation to consciousness and why and how did it affect mankind's view of life? The Bible describes enough of the characteristics to match the description of a conscious individual.

Interestingly this is one area where religion and science seem to agree, at least the Judaeo-Christian traditions, (Islam has a divergent view), for they all have accounts of the seismic event, and both science and religion seem to generally agree on the general nature of the change to being a conscious human being, however, the details are sketchy and much speculation remains such as:

Speculations About Consciousness
- The nature of life before human consciousness
- What is human consciousness
- When did the transformation to human consciousness take place
- The development of Formal Religion as the consequence of consciousness

While scientists seem to somewhat agree that there was at least an advent of human consciousness at some point in the past, they can't come up with a definitive description of the nature of consciousness because they don't understand just what that semi-consciousness state was like or how to describe it. In general, consciousness is described this way.

Consciousness, *at its simplest, is sentience or awareness of internal and external existence. Despite millennia of analyses, definitions, explanations, and debates by philosophers and scientists, consciousness remains puzzling and controversial, being "at once the most familiar and [also the] most mysterious aspect of our lives". Perhaps the only widely agreed notion about the topic is the intuition that consciousness exists. Opinions differ about what exactly needs to be studied and explained as consciousness. Sometimes, it is synonymous with the mind, and at other times, an aspect of mind. In the past, it was one's "inner life", the world of introspection, of private thought, imagination, and volition. Today, it often includes any kind*

John Locke, British Enlightenment philosopher
By Godfrey Kneller - State Hermitage Museum, St. Petersburg, Russia.
https://commons.wikimedia.org/wiki/File:John_Locke.jpg Public domain, via Wikimedia Commons

of cognition, experience, feeling, or perception. It may be awareness, awareness of awareness, or self-awareness either continuously changing or not. There might be different levels or orders of consciousness, or different kinds of consciousness, or just one kind with different features. Other questions include whether only humans are conscious, all animals, or even the whole universe. The disparate range of research, notions, and speculations raises doubts about whether the right questions are being asked.

• Examples of the range of descriptions, definitions, or explanations are: simple wakefulness, one's sense of selfhood or soul explored by "looking within"; being a metaphorical "stream" of contents, or being a mental state, mental event or mental process of the brain; having phanera or qualia and subjectivity; being the 'something that it is like' to 'have' or 'be' it; being the "inner theatre" or the executive control system of the mind.

*• **The origin of the modern concept of consciousness is often attributed to John Locke's Essay Concerning Human Understanding, published in 1690. Locke defined consciousness as "the perception of what passes in a man's own mind".** His essay influenced the 18th-century view of consciousness, and his definition appeared in Samuel Johnson's celebrated Dictionary (1755). **"Consciousness" (French: conscience) is also defined in the 1753 volume of Diderot and d'Alembert's Encyclopédie, as "the opinion or internal feeling that we ourselves have from what we do."***

https://en.wikipedia.org/wiki/Consciousness

For better or worse we also might say that consciousness is the ability to think and act abstractly and rationally beyond meeting the necessities of life. Abstractly meaning that the thought exists solely in the mind and doesn't have any physical reality. This includes

Consciousness: Abstract thinking

- the awareness of the past and the future,
- awareness of self, others, and the world as independent things
- The possession of conscious abstract thoughts of love, hate, compassion, empathy, loneliness, team spirit
- the ability to question, reason, and manipulate our interactions with the world and others
- The ability to foresee the results of interactions with others as beneficial or harmful to self and others and to adjust our actions accordingly

Even these concepts are somewhat nebulous and some aspects can be seen, or imagined, in the actions of animals, especially our pets, but we know there is a world of difference between their life and ours. They certainly don't worry about where their next meal is coming from, or have a "to-do" list for the next five days.

Consciousness is not the opposite of unconsciousness, being unconscious, or being asleep. It refers to an awakening in terms of the realization of self and the ability to change life's situations through unique and newly invented or created actions. To better visualize consciousness we'll define some different levels that are directly observable.

1. **Unconscious.** Asleep, unaware of the world
2. **Animal semi-consciousness** - the robotic life: aware of the world and biological and environmental forces; hunger, pain, food, sex, etc, and living life from moment to moment within the bounds and identities genetically defined for the animal and additionally created or influenced by life situations.
3. **Human consciousness** - the free will life: Added awareness of time as well as self and others and the impacts of actions on self and others, both good and bad. Also, awareness of the ability to learn and adapt/change based on reasoning, and self-determinism.

To better see the difference between man's consciousness and animal semi-consciousness let's use the "Yogi Berra" theoretical consciousness decision-making model.

"When you come to a fork in the road, take it."

If you understand this, your human consciousness is working. If not, let me explain. If you were a bear walking in the woods in search of some wild berries and you came to a fork in the path what would you do? You might sniff for berries in each direction and then randomly choose a path or if you've been going down the mountain, continue on a downward path, or follow the trail you always follow. If you have human consciousness, however, you'll stop and consider, that berries grow on the edges of open fields, so do I see an open field in either direction? Or will the trail going up most likely take me to a clearing on top of the mountain where I can find berries? But I think I also need a potty break and I know there are some outhouses at the bottom of the hill, near that road. And there are always some good picnic leftovers down there, that are as good as a few berries.

The seismic event we're talking about for mankind is the transition from an animal-like consciousness to a more or less human consciousness which gave mankind the ability to examine his life and the consequences of actions, and then come up with ways to change and improve the outcomes along with a recognition of the impacts of those changes on neighbors. Our genes are the product of generations of semi-conscious life. Those genes are still at work directing instincts but we now can control and modify those instincts. We're guessing a bit here as to the exact nature of the before and after conditions, but it gives us a fair representation as described by our second source, a picture in line with the scientific views of mankind, in a sense, waking up from what was an animal like robotic existence.

Besides scientific thinking, analysis, and research, a second source documenting this transition is an ancient written text we know as Genesis in the Bible's Old Testament. And while science, anthropology, physiology, and history may easily confirm through historical documentation and speculate on various theories, that such events as consciousness and religion have occurred, they have no way to postulate specific details of creation or cause.   What Genesis provides are some details that corroborate the advent of consciousness and illuminate or speculate both the cause and effect on humanity, one effect being the birth of religion.

The story in Genesis involves Adam, Eve, the Garden of Eden, the "apple", and the tree of knowledge of good and evil. We won't provide the entire account but just enough to demonstrate the transition event. What this story does is provide an intellectually satisfying and logical account of mankind's transition to consciousness, a satisfying capsule answer to what happened.

> **Genesis 2:15-17** *NASB Then the Lord God took the man and put him into the garden of Eden to cultivate it and keep it. The Lord God commanded the man, saying, "From any tree of the garden you may eat freely; but from the tree of the knowledge of good and evil you shall not eat, for in the day that you eat from it you will surely die."*
>
> **Genesis 3:1-12** *NASB Now the serpent was more crafty than any beast of the field which the Lord God had made. And he said to the woman, "Indeed, has God said, 'You shall not eat from any tree of the garden'?" The woman said to the serpent, "From the fruit of the trees of the garden we may eat; but from the fruit of the tree which is in the middle of the garden, God has said, 'You shall not eat from it or touch it, or you will die.'" The serpent said to the woman, "You surely will not die!* **For God knows that in the day you eat from it, your eyes will be opened, and you will be like God, knowing good and evil.***" When the woman saw that the tree was good for food, and that it was a delight to the eyes, and that the tree was desirable to make one wise, she took from its fruit and ate; and she gave also to her husband with her, and he ate.* **Then the eyes of both of them were opened, and they knew that they were naked; and they sewed fig leaves together and made themselves loin coverings.**
>
> *They heard the sound of the Lord God walking in the garden in the cool of the day, and the man and his wife hid themselves from the presence of the Lord God among the trees of the garden. Then the Lord God called to the man, and said to him, "Where are you?" He said, "I heard the sound of You in the garden, and I was afraid because I was naked; so I hid myself." NASB*

In looking at this story keep in mind that there's a good chance it's an allegory or parable that presents "a truth" just as well as, or perhaps better than if it were described as a "literal" event or published scientific paper. The reason for this is obvious, a parable is much shorter than a scholastic account and thus easily remembered and passed down from generation to generation. It also speaks to and is understood by, a much wider audience than a textbook full of scientific jargon. Parables were the "bumper stickers" of the ancient world. Everyone in the ancient world knew that you didn't have to believe that it was a literal factual account to accept the concept or conclusion of the parable to be true.

Also remember that we are using this parable or allegory because it provides a logical and reasonable interpretation and description of what is accepted by science as a real event that is also one, into which, they have no scientifically based insight. Don't let the talking snake or God's apparent confusion over what happened cause you to miss the message because that is part of the allegory.

- *Allegory*: the expression using symbolic fictional figures and actions of truths or generalizations about human existence, a symbolic representation.
- *Parable*: a usually short **fictitious story** that illustrates a moral attitude or a religious principle
- *Metaphor*: a figure of speech in which a word or phrase literally denoting one kind of object or idea is used in place of another to suggest a likeness or analogy between them (as in drowning in money)
- *Simile*: a figure of speech comparing two unlike things that are often introduced by "like" or 'as' (cheeks like roses)
- https://www.merriam-webster.com/

More importantly, this descriptive interpretation of mankind's transition to a conscious human being provides a great deal of insight into mankind's formation of religions and therefore the nature in which religions influence, either positively or negatively, prosperity and happiness factors.

In condensing this story down to its essence, several significant events took place. The first thing to note is that mankind was first of all living in an idyllic environment from their own viewpoint. The Garden of Eden was not just a physical place but in a larger sense, it defines both an environment in which everything necessary for life was provided and also a carefree manner of life. Mankind lived from moment to moment, without care or concern for where his next meal was coming from, and mankind was said to have casual contact with God. That is mankind had a sense of an external power exerting influence and direction on his life. He felt "guided" through life.

One way to look at the transition to consciousness is to imagine you're waking up from a vivid dream. In that dream world, you had an idyllic life where you found your food just by walking through the fields and you had a friend who talked to you and guided you through your life. You also had a mate, someone who helped you with your activities and gave you the best hugs. You realize you're waking up but you keep on dreaming that same dream, you're still in that dream world trying to solve whatever problem or situation your dream world has created. Half awake, half asleep. But once you fully wake up your dream becomes a distant memory.

For humans waking up into consciousness was perhaps a long time process, days, weeks, years, but the dream world of semi-consciousness was wonderful and you keep wanting to go back to it. As you gradually wake up you keep drifting back and forth into and out of that dream world until you're wide awake. You're living in the same world as your dream, your mate is there, that same person who's been at your side as long as you can remember.

Getting up, you mechanically go through your morning routines and head out to the fields looking for a meal, but something is missing. Where is that friend who talks to you and guides you to all those amazing blueberry patches? You suddenly feel alone, something you've never experienced before and you call out but he doesn't answer. Something's wrong, your mate is still sleeping, not helping find food, and you become agitated. You're alone in the field, where the lions roam. Terror strikes you as you hear a lion roar, you've never felt that afraid in all your life and you turn and run back across the field to your shelter in the trees and your mate is gone. Where did she go, did a lion get her, or is she down at the creek? Am I going mad? Where's my friend and guide when I need him?

This change was probably gradual, over a period of time, thus not as dramatic as pictured above. The change in thinking was real, but perhaps more like the culmination of a teenager becoming an adult. You don't notice the transition, you just notice that as an adult you see life differently. This is the transition the Genesis story was conveying 6,000 years ago and to us today.

Let's make another illustration. If you have a dog that you can take for a walk, unleashed, along a mountain trail, your dog will go running up and down the path and through the woods, sniffing all the wondrous aromas it never experiences at home in the backyard. It's having a wonderful time exploring the woods until it hears you call its name and it comes running back to you. If you've trained it properly. And you may give it a treat. In this case, you're your dog's "God". If you get lost your dog will frantically be looking for you behind every tree until it finds you. Unless it also sees a raccoon of course and then it's off to the races after that raccoon.

According to Genesis, mankind was aware of this life force as "God", someone much brighter and more capable than themselves, but this may simply be literary license in that the writer knew it was God and projected that knowledge onto the characters in the story as a way of stating the reality according to the writer. Remember this story is an allegory or a parable, a short simplistic way to describe a truth. It is therefore free to use simplistic fictional stylized content to present that truth, the truth being the advent of consciousness. It is not necessary that mankind had an actual conversation along the lines of the parable. The objective of the parable is to depict the advent of consciousness and what it meant. Consider that you do talk to your dog, and your dog talks to you. Note also that mankind was not a mindless robot, obeying the commands of his master but had free will to do as he chose, just like your dog.

Elsewhere in Genesis Chapter 2, there is the description of Adam naming all the animals, a depiction that mankind had begun verbal communication while still in the Garden, before human consciousness.

That is, language could have developed before the advent of human consciousness.   This fact gives credence to the slow advent of consciousness, even over generations with conscious and non-conscious humans living and working side by side. Because the Genesis account is not linear but transitions back and forth in time as it amplifies some stories and events it's difficult to make hard decisions as to the timing between events.   But language before consciousness and the slow emergence into consciousness appears to be a real possibility. The other timing issue is the creation of mankind on the sixth day.

> **Genesis 1:26-31** *(NASB) Then God said, "Let Us make man in Our image, according to Our likeness; and let them rule over the fish of the sea and over the birds of the sky and over the cattle and over all the earth, and over every creeping thing that creeps on the earth." 27 God created man in His own image,* **in the image of God He created him; male and female He created them. 28 God blessed them; and God said to them, "Be fruitful and multiply, and fill the earth, and subdue it***; and rule over the fish of the sea and over the birds of the sky and over every living thing that moves on the earth." 29 Then God said, "Behold, I have given you every plant yielding seed that is on the surface of all the earth, and every tree which has fruit yielding seed; it shall be food for you; 30 and to every beast of the earth and to every bird of the sky and to every thing that moves on the earth which has life, I have given every green plant for food"; and it was so. 31 God saw all that He had made, and behold, it was very good.* **And there was evening and there was morning, the sixth day.**

There are several things to point out here. Mankind, both male and female were created in the beginning to multiply and fill the earth and rule over all life on earth. One of the confusing factors is that Adam and the Woman or Eve are considered to be singular individuals, the only residents of the Garden of Eden but from the moment they were put there the mission was to procreate and rule over all life. We can assume they did so for an unknown length of time. You can also not discount that more than one man and woman could have been created and placed in the Garden. The Biblical narrative refers to "them" plural when referring to male and female and does not clarify only one of each.

The later more definitive story of the creation of the woman from man's rib or side is, itself, a parable or metaphor about the hearty structure of the female, she is a part of you, only different, and her complimentary but different nature makes her a helpmate. A helpmate who has a different perspective on life and helps you have a clearer picture of circumstances.

Another factor to note is that the Hebrew word for "Adam" does not refer to a single individual, but the word is the transliteration of the Hebrew word for "mankind" (simply changing the Hebrew letters of the word into equivalent English letters, A. d. a. m., an actual translation would say "mankind"). Thus the English transliteration of the Hebrew as "Adam" does not necessarily refer to a single individual man. This is the case with the Garden of Eden parable where the parable itself deals with single individuals but they represent all of mankind.

> **Adam** '*adam (אָדָם), "man; mankind; people; someone (indefinite); Adam (the first man)." This noun appears in Ugaritic, Phoenician, and Punic. A word with the same radicals occurs in old South Arabic meaning "serf." In late Arabic, the same radicals mean not only "mankind" but "all creation." Akkadian admu signifies "child." The Hebrew word appears about 562 times and in all periods of biblical Hebrew.*
>
> *This noun is related to the verb 'adom, "to be red," and therefore probably relates to the original ruddiness of human skin. The noun connotes "man" as the creature created in God's image, the crown of all creation. In its first appearance, 'adam is used for mankind, or generic man: "And God said, Let us make man(אָדָם), in our image, after our likeness..."*
> Vine's Complete Expository Dictionary of Old and New Testament Words By: W.E. Vine, Merrill F. Unger, William White Jr. THOMAS NELSON / 1996

So Adam and the woman, representing all men and women, were living a moment-by-moment idyllic life in the Garden without care or worry about what tomorrow would bring. We know this from several aspects. One aspect from Genesis 3 (which we didn't quote) is the consequence of them (mankind, which the man and woman represent in the parable), leaving the garden. It's described them as now being conscious, and aware, that the quality of their life was dependent on how well they worked, tended the fields and animals, etc, and that they would be much more aware of consequences and events, the pain of childbirth being an example of something that was only a momentary discomfort when life is lived from moment to moment, very similar to how animals appear to live.

The other significant aspect identified is that while in the Garden they were not fully aware of their own emotions or reactions to the pleasures of sex. But insight into the knowledge of good and evil included now being conscious of the emotions, joys, and pleasures, and they became self-conscious, especially about others sensing their reactions. Clothing then was symbolic of trying to hide their emotions and pleasures by covering themselves, as if that would keep others from seeing the real people underneath the clothing. This was all a new experience, the result of becoming a conscious human being, now aware of their actions and that others would also be aware of them.

Another way of describing this advent of consciousness in terms of the previously semi-conscious state is to examine the animal world. If you're a dog owner all this should make perfect sense. If you are not a dog owner and don't get it, get a dog. Cat's won't work, they don't really like you, they just pretend, to get their way.

It is said that a dog's memory is only seconds long, that he lives his life from moment to moment, and quickly forgets what happened two moments ago. Thus toilet training takes a while until he learns that he heads outside to do his business, which has now become a habit, something he does automatically. Similarly, a dog remembers you through training and recognition but has no concept of time or how long it's been since he's seen you. If you take him to the doggie hotel for two weeks while you go to the beach, he's exceedingly happy to see you again but he doesn't know whether you've been gone for a day, a week, or a year. His excessive happiness might be in associating you with life back at the house as opposed to the boarding facility, and he may get anxious riding in the car because he remembers the boarding facility might be at the end of the ride. But once he gets there, he's just back in his moment-by-moment life. That is, he's not contemplating going outside for his toilet necessities, he just responds when he needs to go.   His genes have been reprogrammed to respond to his needs differently.

The account of a lion's life is similar, lions do what lions do. They kill and eat prey, instincts programmed by genes. They have no thought for the life of the animal, it's just another meal for the pride, a walking snorting "Big Mac". Similarly, a male lion without a pride of his own and a desire built into his genes has been known to kill lion cubs as a natural means of captivating a female lion with cubs and making her part of his newly created pride. The male lion thinks nothing of this, it's just what lions do.

The driving force then to this worry-free, carefree life in the Garden is that they, Adam and the woman, i.e., mankind, do not know about either good or evil.   That is they are clueless that the consequences of their actions affect their life, and can make them better or worse. And they are clueless about their own emotions and the joy of life.

We might further speculate that they didn't know that they could kill their neighbor, take his animals, eat his plot of berries, or consequently help him care for his animals by providing him water when he needed it. Certainly, there were skirmishes between tribes of people, including battles and deaths when two tribes happened to try and occupy the same territory at the same time.   (Identical to the territorial nature of animals and especially predators.) But apparently, they didn't consider that if they went out and found some other tribe and defeated or killed them, they could thus benefit from the enemy's wealth, his animals, and grain. In this sense consciousness came after language, villages, and community life existed, but probably before political power and kingdoms formed.

NOTE: Genesis 4 clearly indicates other people were living in parallel with, and not related to the individual Adam and Eve depicted as representative humans. Mankind was apparently emerging from its pre-consciousness existence everywhere. And while it was a significant event in history it was not much noticed by those living through the event. In every human enclave, there **may have been** both conscious and semi-conscious individuals living side by side.   Both go through the daily routines of living, one aware of life, actions, consequences, and time passing, and the other oblivious to such things.

Now you could say that life without consciousness, described as a moment-by-moment life without care or worry, as we've implied was the case in the Garden, was also a life totally dominated by the genetic programming, both of humans and animals. Before consciousness, humans lived an animal-like existence, operating on genetic instincts, and controls. You could say mankind is living an idyllic life, walking with God, in that he's relying on God to keep the food supplies coming. He is also relying totally on the genetic programming built into his body to determine all that he does.

Once Adam and the woman eat from the Tree of Knowledge, of good and evil, however, everything changes. They are now aware of their own actions and that they have some responsibility for gathering their food. They are aware of the consequences of their actions or non-actions, and that their lives could be affected by their actions.

This is something that never happens with animals. They never get to that state, no matter how smart they appear, how many human words they learn, or how clever they may be at using sticks or rocks to find or locate food. Animals can not escape that moment-by-moment idyllic life in their own small genetically managed world. The chimpanzee who recognizes you, hugs your neck, and learns 100 words is still a chimpanzee, living a chimpanzee life.

When mankind was ejected from the Garden, it was because he had learned about good and evil, the consequences of his actions, and also gained insight into what he could do to gain at the expense of others. He could therefore no longer go back into the garden in the sense that he had a totally different perspective of life and how to live it and could not unlearn what he knew. This is very similar to the passing of children through adolescence and into adults. They can never be children again. This is handled in the allegory as man being expelled from the garden and angels guarding the gates to prevent them from going back.

As Genesis says, Adam was now fearful of God because he had a new worldview that included bad consequences if he didn't do his job. It wasn't that the food supply might dry up, it was that Adam was aware and fearful that it could. This loss of confidence was also tied to a sense of losing God as his confidant, advisor, and supplier of all he needed. That didn't really change, but in seeing the real world he became fearful that it would. And it also included the fear that God would punish them if they did something wrong. Typically the ancient priests and shamans interpreted bad events as coming because they had offended the gods and to make things right again they had to then appease, and please the gods.

This seismic event of the transformation to consciousness, therefore, gives rise to religion. Religion is mankind seeking to beg, persuade, and manipulate the gods or god into doing man favors to keep the food or whatever they need coming and for god to go easy on that punishment thing. Exiting the idyllic life in the garden of the semiconscious moment-by-moment life caused man to search for ways to keep the benefits coming from god. (We're using the "little" god here as opposed to the "big" God because mankind didn't have enough information to make such a distinction at that time.)

So: After consciousness, mankind entered a fearful new world. You can imagine it's what you experience when you begin to wake up and yet continue to live in that last dream. Reality lies mostly in that dream world until you finally wake up sufficiently to toss it aside as only a dream.

Consequences of Consciousness

1. Life before consciousness: a moment-by-moment carefree, worry-free life, relying on genetic programming for directions
2. The consciousness transformation: the wake-up call to real life, decisions, and consequences
3. Life after consciousness:
   a. life in a world with stress, anxiety, worry, and hard work to keep ahead of, and safe from, the rival bands of humans who are now plotting to take all that he has.
   b. Seeking help from the god who kicked you out of the Garden - religion, the search for the lost god
   c. The development of ritual, worship, and rules of engagement with the spiritual world
   d. The development of power politics and the city-state for the protection of property and safety.

This story is conveyed as a factual story, but metaphors and parables are usually told as if they were recounting an actual event. In the story, God has ejected Adam and Eve from the Garden to ensure that they do not eat of the Tree of Life and live forever. The story of mankind with a single couple as the example, Adam and Eve, then continues with the account of their new life and there is no further mention of the Garden. It's as if the Garden never existed, that Adam and Eve did not realize they had been kicked out of the Garden. This reaction and the resetting of the story to the perspective of adults living a normal human life seem to support the metaphorical view of the human transformation into consciousness. It's as if the memory of their earlier life just faded away. Life had not really changed they just were now aware of the risks and threats in the world.

Consciousness also opened a world of possibilities to humans, but its first use was to exploit the genetic intelligence potential of humans without any moral value limitations. The level of violence and human conflict greatly increased and led to the development of clans and city-states for self-protection. Early religions had no moral codes and existed only to exploit the power of the gods in favor of the local clan or tribe. Morality was probably much like the "honor among thieves" gang morality, one strictly for convenience.

We see this immoral and "nasty" cultural aspect in the account of Noah and the flood and it is further amplified by the Old Testament accounts of Israel's encounters with the various clans or city-states in Moses's time and continuing right up to the time of the rise of the Greeks and Romans. And even in our world of strong moral values, we see similar barbarities under Hitler, Stalin, and Mao.

Now also the biblical account of Noah and the flood makes some sense. It's the story of mankind being so bad after consciousness that most of them have to be wiped out and conscious mankind restarted from a better gene pool that responds better, morally toward other humans than the "bad lot" before the flood. The purpose of the flood was to cut off the most violent strand of human nature, which it apparently did. It was like a wakeup call, "I've had enough of the violence and meanness", God says. You could say that the plan worked. People became more civil toward each other, sufficiently so that empires made up of multiple city-states eventually developed. People had to begin cooperating for this to happen. And the impact of mini empires forming was that they imposed an overwhelming authority on the surrounding countryside.   Forcing obedience, and taxation, rather than a sword to kill the men and children and capture the women.

So religion was an immediate reaction to the consciousness translation into real life. Not one of morality and values but one of appeasing the gods and making the gods the servants of the people. Mankind's experience in the garden was what science might even today call walking with god. That is, fully involved and living in the natural animal world existence, free of the plotting and conniving and conflicts human beings have created with their consciousness. The Garden of Eden is still that idyllic life we yearn for, even if we'd be bored to tears within a week.

There is one theory of mankind's conversion to consciousness that is intriguing enough to mention with caution that it is only a theory. It's called "The Bicameral Mind" and proposes that early man's brain was divided into two somewhat independent parts where one side appeared to provide instructions and the other side listened and implemented those instructions. This was thought to be an unconscious process that early man followed instinctively, without thought or reflection on the outcome, a very similar picture to mankind living in the Garden.

The theory further states that as language and life became more and more complex the bicameral mind was replaced by consciousness, rational, logical thinking, evaluating the consequences of actions, and making decisions based on potential outcomes.

The theory was first expressed in the book, referenced below, by Julian Jaynes and has a large number of advocates of his position. The book's analysis and findings rely extensively on the research of early writings and the writer traces the transition from bicameral to conscious thinking over many years and even into Biblical times.

Jaynes, Julian (2000) [1976]. The origin of consciousness in the breakdown of the bicameral mind. Houghton Mifflin. 1976, 2000

This idea of one side of our brain talking to the other side isn't so far from the truth today either. We all talk to ourselves. We'll be thinking, in sentences what we need to do, verbalizing instructions to ourselves about what we need to do about this or that situation.

Many of us are also familiar with the fictionalized depiction of a little devil sitting on one shoulder, trying to get us to do the wrong thing, while a little angel on the other shoulder is trying to talk us into doing the right thing. It's a fictional depiction of something we take as a parable of real life where we're constantly bombarded with good and bad choices in life but can't decide which is good and which is bad. Here too the bad devil, is, in a way, our bad self, our bad old genes, our "old sin nature" to conservative Christians, the old man, that we must counter with good decisions, actions, and principles.

This debate we have with ourselves when we can see multiple choices is, in a way, very similar to the debate going on in the heads of those early members of the human race after the advent of consciousness. A debate they didn't have when "living" in the Garden of Eden, that place where they lived a moment-by-moment existence following a single directive that aligned with their simple but semi-conscious lives. (Semi-conscious and semi-consciousness have been used interchangeably ignoring any potential subtle differences)

Life is simple when you don't have to make decisions that make or break your day, year, or life. Life in the Garden (as a euphemism for the genetically controlled animal-like life before consciousness) was as simple as the life of a pride of lions. That simplicity was destroyed by acquiring the knowledge of good and evil and the self-awareness and self-consciousness that came with it.

While the Genesis account is perhaps a simplistic allegory, it does not contradict what science speculates happened. In fact, because of its general agreement with science, Genesis provides some unique insights into what probably happened. (when accepting the actual variations in ancient word meanings, creative storytelling techniques, and connecting passages in Genesis). And remember the purpose of the Genesis account was to impart some important information to the audience of the original writers and storytellers, so it had to be told and written in a simplified form so that the concepts could be understood by those listeners. If you're struggling with all the discussions of genes and epigenesis and such, you should appreciate the Genesis story as something to more easily understand.

You might think there's not much that early mankind needs to know about this. Why does he have to know about this advent of consciousness? But it is very significant to the fundamental thrust and direction of Judaism and then Christianity which is to teach mankind to control and re-train the malevolent nature consciousness generates.   Other religions have similar intentions but deviate toward avoiding the problem by appealing to little gods for help or escaping the life experience as much as possible.   The next chapter will address religions and the differences, which are significant, and which impact prosperity itself.   The Genesis account of consciousness is the pivotal story that defines the conditions created by consciousness and points the way to a different path for Judaism and Christianity in the future.

The lessons relative to consciousness we have from the Genesis account and the best that science can devise concerning early mankind are as follows.

The Nature and Consequences of Mankind's Consciousness

1. Mankind began living in a semi-conscious, robotic, animal-like, genetically programmed/controlled, moment-by-moment existence without knowledge or insight into his own existence or the ability to manipulate his fellow man for his own benefit. This was a carefree life without stress, worries, or concerns and a time when mankind was in tune with nature. Encounters with other tribes would be mostly peaceful backing away from each other.

2. Something happened however that caused mankind to see life for what it was, consciousness of self, others, and the consequences of actions, both good and bad. The parable says they ate the fruit of a forbidden tree, but this is a parable and its point is that there was a dramatic change in mankind's view of life. The significance of eating fruit is that there was a change from within mankind. The change did not come about from some dramatic external circumstances or events, it was subtle and it was individual. It was not a group or social event.

3. Individuals now saw themselves as a person and that others were viewing them in the same way. A common dispute among my daughters while still pre-teens, sitting in the back of the car on a trip was, "She's looking at me". Consciousness may have come from the increasing contact between groups of people where the need for creative thinking and cooperation was becoming necessary, we don't really know. But there was a significant change.

4. The significant aspect is that mankind was now aware that they could manipulate, lie, steal, and otherwise improve their life at the expense of others. They now recognized both good and evil actions and their consequences and impact on others and themselves. Mankind became a self-centered, self-serving, and malevolent individual who would do whatever he could get away with to advance his personal life.

5. In Genesis Cain, the son of Adam and Eve, displays this arrogant malevolent nature when he tries to tell God what to do and kills Abel just for spite. There is a rebellion against the order of preconscious life.

6. The continual practice of these self-serving and malevolent actions by a significant portion of a tribe caused a transformation of genetic thinking of future members of the tribe and the bad seed genes populated much of the world by Noah's time.

7. It's not clear exactly how this emergence of consciousness took place. The parable seems to say it was an immediate reaction by individuals, but it is a parable written to make a point of a significant change in reality. The change could have come over a lifetime or even gradually over several generations.

8. Genesis says that Cain, a son of Adam and Eve, was exiled and went to live with another community and took a wife clearly stating there were other human enclaves around. (Some speculate Cain's wife was his sister to avoid the other people issue, i.e., where they come from, but that only addresses Cain's wife, the other human enclave is not explained.). Whether they were all emerging into consciousness or only those from Adam and Eve's lineage according to Genesis is not identified.

9. **Religion was an inevitable reaction to consciousness** as malevolent tribes began to impose their will on neighboring tribes. Religion was the attempt to connect to that spirit world that had been known from pre-conscious days and seek protection from the marauding tribes as well as seek help dealing with a world where they now had to depend on themselves and worried about the sources of their next meals.

The next step then is to examine the world's religions for signs that might impact shalom, either positively or negatively and especially to contrast Christianity's views with the others to see if there is any difference. Do the world's religions move or motivate actions that promote prosperity?   Do they deal with the real issues of life created by consciousness or not?

Do not be dismayed at the thoughts of this encounter however, we won't bother you with a course on the beliefs, organizations, and practices of each religion. What we're looking for are the fundamental concepts of life and rules/guidelines for navigation of that view of life. All the other obvious aspects of religions, the spiritual, god or spirit world beliefs, the rituals, and the superficial faces of religion that are most observable to the outside world represent the facade of religion. That facade is what you might learn in a college course. The real interest here is what are the factors that emerge from religions that may affect real life, the prosperity, and happiness of the adherents.

And of course what makes this at all interesting is that we will see a clear relationship between a worldview, the focus or direction of religion, and factors that are the antithesis of that which would promote prosperity. Religion, generated by mankind's unease with the stresses of life, doesn't promote prosperity but generally has the opposite effect, as we shall see.

Luca Giordano - Dream of Solomon
Public domain, via Wikimedia Commons https://commons.wikimedia.org/wiki/File:WGA09004.jpg

11. The Human Nature of World Religions

Religion has played a giant role in life and living for most of mankind since the dawn of history. It is embedded in the life of most people around the world. The meaning and importance of religion in everyday life varies considerably with each specific religion. In most cases, religions have significantly influenced the thinking and approach to life of its followers. Religion, along with our ancient genetic traits, and those newer traits and views of life resulting from human consciousness are equal legs in a 3-legged stool that forms mankind's philosophy and approach to life.

What we have surmised from history is that genetics and consciousness have created a self-centered, self-serving, evil, and malevolent civilization. Using the Bible's metaphorical account of early human life we find a sense of mankind's closeness to God before consciousness, in pre-history. This is somewhat confirmed by archeology and paleontology which have found evidence of man's sense of a spirit world in the burial rites of prehistoric civilizations. Science also confirms the advent of consciousness in humans occurring at some time in the distant past. This experience aligns with the Biblical account of the Garden of Eden and mankind's expulsion from it as a metaphorically accurate picture of what this transformation to consciousness would be like.

This metaphorical picture of consciousness as a coming to understand Good and Evil, the need to work to have food and shelter, that nature can make life hard, and the loss of contact with God in the spirit world provides the right motivation for mankind to create religion. Consciousness has brought with it a whole new way of malicious thinking to man. He now can envision active engagements with other humans to steal their resources and women and kill the men and children to avoid retribution. Tribes of people no longer tend to avoid other tribes, but instead become roaming hordes seeking to rob and plunder their neighbors. Live and let live by avoiding contact is no longer the philosophy. Now life has become a cutthroat world of lust, murder, and mayhem. On a positive note for civilization, collecting together in city-states also emerges as a means to deal with the marauding bands.

Civilization has now become much more dangerous and instinctively mankind turns back to that spirit world and his benefactor from the Garden, God. This is the birth of religion, seeking God's help, not only with the roving bands of terror from adjacent tribes but also with all the other life-threatening natural catastrophes that he can now see or imagine. Mankind, being much more creative as a result of consciousness, seeks to bring God back into the picture for protection from a world full of crazy and evil people and from natural catastrophes as well. The simple connection mankind possessed with God in the Garden has been lost, so mankind improvises with various forms of religion designed to garner the favor of the gods and thus protection from the new wild and scary life. Conscious man is smart and he seizes the opportunity to step in and create a wealth opportunity as a shaman or priest, the earthly connection to God. Man is now free to create whatever kind of religion his tribe is prone to accept and out comes the primitive religions with their multiple gods of flawed superhumans and fictional animal creatures.   Thus religion becomes a valuable philosophical resource for life lessons and the priests become the wise gurus who are looked to for advice on the complicated and complex matters that threaten life.

We have a sketchy connection between consciousness and the beginnings of religion. We understand that the metaphorical exile from the Garden is tied to knowing Good and Evil. Genesis (the Cain story) also indicates mankind "becoming like God", replacing God with themselves, as the new god. Perhaps mankind didn't lose their connection with God but replaced God with themselves. Further, we understand the impact of life on genes and consciousness created a major change in the actions and lives of all of mankind.

Consciousness changes how mankind sees and responds to life. It changes experiences, society, culture, and human philosophy. Over time these changes then become ingrained in our genes so that in the early historical timeframe, from Adam and Eve onward, our lives are guided by a different perspective on life, one that is self-serving, self-centered, evil, malicious, and often naturally malevolent.

From the Bible, God has already set the religion he wants in place as told by the story of Cain and Abel. It's a message of faith and trust in God to provide for mankind with a simple sacrifice of acknowledgment and thanksgiving, but nothing more. From God's perspective, the time is not right for any further guidance. Mankind needs to gain some experience with consciousness before the next step is presented.

What has happened in the timeframe between Adam and Noah however is that consciousness has made mankind about as self-centered, malevolent, and evil as he could become and a major part of that "bad seed" has to be eliminated by Noah's Flood. This resets society a bit and allows civilization to proceed to a time when a fuller presentation of God's plan can be executed.

Man is impatient for results, however, so he takes it upon himself to create religions that he can envision will force or manipulate God into helping with circumstances right now. These are the Human Religions that we see around the world and because of the mayhem that arises out of consciousness, they become powerful influencers of society, on a level with mankind's generic prehistorical genes. We'll look at these religions and assess their ability to impact prosperity because they are the current competitors to Christianity. What we mean by the "thinking" of the World religions is the theology and philosophy that impact how their followers orient to life. It is the thinking espoused by these religions that they pass along to the progeny of the followers.

This thinking of human religion is not without good intentions, old genes and consciousness have turned civilization into a wild and scary place to be. The objective of religion is to try and influence mankind's behavior by modifying how the followers view and respond to life and the spiritual world. Conversely, religion also tries to manipulate God or gods into helping mankind with man's problems, including help with marauding bands of thieves and murderous tribes. Over time that thinking modifies or adjusts the genetic programming of consciousness based on the theology and philosophy presented. Mankind eventually elevates himself above God and believes he can tell God what to do. We have only to look at the story of Cain and Abel in Genesis to see the self-centered thinking of Cain acting like an equal or even a superior to God. (Story in chapter 13)

Mankind thus has three factors that form his basic thinking, pre-consciousness genes from pre-history, consciousness (knowledge of good and evil), and the influence of religion. Life then introduces biases or choices that determine how one's life turns out. This is the starting point in defining mankind's self-serving, self-centered, malevolent self that produced the early historical world of mankind.

The basis of human philosophy and thinking about how to handle life is then a derivative of these influences plus primary life experiences.

Philosophy: a theory or attitude held by a person that acts as a guiding principle of behavior

The Basis of Human Philosophy and Thinking

1. *Genes: basic instincts*
2. *Consciousness: An expanded view of alternatives and consequences*
3. *Religion: rules for life and gaining god's help to defeat your neighbor*

These foundations of thinking are then modified by what we learn from our environment, our friends, and our peers. All the influences in your life are competing for prominence and control of your life. Your personal experiences act as influencers on the basic built-in drivers of your thinking. If you think life is complicated, your "now" Philosophy of Life can be just as confusing. And all of the factors that figure into your philosophy, even religion, can be malevolent and lead to a dumpster fire life. Don't overthink this, the point is to recognize that our decision making is influenced by lots of factors that can be either positive or negative and religion is a big factor in our choices, even if you are not a religious person at all. It seeps in through your friends and community. If you have no religious beliefs then you are your own religion.

Concerning religion, it matters little whether a religion is true or not, believers will make that religion a major aspect of their life. And then the tenants and philosophy of that religion will play a big role in forming the nature and characteristics of the believer's life, and the life of everyone in that society or culture who follows that particular belief system. A formal definition of religion usually looks something like this.

Religion

Religion may be defined as a cultural system of designated behaviors and practices, world views, texts, sanctified places, prophecies, ethics, or organizations, that relates humanity to supernatural, transcendental, or spiritual elements.
https://en.wikipedia.org/wiki/Religion

Before the Protestant Reformation in the 16th century, the idea of religion as a separate aspect of life independent of kings and governments was unknown. Religion was a routine part of life, like eating and sleeping. Life was short, hard, and often fearful so, put yourself back in the Middle Ages and you can maybe envision the idea of keeping the gods or God close to you, as fully involved in your life on a moment-by-moment basis. This tightness between governments, religion, and society was the barrier that Christianity faced as it emerged in the Roman Empire. A unique claim of Christianity was that individuals had the right to the religion of their choice, even if it was at odds with the established government religion. When Christianity did conquer Rome it took on that same tight connection between governments and ordinary life as had existed under Roman rule. That connection became control which led to the Reformation of the 16th century that fractured that tight connection and power politics, almost. Individual countries sided with either the reformers or the establishment Catholic Church, based in Rome. The result was the basis for many of the small wars over several hundred years. Eventually, religious freedom won out and people were free to follow the religion of their choice. Religion had been separated from governments, and people had to decide on their own what type of Christianity, or some other religion, to follow.

This Western / Christian concept of religion as a separate and selectable aspect of life is somewhat alien to the rest of the world who follow the official religion of their government or society without question. When religion is ubiquitous and self-serving, and offers little or no perceived benefits to living, it becomes a dead religion, relegated to holidays and ceremonial rituals, followed because of tradition. It's just part of life but without real value to those who observe it, ritual without reality. We will see that in later discussions of the world's religions but we can see this same phenomenon occurring within Christian nations today as religion is seen to be optional.

Worship (noun)

1. *reverence offered a divine being or supernatural power, also: an act of expressing such reverence*
2. *a form of religious practice with its creed and ritual*
3. *extravagant respect or admiration for or devotion to an object of esteem*
https://www.merriam-webster.com/dictionary/worship

Worship is what religious people do to follow their beliefs. So religions have two aspects, a description of the spiritual world and how it interacts with the physical world, and, worship, how mankind does or should interact with that spiritual world. What is missing is the motivation for mankind to do anything at all. Many people believe in the existence of a spiritual world but see it as something that can never be known and also something that has little or no involvement with their day-to-day lives in the physical world. (We will see some major religions along these lines)

However, the religious motivation for serious worship comes from the belief that this spiritual world does indeed come into contact with the physical world and can personally influence our lives directly, both in this life and the next. This belief is at the heart of most of the world's religions, it directly follows that the purpose of worship is not merely to show respect or reverence through our actions, but to influence the gods or God or spirits of this unseen but powerful world to work their magic, to make life better for us, to fix our problems. This manipulation of the spirit world is the fundamental objective of religion and most all the religious activities we observe around the world are performed for this reason (with a few notable exceptions).

Objective of Religion
The primary objective of religion and worship is to influence (manipulate) the spiritual world and its gods or God into giving us what we want and/or need, and to help us with our problems.

In other words "worship" has a purpose, influencing the gods. Rain is important, it gives a good crop, as is protection from the lions and protection from the neighboring tribes.   As with any discipline, undertaking, or interest, there are many different human responses to a religion of choice or heritage.   There is another aspect of worship that we associate with admiration for exceptional people. Usually, someone who has exceptional talent in a given field, sports figures for example.   Of course, they are admired for expertise in their particular sport but that expertise easily gives them the appearance of expertise in other areas of life. The resulting worship usually comes in the form of emulation of the object's personality, dress, beliefs, or life. If they have a certain type of car, then "I've got to have one just like it". If they tell me to eat "Wheaties" (the cereal) for breakfast, I'll do it. This type of worship doesn't translate well to religion, especially the early religions, because the gods were silent. Instead, that worship of example is transferred to the priest or shaman. The shaman eats "Wheaties" for breakfast, I will too. The hope still is that eating Wheaties probably is a good way to appease the gods and get what I want because the shaman does it.

Even if you are not religious yourself or are just going along to get along, your worldview and even your values and cultural norms are most likely colored by the dominant religion in which you live. An atheist can be a morally upright citizen, not because of his atheist foundational philosophies, there aren't many of those around, but because he is influenced by his peers or parents or by his genes, modified by hundreds of years of ancestors who may even have been religious. He may not believe in or practice the worship regime but still lives within the norms and standards rules. The Hindu Indian atheist doesn't publicly bother the cows, even if he secretly eats steak when he can. The Hindu agnostic on the other hand probably won't eat beef because, "it can't hurt, and you never know". I don't believe there are any Outback Steak Houses in India!

So religions have a general and almost universal course of action, their objective, which will be followed to varying degrees by both active and passive adherents of the religion. What differs between religions are the details that describe the gods themselves and the spirit world, including their motivations, objectives, and characteristics, and, the information and directions being given to mankind to interact with this spiritual world.

The earliest religions had little in the way of rules for daily life. Gradually, as the rituals and ways to manipulate the gods grew, life habits and dress changed to comply with those efforts, and the culture of the people reflected their religion and religious beliefs. This combination of spiritual worship, with customs and daily life, modified to appeal to the gods or spirit world, is a common theme among most religions and forms a worldview of the religion. This worldview is a major influence and motivator in the individual life of the follower. What we will see is that the world views of most of the world's religions are similar in that they share a common objective that we stated for religion, influence and manipulate the spirit world.

Christianity, in principle, does not share this common human religious objective to influence and manipulate God, as we shall see. In practice of course it's easy for human nature (genes) to step in and add that "influence and manipulation of God" aspect back into practicing Christianity. The inclusion of the desire to influence and manipulate God, of course, does not make it real, or part of Christianity as documented in the Bible.

Usually, the world's religions are characterized by differences in worship because that is what is observable, the different ways each religion is trying to manipulate the gods or God and gain favor. That is what is meant by the common idea of "many paths to God". That all religions are good, that each is seeking "God" in their own way, and that each one of us can follow any path, even our own. The many paths to God seem like a very natural, live-and-let-live, strategy since we have little or no capability to prove the veracity of any religion, until we encounter those religions sacrificing their young men, women, and children on a stone altar, to the gods.

The casual view of all religions then is based on their ritual approaches to "God" and one other factor, the primary cultural norms and standards associated with the religion. The cultural views are derived from the religion's literature, either written or oral, and evolving practices of the religion over time. So there are two key philosophical directives from religion, one deals with how life works, and the other deals with how we should work with life. These are the two aspects of a religion's philosophy of life, their "World View" that make a difference in prosperity, "How Life Works" and "How We Need to Work with Life".

What's not so obvious is that the "World View" of each religion, its philosophy of life derived from its religious beliefs, is embedded into the culture of the society that it dominates. This worldview is like a river carrying the culture and its daily activities down a certain stream, in a certain direction. The worldview provides a distinctive direction to life that causes its adherents to proceed down a particular path, a particular philosophy of life that colors and flavors the culture and individual lives of the followers. The movie "Fiddler on the Roof" does an excellent job of demonstrating the embedded worldview of Judaism in the lives of its followers. And you see in this movie just how religion is interwoven into the fabric of life in the late 19th and early 20th centuries.

What we're not saying is that religions other than Christianity have no positive moral or life values or that the adherents to other religions are inherently bad people because that is certainly not the case. What we're saying is that their religious worldviews direct them down different life paths from the one that comes from basic Christianity and those different life paths produce different results in the areas of peace, prosperity, and happiness.

We're also not saying that people from other religions and cultures can't achieve high levels of prosperity and happiness either. Some people can succeed in any endeavor despite mediocre coaching and training and others may succeed by living and adopting some of the aspects of the Christian Western World, something we've seen in our assessments of world prosperity.

Going back to a sports analogy, the quarterback who doesn't set his feet firmly on the ground before he throws a pass is off balance, and that significantly reduces the chance of an accurate and completed pass. This may be out of necessity, his offensive line may not be able to protect him from the opposing team, and he's learned to pass while off balance, on one foot to avoid being flattened on the ground. But the better quarterback has learned to read the defenses and quickly set his feet and pass. As we examine various religions we will see many examples of advice and wisdom that is "off balance", not wrong or evil necessarily but just "off balance" enough to impact prosperity.

Now, there are many other examples of differences between religions that might be laid down as rules that can affect prosperity. But there is also an overriding force, a theological or philosophical direction, to religious beliefs that sets up an environment to generate these kinds of specific laws and rules.

This means that there is no necessity to work through each of the current major religions for rules that may or may not affect prosperity.

We're not going to end up with a list of a hundred or so rules across the major religions with a prosperity rating for each rule and then add up all the points. We only need to look at the overall theology, philosophy and orientation to life that each religion offers to see the causes of dramatic differences in prosperity outcomes. There are, of course, a few complications that we will address, even when it comes to Christianity, due to the very nature of religion itself and especially how religion got started in the first place.

First of all, there are three fundamental views of the spirit world taken by all the world's religions. These views appear to be three evolutionary stages of religious thinking where each new stage is an evolution in thinking about the spirit world and a god or gods. That is not necessarily the case, however, as logical as it may appear. All three fundamental views developed about the same time and still exist today.

Categories of Religions

1. **Simple Folk Religions:** These comprise Primitive, Native, Small Group, and Casual Religions. There is an unseen spirit world that affects our local events and the transition of the dead into that spirit world but we can't do much about it so there's little ritual or attention paid except for special occasions. This view is open to the widest fanciful religious concepts, witches, hobgoblins, and all sorts of spiritual creatures, that come directly from the mind of its followers.

2. **"Flawed human silent gods" Religions:** These are religions that develop a concept of a god or gods who impact local events and the transition of the dead into the spirit world so they must be appeased and sought out for help with worldly problems as well as the transition to the spirit world after death. This includes Hinduism, and Buddhism, a mental gymnastics approach to Hinduism. Other early religions fall into this category such as the Greek, Roman, and Egyptian religions and all those associated with various local cultures encountered by the Hebrews in the Biblical Old Testament. It would also include the religions of Central and South America, the Incas and Aztecs.

3. **All-Powerful Creator God Religions:** These represent the advent of the all-powerful Creator God who is interested or somewhat interested in mankind's welfare and prosperity. Judaism, Christianity, and Islam represent this phase of religious thinking. Some Hindu apologists claim this view as true Hinduism as well with the explanation that all the

strange little Hindu gods are but local ritual representations of an all-powerful Creator God, but that's just admitting that all the Hindu documentation is an allegory or parable without any documentation on the claimed new reality.

Religion is a universal aspect of almost all cultures throughout the world. Mankind has accepted and embraced religion from the dawn of civilization. And the world's religions provide a wide diversity of beliefs, structures, and actions. It is as if religion is a natural result of man becoming a conscious or super-intelligent creature.

Modern men and women today can easily look back on our primitive relatives and question, if not scoff at, their ignorance of the world and their "God is everywhere" wonder of it all. That ball of fire in the sky by day and the lesser light by night, the millions of dots of light that move across the heavens, and the nature of life and the earth. How could they not believe in magic, magical super creatures, and magical events?

In our own stage of innocence, however, just a hundred years or so ago, we viewed the same natural things under the light of a candle and with a handheld magnifying glass and proclaimed that we now understand it all. A little over a hundred or so years ago our older selves knew very little about the reality of the universe, physical matter, or the design and construction of life compared to our current understanding. Today when a thoroughly modern man gazes at the heavens and sees a beginning to the universe, or sends subatomic particles racing around a 10-mile-long tunnel at near the speed of light to collide with another particle to understand the nature of matter, energy, and the universe, or peers into a microscopic living community of chemical machines that work together to form each single living cell in our bodies, we again tend to see an intelligent designer behind it all.

But these recent revelations of an underlying beginning, complexity, design, and order to life and the universe over the last hundred or so years are still a rare exception to the way a large majority of people, and scientists, view the world and life. Many of the complexities of the universe, genetics, and the true nature of life at the cellular level were not revealed or known until well into the last half of the 20th century (1950 to 2000) and even later. So some scientists are stuck defending their "old, pre-1980s science because that is what they were taught in school. And the vast majority of the non-scientific community in the world is oblivious to the current scientific debate, hardly caring whether Darwinian evolution created life or whether there are an infinite number of universes and we just happen to live in the one-in-a-billion that can abundantly support life. (The Multiverse is one of the scientific theories, without any scientific evidence, proposed as an alternative to the Big Bang theory.)

The Pew Research Center on Religion & Public Life and a study published on 18 Dec 2012 assesses the world's religious structure. Two aspects of the distribution of religious affiliation from that study tell the story.

The Pew Research Center on Religion & Public life 18 Dec 2012			
Oldest to Newest religions	Religion claimed	% of World population	% Living as majority in a country
1	Folk - structured	5.9	<1
1.a	Folk - unstructured and unaffiliated in China, Japan, N Korea, ...	16.3	71
2	Hinduism	15	97
4	Buddhism	7.1	28
3	Judaism	0.2	41
5	Christian	31.5	87
6	Islam	23.2	73
	All Other	0.8	0

Of particular note is that the 16.3%   who are unaffiliated with any religion are a majority in six countries, China, the Czech Republic, Estonia, Hong Kong, Japan, and North Korea. China, Japan, and North Korea are the largest countries in this group. In reality, in China and Japan, it's not that they have no religious interests but that they look upon religion as more of a historic and cultural interest for holidays and funerals. Both China and Japan have mixed the local Folk traditions with the rituals from Buddhism while ignoring the doctrines or teachings of Buddhism itself.

The study also noted that many of the unaffiliated were not atheists, however. Many held some beliefs in a spiritual world and a god but just didn't participate in any formal religion.

http://www.pewforum.org/2012/12/18/global-religious-landscape-exec/

For all their differences, however, the world's religions have some very common attributes, perhaps because man is involved in the process of at least documenting and also creating many aspects of these religions. Simplistically religion, as we previously stated, is defined as:

Religion

Religion may be defined as a cultural system of designated behaviors and practices, world views, texts, sanctified places, prophecies, ethics, or organizations, that relates humanity to supernatural, transcendental, or spiritual elements.

https://en.wikipedia.org/wiki/Religion

Worship what religious people do (noun)

1. *reverence offered a divine being or supernatural power also: an act of expressing such reverence*
2. *a form of religious practice with its creed and ritual*
3. *extravagant respect or admiration for or devotion to an object of esteem*

https://www.merriam-webster.com/dictionary/worship

Now the first thing to notice is that religion is characterized by a belief system and worship is characterized by both an emotional feeling and by logical thinking that sees both a need to have some help and the existence of a spirit world with sufficient powers to help. All of this comes from the advent of consciousness, the exile from the Garden of Eden, and the idyllic carefree life.

First of all, religion as a belief system means that adherents to a particular religion have come to believe and accept the tenets, principles, rules, regulations, and rituals of the religion. To believe means to trust in or have faith in the practices of the system, and to accept the religious system as true.   We, mankind, therefore, are an essential element in religion. It is what we believe and practice, so for a religion to exist it must capture or align itself with our thinking. That is we, humanity must buy into the precepts, the belief system, and the worship. To paraphrase Pogo, an old newspaper comic strip character, "We have met religion and it is Us". Human viewpoint and human sensibilities are both involved in and influence religion as it has evolved. And for this reason, religion is usually tightly coupled with the culture of its followers, so much so that religion often seems strange, and foreign to other cultures.   The third factor in religion is that there is an objective.

Objective of Religion
The primary objective of religion and worship is to influence (manipulate) the spiritual world and its gods or God into helping us with our needs and our problems.

The problem with the objective is that no one knew how to make that happen.   Just as nature abhors a vacuum, a fourth aspect of religion emerged to take on the challenge of how to manipulate the spiritual world. This is a priesthood of religious professionals who assume a superior knowledge of every aspect of the religion.   They claim a superior knowledge of the belief system and serve to direct the masses in worship. These priests or gurus or shamans or enlightened ones serve as guides to worship and ritual and thus become intercessors between man and the gods or spirits that lie beyond the visible world.   These members of the priesthood become the ones reputed to know best how to manipulate the spirit world to their own and other adherents' favor. So much so that they develop a reputation for actually being able to control the spiritual world and the gods.   They are indeed powerful men with great status in the community and whom most fear lest the shaman turns the gods against one's self for crossing the shaman.

Worship or practicing a particular religion is seen as a way to both protect one from dangers and disasters and to prosper oneself in life. Worship also professes to have value in aiding one to attain status in the afterlife or spirit world when one dies.

Simplistically then we can say that all religions, more or less, have these characteristics.

Characteristics of Religions
1. A god or gods and a spiritual world beyond what man can see
2. A sense of good and evil and the consequences
3. Human guides (priests, shamans, gurus, enlightened ones, etc) to help man understand good and evil and to interact with this spirit world
4. A set of beliefs, rituals, and practices intended to help communicate with the gods and/or spirit world and gain both favor and enlightenment.

So, ignoring some complex details of beliefs and rituals, one thing all religions have in common is a set of beliefs and ritual actions directed at manipulating the god figure(s) and getting what you, the believer and worshiper, want from your religion's god or gods. The actions taken or rites or rituals represent the distinctive outward characteristics of a religion, and what the believer wants is a better life.

This is certainly a gross simplification of the world's religions and one may argue that it doesn't accurately fit any of them but what we want to see here are the primary focus and the similarities. A detailed academic study quickly gets wrapped up in the details of each of these religions, the trees and the leaves so to speak, so that the objective or world view or life's road advocated by the religion, the forest so to speak, is not revealed. More simply, the details of religions present what people do, but not what their objectives are. In Islam, Muslims are expected to make a pilgrimage to Mecca at least one time in their lifetime. But that knowledge does not say anything about what the pilgrim expects to gain from that effort and the same can be said for all the other rituals. So we learn nothing about the objectives and purpose of religion by looking at the rituals or organizations. But it is the forest; the nature, focus, and direction of man's religions that we want to examine and understand because these fundamental aspects of religion are key to clearly seeing the differences, or similarities between them, especially concerning prosperity and happiness.

Goddess Durga and a pantheon of other gods and goddesses being worshipped during Durga Puja Festival in Kolkata, India

12. The Silent God Religions

One way to look at the world's religions is to group them by the type of god they envision. This might be broken down into two categories that somewhat align with the perceived age of religions that mankind has experienced. These two categories are the Little or Silent God religions and what we're calling the Big God religions. We'll discuss the Little or Silent God religions in this chapter. The next chapters and section will spend more time on the Big God religions, Judaism and Christianity as they and their Philosophy and Theology are intertwined and collectively have been a major influence on Western Prosperity. A discussion of Islam follows. Islam is the third Big God religion, but with a different philosophy, and some interesting connections to Judaism and Christianity.

The Pew Research Center on Religion & Public life		18 Dec 2012		
Oldest to Newest religions	Religion claimed (Old Religions Added)	% of World population	% Living as majority in a country	Type of God(s) Envisioned
1	Folk - structured +Egyptian, Greek, Roman, Aztec / Incas	5.9	<1	Nebulous, Silent, Malicious, Humanoid
1.a	Folk - unstructured and unaffiliated in China, Japan, N Korea	16.3	71	Godless Silent
2	Hinduism	15	97	Nebulous, silent
4	Buddhism	7.1	28	Godless?, silent
3	Judaism	0.2	41	All Powerful Creator
5	Christian	31.5	87	All Powerful Creator
6	Islam	23.2	73	All Powerful Creator
	All Other	0.8	0	

Types of Gods envisioned by religions

1. **Nebulous godless spirit world**: Worship of a spirit world with little direct understanding or contact and only a primitive view of the dead passing into that spirit world.
2. **Silent gods seen in nature**: Worship of passive non-communicating gods seen in large objects of nature such as the sun, moon, sea, volcanos, trees, etc.
3. **Malicious and Flawed humanoid little gods**: Worship of malicious, flawed, and unhelpful gods with human or half-human characteristics and who suffer from human flaws, weaknesses, and flawed lives in the spirit world that mirror human life
4. **Single All-Powerful Creator God**: Worship of a single powerful God who has created the world for mankind

The Folk Religions

The beginning religions included ritual sacrifices designed to appease the spirits, seen as objects in nature from the sun to animals to natural elements. The spirits in nature gradually progressed from a mix of half-man and half-animal creatures into superhuman creatures who acted just like mankind with flaws and imperfections along with their superpowers.

We can categorize these early phases as Folk Religions. The Indians of North America, small/isolated group tribal religions, and the folk religious traditions in China and Japan are typical. They are primarily traditional rituals, especially around the last rites for the dead. Variations include building ritual buildings that reach the skies, potentially to get close to the spirit world. These are seen in the Biblical story about the tower of Babel, the pyramids of Egypt, and the Inca /Aztec temples in the Americas. The Inca and Aztec religious trends are similar to what the Israelites encountered in various tribes of peoples on their way from Egypt to their promised land and for much of their early life as a nation. A mix of gods ranging from nature as well as superhuman but flawed god-men and god-women. And as much as anything the flawed, fickle nature of their gods led them to try anything to get their attention, approval, and favor. Human sacrifices became common and grew worse as their gods seemed to ignore them.

The Egyptian religion

The Ancient Egyptian Religion is perhaps the largest and most documented of the Folk religions. It flourished for almost four thousand years until Egypt fell under first Greek and then Roman control, followed by Christianity and then Islam, which phased out most remaining practices.

> *The Ancient Egyptian religion was a complex system of polytheistic beliefs and rituals that formed an integral part of ancient Egyptian culture. It centered on the Egyptians' interactions with many deities believed to be present in, and in control of the world. Rituals such as prayer and offerings were provided to the gods to gain their favor. Formal religious practice centered on the pharaohs, the rulers of Egypt, believed to possess divine powers by virtue of their positions. They acted as intermediaries between*

their people and the gods and were obligated to sustain the gods through rituals and offerings so that they could maintain Ma'at, the order of the cosmos, and repel Isfet, which was chaos. The state dedicated enormous resources to religious rituals and to the construction of temples.

Individuals could interact with the gods for their own purposes, appealing for help through prayer or compelling the gods to act through magic. These practices were distinct from, but closely linked with the formal rituals and institutions. The popular religious tradition grew more prominent over the course of Egyptian history as the status of the pharaoh declined. Egyptian belief in the afterlife and the importance of funerary practices is evident in the great efforts made to ensure the survival of their souls after death – via the provision of tombs, grave goods, and offerings to preserve the bodies and spirits of the deceased.

The religion had its roots in Egypt's prehistory and lasted for 3,500 years. The details of religious belief changed over time as the importance of particular gods rose and declined, and their intricate relationships shifted. At various times, certain gods became preeminent over others, including the sun god Ra, the creator god Amun, and the mother goddess Isis. For a brief period, in the theology promulgated by the pharaoh Akhenaten, a single god, the Aten, replaced the traditional pantheon. Ancient Egyptian religion and mythology left behind many writings and monuments, along with significant influences on ancient and modern cultures.
https://en.wikipedia.org/wiki/Ancient_Egyptian_religion

The next phase of religious thinking was the evolution of the gods into super-humans or half animals half-humans, all with superpowers and human weaknesses and vices.   The Egyptian Religion promoted its pharaoh leader as a human god although the pharaohs were as much priests, as gods.   The Greeks and Romans excelled at the superhuman approach, creating a pantheon of human-form superheroes (with tragic flaws), while the Hindu religion triumphed at the half man half animal approach.   In all cases, the primary focus is to appease the gods and to extract some action from them that benefits the faithful who show their reverence through rituals thought to win the gods' approval.   Included in this category are the religions associated with tribes and nations in the Middle East that preceded the Greeks and Romans and that surrounded and infiltrated their traditions into the lives of the Hebrews.

Inca and Aztec religions

Independently in the Americas, the Inca and Aztec religious trends were similar to what the Israelites encountered in various tribes of peoples on their way from Egypt to their promised land, and for much of their early life as a nation in the 1,400 to 1,000 BC era. A mix of gods ranging from nature as well as superhuman but flawed god-men and god-women. And as much as anything the flawed, fickle nature of their gods led them to try anything to get the gods' attention, approval, and favor. Human sacrifices became common and grew in intensity and cruelty as their gods seemed to ignore them. The Incan and Aztec cultures were both elaborate civilizations that completely passed from history, perhaps a victim of their own religion, not just the human sacrifices, but a victim of the culture of those sacrifices that allowed their society to become too dysfunctional to continue.

In any event, the early religions saw gods in the air, sun, moon, water, etc and they saw gods who were powerful but possessed human foibles just like us. God has been brought down to earth, but these more human gods still control man's environment so they must be appeased or manipulated into giving a person what he wants. The birth of a human spiritual guide or shaman, witch doctor, or priest comes with this need to control the gods. To make it all seem real, the many rituals and rites are created by the shaman who claims some direct connection or communication or special wisdom concerning the gods. The shaman or priest creates the rituals thus making himself appear to have mystical powers. And subsequently, those priests use that "authentication" to create other rituals to further demonstrate their powers.

These spiritual leaders thus gain considerable power in their communities and work diligently to keep it. And they have a ready answer if they fail to heal or bring rain, or victory in battle. "The gods were not appeased, nor pleased, give more, sacrifice your firstborn, give me, your shaman, your best ox or lamb."

These folk religions include those of almost all the existing primitive civilizations still found in remote parts of the world today. And they include today's Chinese and Japanese folk beliefs as well as those of the

Incas and Aztecs in central and South America whose violent and brutal human sacrifices equaled those of the tribes of peoples encountered by early Israel depicted in the Bible.

The essence of Folk religions is to project concepts of an unseen spiritual world of semi-powerful creature gods who more or less controlled or at least could influence the life of mankind and therefore had to be worshiped and treated with respect. The priests served to keep the stories coming to maintain their own lifestyle and power position. But there was little in the way of guidance on life otherwise. The lessons learned from the Folklore gods usually had little application to the lives of real people trying to survive in the ancient world. Roman Generals had priests examine sheep entrails for signs and directions on how or when to wage a war. The priests were quick-witted and always had answers that satisfied the Generals, or else they died.

When we look at the existing mix and popularity of religion today we see a mix of all of these religious traditions. We also see physical/cultural isolation as playing a part in the continued existence of the many gods / primitive religions alongside the more modern single creator God religious view. We also see two religions that span the gap between the folk religions or traditions and the modern creator God religions. Both Hinduism and Buddhism are proactive extensions of folk traditions that seek to guide their followers with some specific approaches to dealing with the religious and spiritual world they see.

Hinduism

Hinduism carries with it the folk traditions of many human/animal flawed gods and expands on life after death in the spirit world with a rather interesting twist, reincarnation and the need for perfection in life. If you are less than perfect you will be reincarnated, and reborn into the physical world to see if you can do a better job at being perfect. If you're particularly bad you might come back as an animal or an insect. If you've been fairly good in your last life you might come back as a privileged human and thus better able to keep advancing until you are so perfect that you reach nirvana where reincarnation is ended and your spirit is blended into a global spirit world where your identity of self disappears.

Like most religions, Hinduism has no real guidance on how good you have to be. Secondly, it has many gods, many sects, and many gurus, with a wide variety of approaches to life that deal with how to raise the level of your life, that is to qualify for Nirvana, their concept of the end of the reincarnation cycle.

Hinduism has emerged from the world of Folk religions with a large following, perhaps because they lacked the violent human sacrifices found elsewhere and secondly perhaps because it was somewhat isolated from the rest of the world by distance.

Hinduism might be described as a religion with a foot in each camp. Its roots are in the folk religion camp with gods everywhere, but it also tries to consider human nature and has developed various philosophies for handling that human nature.

Hinduism: *Hindus believe that all living creatures have a Self. This true "Self" of every person, is called the ātman. The Self is believed to be eternal. According to the monistic/pantheistic (non-dualist) theologies of Hinduism (such as Advaita Vedanta school), this Atman is indistinct from Brahman, the supreme spirit or the Ultimate Reality. The goal of life, according to the Advaita school, is to realise that one's Self is identical to supreme Self, that the supreme Self is present in everything and everyone, all life is interconnected and there is oneness in all life. Dualistic schools (Dvaita and Bhakti) understand Brahman as a Supreme Being separate from individual Selfs. They worship the Supreme Being variously as Vishnu, Brahma, Shiva, or Shakti, depending upon the sect. God is called Ishvara, Bhagavan, Parameshwara, Deva, or Devi, and these terms have different meanings in different schools of Hinduism. Hindu texts accept a polytheistic framework, but this is generally conceptualized as the divine essence or luminosity that gives vitality and animation to the inanimate natural substances. There is a divine in everything, human beings, animals, trees, and rivers. It is observable in offerings to rivers, trees, tools of one's work, animals and birds, rising sun, friends and guests, teachers and parents. It is divine in these that makes each sacred and worthy of reverence, rather than them being sacred in and of themselves. This perception of divinity manifested in all things, as Buttimer and Wallin view it, makes the Vedic foundations of Hinduism quite distinct from animism, in which all things are themselves divine. The*

animistic premise sees multiplicity, and therefore equality of ability to compete for power when it comes to man and man, man and animal, man and nature, etc. The Vedic view does not perceive this competition, equality of man to nature, or multiplicity so much as an overwhelming and interconnecting single divinity that unifies everyone and everything.
https://en.wikipedia.org/wiki/Hinduism

This description does not do justice to the complexity of Hinduism. It is generally not a single religion with one set of beliefs, but a collection of religious thoughts that can conflict with each other. But what should be obvious is that it comes from multiple individual folk religions with a multitude of gods and a multitude of ways to manipulate the gods for the believer's benefit.

Hinduism also begins to address the consequences of human failures, weaknesses, and being a downright bad person with philosophies on how one should live their life. At the same time, they connect human failures to what happens after death, reincarnation into either a better person and life or into a lower class person or an animal or an insect.

So Hinduism adds two significant elements, life after death and the quality of that second or third, etc life is determined by the quality of the current life in terms of aspects of good and bad. That is you have to earn your way into heaven and out of the endless reincarnations. How you do that, how good you have to be is an unknown however, so the striving for it either ceases in exhaustion or turns you into one of the many mystics making your life as numb or meaningless as possible to avoid doing anything bad. Or on the other hand, beating and torturing your body relentlessly so as to already be punished enough in this life that somehow you get into heaven.

Thus Hinduism is a religion of endless ritual appeasing the various gods for favors in life just like the primitive religions while also trying to comply with a multitude of conflicting rules from different versions on how to be perfect to escape reincarnation. This certainly makes Hinduism seem like a very old religion, but its current framework and traditions are much younger than you probably imagine. Here is a synopsis of the evolution of Hinduism. To clarify the dates with our own calendar we'll define just what the referenced BCE date means. The short answer is that the BCE dates are identical to our BC/AD dates.

Common Era or Current Era (CE)[1] is one of the notation systems for the world's most widely used calendar era. BCE (Before the Common Era or Before the Current Era) is the era before CE. BCE and CE are alternatives to the Dionysian BC and AD system respectively. The Dionysian era distinguishes eras using AD (anno Domini, "[the] year of [the] Lord")[2] and BC ("before Christ"). Since the two notation systems are numerically equivalent, "2019 CE" corresponds to "AD 2019" and "400 BCE" corresponds to "400 BC". Both notations refer to the Gregorian calendar (and its predecessor, the Julian calendar). The year-numbering system utilized by the Gregorian calendar is used throughout the world today and is an international standard for civil calendars.
https://en.wikipedia.org/wiki/Common_Era

Origin of Hinduism

The Vedic period, named after the Vedic religion of the Indo-Aryans,\ lasted from c. 1500 to 500 BCE.\ The Indo-Aryans were pastoralists\ who migrated into north-western India after the collapse of the Indus Valley Civilization.

During the early Vedic period (c. 1500–1100 BCE) Vedic tribes were pastoralists, wandering around in northwest India. After 1100 BCE the Vedic tribes moved into the western Ganges Plain, adapting an agrarical lifestyle. Rudimentary state forms appeared, of which the Kuru-Pañcāla union was the most influential. It was a tribal union, which developed into the first recorded state-level society in South Asia around 1000 BCE. This, according to Witzel, decisively changed the Vedic heritage of the early Vedic period, collecting the Vedic hymns into collections, and shifting ritual exchange within a tribe to social exchange within the larger Kuru realm through complicated Srauta rituals. In this period, states Samuel, emerged the Brahmana and Aranyaka layers of Vedic texts, which merged into the earliest Upanishads. These texts began to ask the meaning of a ritual, adding increasing levels of philosophical and metaphysical speculation, or "Hindu synthesis".

Vedic religion: Historical Vedic religion

The Indo-Aryans brought with them their language and religion. The Vedic beliefs and practices of the pre-classical era were closely related to the hypothesised Proto-Indo-Europe In the later Vedic period, it co-existed with local religions, such as the mother goddess worshipping Yaksha cults. The

Vedic was itself likely the product of "a composite of the indo-Aryan and Harappan cultures and civilizations". David Gordon White cites three other mainstream scholars who "have emphatically demonstrated" that Vedic religion is partially derived from the Indus Valley Civilizations. Their religion was further developed when they migrated into the Ganges Plain after c. 1100 BCE and became settled farmers, further syncretising with the native cultures of northern India.

The composition of Vedic literature began in the 2nd millennium BCE. The oldest of these Vedic texts is the Rigveda, composed between c. 1500-1200 BCE

The first half of the 1st millennium BCE was a period of great intellectual and social-cultural ferment in ancient India. New ideas developed both in the Vedic tradition in the form of the Upanishads, and outside of the Vedic tradition through the Śramaṇa movements. For example, prior to the birth of the Buddha and the Mahavira, and related Sramana movements, the Brahmanical tradition had questioned the meaning and efficacy of Vedic rituals, then internalized and variously reinterpreted the Vedic fire rituals as ethical concepts such as Truth, Rite, Tranquility or Restraint. The 9th and 8th centuries BCE witnessed the composition of the earliest Upanishads with such ideas Other ancient Principal Upanishads were composed in the centuries that followed, forming the foundation of classical Hinduism and the Vedanta (conclusion of the Veda) literature.
https://en.wikipedia.org/wiki/Hinduism#Origins

To put Hinduism in perspective its development took place over a period from approximately 2000 BC to 500 BC. In comparison, the Biblical Old Testament records place these approximate dates on events. (Best estimates of genealogies and external historical sources)

Approximate Biblical Timeline
- 4000 BC: Adam and Eve
- 2500 BC: Noah and the flood
- 2000 BC: Abraham, the father of both the Jews and the Arabs
- 1446 BC: Moses and the Exodus from Egypt form the nation of Israel
- 1000 BC: Kings David and Solomon and the golden era of Israel

These dates are nebulous, as are the Hindu dates, but the Biblical record is at least contemporary and may predate Hinduism by hundreds if not thousands of years. Yet the Bible speaks of a single creator God with compassion and actual interest in the welfare of His creation, including mankind, to the extent that He, God will take care of both the needs of daily life but also life after death. This is an adult God so to speak who does not need adoration and praise from his people to take care of them. This is compared with the Hindu multi-god man/beast combinations and reincarnation as punishment for sins with no account of how to escape, or the level of goodness that must be achieved to escape. So even if these religious traditions are contemporary with one another the single all-powerful creator God of the Hebrews is a significant departure from the Hindu folk religion concepts of the time.

Unfortunately, many scholars place dates on events based on two major factors, the evolution of the language and the earliest dated texts found. The result is that they tend to compress the above Biblical events into the historical timeframe of the oldest manuscripts. Given that the oldest copies of the Old Testament are from the 600 BC era scholars tend to think that Abraham was from that 600 BC era as well, simply because the language used to create the written text of Abraham's story was 600 BC language.

The scholars also pick at the language, for example citing 600 BC language constructs as verifying a 600 BC date for events that are dated by historical reference as occurring much earlier. They forget or ignore, of course, two major influencing factors. First, those language constructs are updated as newer copies of written texts are created. Secondly, the initial means of recording stories and events were verbal, and those verbal recordings changed over many years up until the time that the stories could be reliably documented, stored, and copies created. Changing language constructs do not harm the accuracy and authenticity of the Old Testament record. It's no more than the change of English texts where "thy" is now documented as "your".

By the same measure, many modern scholars say that the New Testament was not written until the fourth century AD because the oldest New Testament texts found were from after 300 AD. That's like saying that 500 years from now Thomas Jefferson will have thought to be alive in 2025 because that's the date of the oldest copy of one of his books available.

Likewise of course the dates given above for phases of the Hindu religion are similarly suspect, so most likely, Hinduism is roughly contemporary with the Jewish and Christian biblical history. The one major difference that should be noted is that Hinduism was the result of several different cultures and religious thoughts being merged over hundreds if not thousands of years. Contrast this with the Biblical record of Judaism which develops along a single line of reasoning and tradition.

In summary, then the Folk or primitive religions, including Hinduism have endured as long as the civilizations that accepted them have endured, with little change in their beliefs or practices over thousands of years. Hinduism might more logically be looked at as a collection of many different folk religions rather than one homogeneous religion. This is perhaps also the case with the folk religions of China and Japan which are not much more than ancestor worship without a formal set of rituals or spiritual doctrines. What has happened in China and Japan however is that some of the ritual traditions from Buddhism have become accepted, giving the Chinese and Japanese people a bit more in the way of traditions and rituals to hold onto, in addition to the ancestor worship traditions.

Buddhism

Buddhism is a second-generation folk religion and an update to Hinduism in the sense that it provides an intellectual, behavioral approach to reaching Hindu nirvana, that state of spiritual nothingness that Hindus seek. Hinduism has multiple paths to nirvana but they tend to follow one of two opposite extremes of asceticism, extreme avoidance of worldly pleasures (often associated with self-torture or physical punishment), or, contrarily fully indulging in worldly pleasures as your sole objective to burn them out of your desires, so to speak. Buddhism sees itself as a somewhat middle ground in Hinduism in that it seeks to avoid all worldly pleasures through the mental discipline of self-control and self-denial. Two views of the essence of Buddhism come from the following source.

"The Essence of Buddhism." David Tuffley. Apple Books. https://itunes.apple.com/us/book/the-essence-of-buddhism/id401059291?mt=11

A. *The Tenants of Buddhism*

1. *The greatest achievement is selflessness.*
2. *The greatest worth is self-mastery.*
3. *The greatest quality is seeking to serve others.*
4. *The greatest precept is continual awareness.*
5. *The greatest medicine is the emptiness of everything.*
6. *The greatest action is not conforming with the worlds ways.*
7. *The greatest magic is transmuting the passions.*
8. *The greatest generosity is non-attachment.*
9. *The greatest goodness is a peaceful mind.*
10. *The greatest patience is humility.*
11. *The greatest effort is not concerned with results.*
12. *The greatest meditation is a mind that lets go.*
13. *The greatest wisdom is seeing through appearances.*

B. *The Four Noble Truths*

1. *If you are alive you will suffer, and pleasures will make that suffering greater*
2. *The cause of suffering is attachment to worldly things, including self, social life, relationships, human life, and culture*
3. *You can end suffering by mentally killing self and ego*
4. *You can end suffering by following the eight-fold path*
   (1) *Right View*
   (2) *Right Intention*
   (3) *Right Speech*
   (4) *Right Action*
   (5) *Right Livelihood*
   (6) *Right Effort*
   (7) *Right Mindfulness*
   (8) *Right Concentration*

Excerpt From: David Tuffley. "The Essence of Buddhism." Apple Books. https:// itunes.apple.com/us/book/the-essence-of-buddhism/id401059291?mt=11

The book, "The Essence of Buddhism" also has a direct quote from the Buddha as its sub-title that summarizes Buddhism's approach or philosophy of life considered necessary to solving the Hindu complex problem of reincarnation and finally achieving nirvana.

"But if you do not find an intelligent companion, a wise and well-behaved person going the same way as yourself, then go on your way alone, like a king abandoning a conquered kingdom, or like a great elephant in the deep forest. – The Buddha."

The bottom line is that Buddhism is attractive in the sense that it talks about doing good and being mentally tough in controlling your life. But it also tells you that life and pleasures in life, including just smelling the roses or listening to a symphony orchestra or a country band are bad. And even beyond that, it emphasizes withdrawing from life altogether.

If you become a Buddhist monk you have a chance at escaping reincarnation. If you can't be a monk then do the best you can, but good luck at that, you'll never make it. But you can donate money or gifts to a monastery and gain some credits toward nirvana by association with the monks who are far closer to perfection than you'll ever be.

And of course, there is the anomaly that Buddhism is trying to reach a stage of perfection that must have been defined by some higher creature, a god, that they fail to recognize. And again they want you to abstain from all those pleasures and capabilities in life that are designed into the world and human life by that same god. And they chant and pray (chant mantras) and ring bells to those self-same but nameless and unknown human gods, humans who have become perfected and postpone Nirvana to help others become perfect.

Buddhist mantras Definition:*A mantra (Sanskrit: मन्त्र,*

romanized: mantra, /ˈmʌntrə/; Pali: mantaṃ) or mantram is a sacred utterance, a numinous sound, a syllable, word or phonemes, or group of words in Sanskrit, Pali and other languages believed by practitioners to have religious, magical or spiritual powers. Some mantras have a syntactic structure and literal meaning, while others do not.

Function and structure of Mantras

One function of mantras is to solemnize and ratify rituals. Each mantra, in Vedic rituals, is coupled with an act. According to Apastamba Srauta Sutra, each ritual act is accompanied by one mantra, unless the Sutra explicitly marks that one act corresponds to several mantras. According to Gonda, and others, there is a connection and rationale between a Vedic mantra and each Vedic ritual act that accompanies it. In these cases, the function of mantras was to be an instrument of ritual efficacy for the priest, and a tool of instruction for a ritual act for others.

Over time, as the Puranas and Epics were composed, the concepts of worship, virtues and spirituality evolved in Hinduism. Religions such as

*Jainism and Buddhism branched off, and new schools were founded, each continuing to develop and refine its own mantras. In Hinduism, suggests Alper, the function of mantras shifted from the quotidian to redemptive. **In other words, in Vedic times, mantras were recited with a practical, quotidian goal as intention, such as requesting a deity's help in the discovery of lost cattle, cure of illness, succeeding in competitive sport or journey away from home. The literal translation of Vedic mantras suggests that the function of mantra, in these cases, was to cope with the uncertainties and dilemmas of daily life**. In a later period of Hinduism, mantras were recited with a transcendental redemptive goal as intention, such as escape from the cycle of life and rebirth, forgiveness for bad karma, and experiencing a spiritual connection with god. The function of mantras, in these cases, was to cope with the human condition as a whole. According to Alper, redemptive spiritual mantras opened the door for mantras where every part need not have a literal meaning, but together their resonance and musical quality assisted the transcendental spiritual process. Overall, explains Alper, using Śivasūtra mantras as an example, Hindu mantras have philosophical themes and are metaphorical with social dimension and meaning; in other words, they are a spiritual language and instrument of thought.*

According to Staal, Hindu mantras may be spoken aloud, anirukta (not enunciated), upamsu (inaudible), or manasa (not spoken, but recited in the mind). In ritual use, mantras are often silent instruments of meditation.

https://en.wikipedia.org/wiki/Mantra

The veracity of the above-referenced detail on mantras and their application to Buddhism may be questioned, but it shows the complex fabric and multiple thoughts and traditions that have emerged. It also demonstrates that saying that Buddhists pray to a higher spirit or a god is not quite how they see it. What we call prayer they call mantras which are repeated chants. These chants have multiple functions including appeals for help from humans who have reached perfection but have delayed Nirvana in order to help others attain perfection. So are these perfect humans, who may or may not be alive, gods? They are certainly humans, or at least similar to Judaeo Christian angels, but also similar to the little gods of Hindu and other folk religions. Notice also that at least some of the motivation for mantras chanted to these perfect humans is to aid one in attaining perfection.

All Buddhists might not acknowledge this perfection objective of mantras because of the complexity, depth, and variations among various Buddhist sects, including some in monasteries. Some may claim it is to help clear their thoughts to continue the Buddhist path to perfection, but the end is the same. They are striving, to the point of denying life itself, to become perfect. And this is a goal of mankind from his exile from the Garden and transition into a conscious human being. It is an essential part of human religious thinking.

Most of all, at the practical level, the Buddhist approach is to withdraw from life, especially life with others and their imperfections. And of course, since you'll never reach a level of perfection, you'll never be at peace with yourself. Buddhism then is the ultimate anti-prosperity and anti-happiness philosophy of life. It is most assuredly anti-prosperity not just because it has disdain for prosperity and the things of life but because it teaches a strictly anti-social lifestyle. As the quote from Buddha says avoid people who are not marching in lock step with your own drummer, which excludes most everyone else. Real shalom prosperity comes from a cooperative effort with your neighbors who may be drastically different from yourself. So the culture that promotes and teaches respect for and, the indulgence of your neighbor enables a cooperative effort, one that collectively creates the greatest prosperity.

And of course, Hinduism and Buddhism both set their followers on a hopeless path of achieving an undefined perfection. While Hinduism pursues appeasing the gods as an alternative way out, Buddhism puts the full burden on your own back. They both detract significantly from achieving both prosperity and happiness in life. This is emphasized by the focus on self, getting one's self to nirvana, at the exclusion of everyone else. To be clear this "me, me, me" approach to life is not found in every adherent of Hinduism or Buddhism as many of the followers are more casual observers, following the ritual and picking and choosing whatever aspects suites them. But when the overriding cultural approach is flavored by those religions, that "me, me, me" flavor seeps into everyone's life.

Taoism and Confucianism

Two other minor second-generation religions (after Buddhism) are born out of the Chinese Folklore traditions, Taoism and Confucianism. Taoism emerges first and while holding onto the polytheistic Folk Lore traditions, it follows the intellectual, knowledge-based path to perfection much like Buddhism which it predates by 500 or so years. It lacks the idea of the Hindu Nirvana and reincarnation so the idea of perfection through knowledge, right actions, and self-discipline is more focused on the influence of prosperity and happiness in life. Confucianism follows Taoism by about 500 years and emerges at about the same time as Buddhism. It basically takes Taoism and drops the polytheistic aspects, and Confucius, like Buddha, (both being claimed to be actual humans), is the model for self-training, self-discipline, and achievement of a perfect state.

Shintoism

A fourth second-generation religion is actually a combination of a primitive religion and a second-generation religion. Shinto or Shintoism evolves from its Folk Lore roots to combine with Buddhism, and in Japan where it originated most are adherents of practices from both religions. Shinto itself is primarily a Folk Lore tradition where many followers also practice Buddhist traditions and rituals, but the Buddhist additions are less intellectual and more ritualistic than Buddhism elsewhere.

Greek/Roman pantheon

A fifth second-generation religion, the Greek/Roman pantheon of gods, has its roots in a mix of Folklore traditions in the Middle East including the Egyptian religion. These Folklore religions were contemporaries of Judaism and the Old Testament has much to say about them as they were in constant contact with the people of Israel. The Greek/Roman religion takes the Folk Lore nebulous concepts of god and gods and formalizes it into a strong cadre of superhuman beings. Temples, priests, and rituals are firmly established as traditions, and social life is often centered around temple activities. Rituals are used to try and manipulate the gods to be favorable to you in life. This becomes the primary religion of the Roman world.

Zoroastrianism

A sixth second-generation religion is Zoroastrianism. It comes from Folk Lore roots with ties to Hinduism and is the creation of the prophet Zoroaster approximately during the 6th century BC. Zoroaster refined the folklore religion in the middle east, especially Iran by moving to a monotheistic concept and revising some of the rituals. It has similarities with Judaism in creation, judgment and heaven and hell and is often said to have influenced Judaism however the reverse seems to be the truth as Judaism has a much older historical record.

The nation of Israel was a prominent player in the middle east both economically and militarily for over 500 years before Zoroaster and Israel's monotheistic creator God religion was well known, even to some of the powerful rulers of the time that had conquered Israel such as the Persians and the Babylonians. Since the Persian empire was a pre Iranian empire that included most of what is modern-day Iran the influence of Judaism on Zoroaster is more likely the case.

Zoroastrianism also may have had an influence on Islam given it was the state religion of the Iranian empires for a thousand years prior to the advent of Islam and performed much the same objectives as that of Mohammad in that it reformed the area's folk religions with their many gods by categorizing them as to their worthiness of worship (some were and some weren't) and by proclaiming one to be the supreme creator God of the universe.

Zoroastrianism: With possible roots dating back to the second millennium BCE, Zoroastrianism enters recorded history in the 5th century BCE. Along with a Mithraic Median prototype and a Zurvanist Sassanid successor, it served as the state religion of the pre-Islamic Iranian empires for more than a millennium, from around 600 BCE to 650 CE. Zoroastrianism declined from the 7th century onwards following the Muslim conquest of Persia of 633–654. Recent estimates place the current number of Zoroastrians at around 110,000-120,000, with most living in India and in Iran; their number has been thought to be declining. Besides the Zoroastrian diaspora, the older disputed Mithraic faith Yazdânism is still practised amongst Kurds.

The most important texts of the religion are those of the Avesta, which includes as central the writings of Zoroaster known as the Gathas, enigmatic ritual poems that define the religion's precepts, which is within Yasna, the main worship service of modern Zoroastrianism. The religious philosophy of Zoroaster divided the early Iranian gods of the Proto-Indo-Iranian tradition into ahuras and daevas, the latter of which were not considered worthy of worship. Zoroaster proclaimed that Ahura Mazda was the supreme creator, the creative and sustaining force of the universe through Asha, and that human beings are given a right of choice between supporting Ahura Mazda or not, making them responsible for their choices. Though Ahura Mazda has no equal contesting force, Angra Mainu (destructive spirit/mentality) is considered the main adverserial force of the religion standing against Spenta Mainyu (creative spirit/mentality), whose forces are born from Aka Manah (evil thought). Middle Persian literature developed further Angra Mainyu into Ahriman and advancing him to be the direct adversary to Ahura Mazda. https://en.wikipedia.org/wiki/Zoroastrianism

The essence of the Folk and unknown gods / multiple gods religions including Hinduism and Buddhism and all their derivatives then is:

Folk and multiple unknown god Religions

1. The gods are mostly unknowable and uncommunicative with mankind. Their philosophy of life is mostly devoted to rituals designed to achieve nirvana/heaven. Culturally some wisdom is grudgingly dispensed through priests with Buddhism dispensing some wisdom for living while still requiring a monastic life to become qualified for nirvana.
2. Life is tough and the gods could care less
3. The gods can possibly be manipulated to help through rituals and sacrifices and intercessory shaman, gurus.
4. The gods/spirit world demands perfection
5. Your sins keep you from nirvana/heaven
6. Your sins can make your next life (reincarnation) miserable
7. The gods/spirit world provide NO direction for achieving perfection and entering nirvana/heaven
8. Gurus/shamans/priests provide a multitude of rituals and actions to gain the god's favor and support, and to achieve perfection and eventually enter nirvana/heaven
9. Buddha's advice is to avoid everyone different from yourself and think perfect thoughts but Buddhism also acknowledges the need to manipulate the unknown spirit world with rituals and homage through a "set aside" monastic life AND by supporting the monastic life of others.

The three remaining world religions on our list invoke a single all-powerful creator God and we sometimes think of these as modern religions which have evolved from the Folk Religion's multiple images of little gods. But Judaism is as old or older than Hinduism and both Christianity and Islam trace their roots back to Judaism.   So this view of a single all-powerful creator God is more like a separate branch of religious thought rather than an evolutionary step.

Two final notes on the primitive religions.   First of all modern followers of these religions, when faced with the contrast between a single all-powerful creator God and the many small, flawed, and silent mini gods, are prone to give their religion a fresh coat of paint, a new appearance to the modern eye.   Hindu progressives now say that Hinduism certainly believes in the single all-powerful creator God and that the individual mini gods are but local training aids to help communicate Hinduism. Buddhism hides its silent gods within its closed monasteries and probably has similar apologists but their religion has not had the same direct and large interaction with Christianity through the British Empire as has occurred in India.

Secondly, while we haven't made an issue of it, primitive religions are not without some aspects of morality and a virtuous life.   Buddhism in particular has several principles that we, who live under the influence of Judaeo-Christian moral standards, would consider valuable wisdom and guidance.   Hinduism may have some teachings as well but India having been under British rule for some time has adopted a number of Christian values of government and morality so it would be hard to separate that impact from Hinduism's fundamental values.

Morality is generally thought of as something like broad standards for community life, often with legal implications, so perhaps "Philosophy of Life" is a more complete description of influences on human interactions. This includes morality, as well as interactions with others which we might think of as manners and good social etiquette. And certainly, a philosophy of life, including morality can come from the needs of any society to develop a better operating system for social and business interaction.

A Philosophy of Life and morality developed apart from religion has failed catastrophically in the French Revolution, Communist Russia, and China, however, because it has overturned cultural roots and possessed no superior intellectual claims.   The new culture was also easily changed by the whims of whoever possessed the power and devised the rules to benefit themselves.   By extension, Socialist countries have failed similarly for the same reasons.   They created a flawed morality and culture created by flawed human socialist thinking.   At least with the Folk religions, the culture, philosophy of life, and morality arose from trial and error agreement within the culture.   Trial and error morality doesn't say anything about absolute morality however, just that the community had come to agree on it. The harsh punishment of minor sins by Islam and by folk religions with barbarian ideals is not a standard we in the Christian West would easily accept.

Communism, socialism, and modern human philosophies all fail because they fail to understand the complexity and nature of human beings.   And in doing so derive governments that may satisfy their own need for power and control, but ignore the impact on complex human consciousness.   This is best explained by a Judaeo Christian philosophy that says:

> *1 Corinthians 9:9-10 (NASB) For it is written in the Law of Moses, "YOU SHALL NOT MUZZLE THE OX WHILE HE IS THRESHING." God is not concerned about oxen, is He? 10 Or is He speaking altogether for our sake? Yes, for our sake it was written, because the plowman ought to plow in hope, and the thresher to thresh in hope of sharing the crops.*

First of all, this passage points out directly that the truths of the Bible are much deeper than just a surface reading and in fact, the deeper truths are the more important ones.   On the surface, you could say the Ox is working and gets hungry, let him eat a few grains. And you could certainly say this means we should treat animals humanely. But that's not the point being made.   This is a metaphor that is explained as a truth of human nature and a principle of economics and life. Mankind naturally expects to profit by the works of his hands.   And the obvious implication is that society will work better if this is the case.

This is an example of principles within Judaism that are expanded by Christianity. The principle was there, hidden within a metaphor in the Jewish Bible, but specifically called out in the Christian New Testament.

Secondly, this captures the essence of the prosperity of Western culture and why Communism, socialism, slavery, and similar human philosophies of life fail miserably, they don't consider human nature. But there's something even deeper, work is an essential part of life that gives us satisfaction, and shalom prosperity, no matter what it is, just as long as we feel challenged by it and succeed at it. This is a Principle of Life from Ecclesiastics in the Hebrew Bible that is expanded and confirmed in the New Testament. This is also one of the subtle principles that propelled prosperity under Christianity over the last three hundred years of Christian dominance in the Western World. We'll see this take place in our examination of the Middle Ages in Volume II.

This parable of the Ox also demonstrates the failure of human religions to move beyond their own human-created metaphors of God and gods and see the All-Powerful Creator and Mentor God identified first in Judaism. They worship the idols made from hands. In every case, there are probably examples of metaphors of wisdom. Certainly, Buddhism and Taoism contain some level of that sense of wisdom in their philosophies since they were the result of human philosophers thinking about life. But they are still human religions as their view of God is still nebulous at best.

These human philosophies are certainly hit and miss, like the advice of the 100-year-old woman who smoked cigars and ate a package of cookies every day, crediting that to her age.

Abraham's Journey from Ur to Canaan
by József Molnár, 1850 (Hungarian National Gallery, Budapest)

SECTION E: THE BIG GOD RELIGIONS

13. Judaism: Thinking Differently

Judaism is the precursor to Christianity. It shares much of its Theology and Philosophy of Life with Christianity. It also has its heritage in the prehistoric past before human consciousness along with all the primitive folk religions. But it differs significantly from those primitive folk religions and from those that grew out of them in two distinct ways. While it begins life along with all the primitive religions in that prehistoric mix before man became a conscious human being, it establishes a unique view of God as an All-powerful creator and mentor God who designed and created the world and mankind. God as the designer and builder of the world is viewed as a benevolent God who cares for his creation and the primitive pre-Judaic approach is to trust God to do the right things for his people. This becomes the Faith of Abraham and the only "religious" ritual given is that of a thanksgiving offering illustrated by Abel's animal sacrifice. This ritual is not designed to manipulate or appease God but to thank Him for the provisions and resources for life he has provided. It also serves as a reminder of who God is. This leads to the second big distinction, Judaism from the beginning of the pre-Judaic forerunner accepts God's decisions and judgments on matters of life, it does not attempt to manipulate God with praises or rituals to get Him to do their bidding.

There's a song in Fiddler on the Roof that demonstrates that faith and trust, "If I were a Rich Man". The song is performed by Tevye (played by actor Chaim Topol), the main character in the musical, and reflects his dreams of wealth. But it is sung as a comedic wish that he knows will never come true. That is Tevye dreams of riches but knows the future is always in God's hands to decide such things.

Fiddler on the roof - If I were a rich man (with subtitles)
YouTube·guru006·Aug 19, 2006 Fair Use

... Oh, Lord, you made many, many poor people
I realize, of course, it's no shame to be poor
But it's no great honor either
So, what would have been so terrible if I had a small fortune?

✦

... If I were a rich man
Ya ba dibba dibba dibba dibba dibba dibba dum
All day long, I'd biddy biddy bum
If I were a wealthy man
✦

I wouldn't have to work hard
Ya ba dibba dibba dibba dibba dibba dibba dum
... If I were a biddy biddy rich yidle-diddle-didle-didle man
✦

I'd build a big, tall house with rooms by the dozen
Right in the middle of the town
A fine tin roof with real wooden floors below
There would be one long staircase just going up
And one even longer coming down
And one more leading nowhere, just for show
✦
✦

And it concludes with....

Lord, who made the lion and the lamb
You decreed I should be what I am
Would it spoil some vast eternal plan
If I were a wealthy man?

Placing one's faith and one's future in an All-powerful Creator God was the path demonstrated by Abraham that became the mantra for both Judaism and Christianity.

This pre-Judaic religion is based on faith in God to guide their lives. There were no rituals designed to manipulate God into giving them things. That faith also caused them to collect and tell the stories of God creating the world and mankind, and how consciousness eventually descends on man, making him fearful of life and creating religions that seek to manipulate God to get God to do their bidding.   We'll see this view enlarged in the Genesis story of Abel's sacrifice.

The collection of the Genesis stories tells of the advent of consciousness and the malevolent, self-centered, and self-serving society that results as seen through the eyes of Adam and his descendants, Noah, and up through the stories of Abraham and his descendants. The stories are memorized and passed down to each new generation until they can be recorded in written form by Moses as the nation of Israel is being formed after the Exodus in about 1,400 BC. The pre-Judaic stories are also unique in their historical nature, and they survived over an extended period until they could be preserved in writing, a unique situation among the primitive religions. This essentially is the book of Genesis.

> **The Book of Genesis** (from Greek Γένεσις Génesis; Hebrew: בְּרֵאשִׁית,
> Bərēšīt, "In [the] beginning") is the first book of the Hebrew Bible and the
> Christian Old Testament. Its Hebrew name is the same as its first word,
> Bereshit ("In the beginning"). Genesis is an account of the creation of the
> world, the early history of humanity, and of Israel's ancestors, and the
> origins of the Jewish people.
>
> Tradition credits Moses as the author of Genesis, as well as the books of
> Exodus, Leviticus, Numbers, and most of Deuteronomy, but modern scholars,
> especially from the 19th century onward, see them as being written hundreds
> of years after **Moses is supposed to have lived, in the 6th and 5th
> centuries BC**. Based on the scientific interpretation of archaeological,
> genetic, and linguistic evidence, most scholars consider Genesis to be
> primarily Judeo-Christian mythology rather than historical.
>
> It is divisible into two parts, primeval history (chapters 1–11) and
> ancestral history (chapters 12–50). The primeval history sets out the
> author's concepts of the nature of the deity and of humankind's relationship
> with its maker: God creates a world that is good and fit for mankind, but
> when man corrupts it with sin God decides to destroy his creation, sparing
> only the righteous Noah and his family to re-establish the relationship
> between man and God. The ancestral history (chapters 12–50) tells of the
> prehistory of Israel, God's chosen people. At God's command, Noah's
> descendant Abraham journeys from his birthplace (described as Ur of the
> Chaldeans and whose identification with Sumerian Ur is tentative in modern
> scholarship) into the God-given land of Canaan, where he dwells as a
> sojourner, as does his son Isaac and his grandson Jacob. Jacob's name is
> changed to "Israel", and through the agency of his son Joseph, the children of
> Israel descend into Egypt, 70 people in all with their households and God
> promises them a future of greatness. Genesis ends with Israel in Egypt, ready

for the coming of Moses and the Exodus. The narrative is punctuated by a series of covenants with God, successively narrowing in scope from all mankind (the covenant with Noah) to a special relationship with one people alone (Abraham and his descendants through Isaac and Jacob).

In Judaism, the theological importance of Genesis centers on the covenants linking God to his chosen people and the people to the Promised Land. Christianity has interpreted Genesis as the prefiguration of certain cardinal Christian beliefs, primarily the need for salvation (the hope or assurance of all Christians) and the redemptive act of Christ on the Cross as the fulfillment of covenant promises as the Son of God.
https://en.wikipedia.org/wiki/Book_of_Genesis

> NOTE: The late dating of events and presumptions of mythology vs historical fact comes from a lack of age-relevant manuscripts and ancient physical artifacts of civilization. (Example Sodom did not exist because archeological evidence has not been found, etc.) But the lack of physical evidence is not proof as new evidence in support of the historical Biblical record is continually being unearthed, archeological pun intended. We'll assume the validity of the historical accounts with Moses living about 1,000 years earlier because it is a better fit with other historical and archeological records.

Genesis contains the story of both God and mankind from the beginning until the Exodus and the establishment of Judaism and the nation of Israel, a period of about 2,500 years after the Adam and Eve story. Remember that the Genesis accounts are still approachable as a parable of a real situation, even though these stories contain references and seemingly historical accounts of potentially real people, and seemingly real-life situations that describe life at that time similar to the "wild wild west", lawless and requiring citizen action to protect one's property. Giving a dialogue to characters in such a parable is a vehicle to quickly indicate the thoughts and intents and thinking of people but not necessarily represent an exact conversation. The objective of the Old Testament Genesis text, as passed down verbally, was to get the point across to the listener beginning as far back as Adam and Eve, some 2,000 or so years before Abraham and another 500 years before Moses. Moses is said to have codified or written down the beginning books of the Judaeo Christian Old Testament Bible, about 1,400 BC. The first 5 books of the

Bible, Genesis, Exodus, Leviticus, Numbers, and Deuteronomy constituted the Bible up and through the Exodus and the creation of Israel and Judaism. These five books established who God was and how he was working with mankind. They were mainly Theology and a little Philosophy with lots of parables and metaphors to simplify the concepts. The advent of Judaism added to the simple Theology and Philosophy of Abraham and created the cultural and religious rituals of Judaism designed to last until the fulfillment of a Jewish Messiah who would re-arrange Judaism and take the message to the world.

The original text was written in Hebrew but a Greek translation became the version best understood and therefore matches up well with the New Testament Greek.

The Septuagint

The Hebrew Bible was translated into Koine Greek in the third century BC, Koine Greek is a well-documented and understood language, especially at that time in the Roman world. Its great value is that the translation was done by Hebrew Biblical scholars and it was translated into an equally well-known and very expressive language Koine Greek, which just happens to be the language of New Testament Christianity.

The Septuagint (/ˈsɛptjuədʒɪnt/ SEP-tew-ə-jint), sometimes referred to as the Greek Old Testament or The Translation of the Seventy (Ancient Greek: Ἡ μετάφρασις τῶν Ἑβδομήκοντα, romanized: Hē metáphrasis tôn Hebdomḗkonta), and often abbreviated as LXX, is the earliest extant Greek translation of the Hebrew Bible from the original Hebrew. The full Greek title derives from the story recorded in the Letter of Aristeas to Philocrates that "the laws of the Jews" were translated into the Greek language at the request of Ptolemy II Philadelphus (285–247 BCE) by seventy-two Jewish translators—six from each of the Twelve Tribes of Israel.

Biblical scholars agree that the first five books of the Hebrew Bible were translated from Biblical Hebrew into Koine Greek by Jews living in the Ptolemaic Kingdom, probably in the early or middle part of the third century BCE. The remaining books were presumably translated in the 2nd century BCE. Some targumim translating or paraphrasing the Bible into Aramaic were also made during the Second Temple period.

Few people could speak and even fewer could read in the Hebrew language during the Second Temple period; Koine Greek and Aramaic were

the most widely spoken languages at that time among the Jewish community. The Septuagint therefore satisfied a need in the Jewish community.
   https://en.wikipedia.org/wiki/Septuagint

Koine Greek: *ἡ κοινὴ διάλεκτος, romanized: hē koinè diálektos, lit. 'the common dialect'),[a] also known as Hellenistic Greek, common Attic, the Alexandrian dialect, Biblical Greek, Septuagint Greek or New Testament Greek, was the common supra-regional form of Greek spoken and written during the Hellenistic period, the Roman Empire and the early Byzantine Empire.* **It evolved from the spread of Greek following the conquests of Alexander the Great in the fourth century BC and served as the lingua franca** *of much of the Mediterranean region and the Middle East during the following centuries. It was based mainly on Attic and related Ionic speech forms, with various admixtures brought about through dialect leveling with other varieties.*

   *A **lingua franca**, also known as a bridge language, common language, trade language, auxiliary language, vehicular language, or link language, is a language systematically used to make communication possible between groups of people who do not share a native language or dialect, particularly when it is a third language that is distinct from both of the speakers' native languages.*
   https://en.wikipedia.org/wiki/Koine_Greek

   Note: perhaps insightful concerning the language of Jesus, the New Testament writers and Apostles.

The impact of this view of God is that the pre-Judaic followers have a true God who is available as needed when things get tough and they can live their lives focused on day-to-day life.   The picture of God presented begins with the creation of the world and man in Genesis 1:1. The parable/ metaphor form provides an easy way to explain what happened in a form understandable to humans 6,000 years ago, at the time of Adam.

Genesis 1:1 - 2:4 (NASB) 1 In the beginning God created the heavens and the earth. 2 The earth was formless and void, and darkness was over the surface of the deep, and the Spirit of God was moving over the surface of the waters. 3 Then God said, "Let there be light"; and there was light. 4 God saw that the light was good; and God separated the light from the darkness. 5 God called the light day, and the darkness He called night. And there was evening and there was morning, one day.

6 Then God said, "Let there be an expanse in the midst of the waters, and let it separate the waters from the waters." 7 God made the expanse, and separated the waters which were below the expanse from the waters which were above the expanse; and it was so. 8 God called the expanse heaven. And there was evening and there was morning, a second day.

9 Then God said, "Let the waters below the heavens be gathered into one place, and let the dry land appear"; and it was so. 10 God called the dry land earth, and the gathering of the waters He called seas; and God saw that it was good. 11 Then God said, "Let the earth sprout vegetation, plants yielding seed, and fruit trees on the earth bearing fruit after their kind with seed in them"; and it was so. 12 The earth brought forth vegetation, plants yielding seed after their kind, and trees bearing fruit with seed in them, after their kind; and God saw that it was good. 13 There was evening and there was morning, a third day.

14 Then God said, "Let there be lights in the expanse of the heavens to separate the day from the night, and let them be for signs and for seasons and for days and years; 15 and let them be for lights in the expanse of the heavens to give light on the earth"; and it was so. 16 God made the two great lights, the greater light to govern the day, and the lesser light to govern the night; He made the stars also. 17 God placed them in the expanse of the heavens to give light on the earth, 18 and to govern the day and the night, and to separate the light from the darkness; and God saw that it was good. 19 There was evening and there was morning, a fourth day.

20 Then God said, "Let the waters teem with swarms of living creatures, and let birds fly above the earth in the open expanse of the heavens." 21 God created the great sea monsters and every living creature that moves, with which the waters swarmed after their kind, and every winged bird after its kind; and God saw that it was good. 22 God blessed them, saying, "Be fruitful and multiply, and fill the waters in the seas, and let birds multiply on the earth." 23 There was evening and there was morning, a fifth day.

24 Then God said, "Let the earth bring forth living creatures after their kind: cattle and creeping things and beasts of the earth after their kind"; and it was so. 25 God made the beasts of the earth after their kind, and the cattle after their kind, and everything that creeps on the ground after its kind; and God saw that it was good.

26 Then God said, "Let Us make man in Our image, according to Our likeness; and let them rule over the fish of the sea and over the birds of the sky and over the cattle and over all the earth, and over every creeping thing that creeps on the earth." 27 God created man in His own image, in the image of God He created him; male and female He created them. 28 God blessed

them; and God said to them, "Be fruitful and multiply, and fill the earth, and
subdue it; and rule over the fish of the sea and over the birds of the sky and
over every living thing that moves on the earth." 29 Then God said, "Behold, I
have given you every plant yielding seed that is on the surface of all the
earth, and every tree which has fruit yielding seed; it shall be food for you;
30 and to every beast of the earth and to every bird of the sky and to every
thing that moves on the earth which has life, I have given every green plant
for food"; and it was so. 31 God saw all that He had made, and behold, it was
very good. And there was evening and there was morning, the sixth day.

    Genesis Chapter 2 The Creation of Man and Woman: *1 Thus the*
heavens and the earth were completed, and all their hosts. 2 By the seventh
day God completed His work which He had done, and He rested on the
seventh day from all His work which He had done. 3 Then God blessed the
seventh day and sanctified it, because in it He rested from all His work which
God had created and made. 4 This is the account of the heavens and the earth
when they were created, in the day that the LORD God made earth and
heaven.

Consciousness

Consciousness was an awakening to self and the consequences of actions, a key event in mankind's life that opened his mind to the world but also brought in the malevolent, self-centered, self-serving thinking. It's like a switch went off in mankind's head and the focus of thinking and intellect switched from a connection to God to a connection to mankind's inner self and he now began to think differently, to think for himself. There was a downside to this change however, he now saw the realities of life, and also that he could manipulate life to his benefit. He also then thought he could control God as well.

Impact of Consciousness (knowing good and evil)

- Consciousness ends mankind's moment-by-moment worry-free life
- Consciousness makes mankind fearful of life's possibilities, and death
- Consciousness gives mankind a sense of both good and evil as options for dealing with life. He doesn't see evil as evil but just a means to an end
- Consciousness masks mankind's sense of connection with the God
- Consciousness also lets mankind see that both nature and evil men can make their lives miserable and think that God can help.
- Consciousness then causes mankind to seek ways to gain God's favor

Mankind's earliest religions were derived from these conditions in which mankind found themselves, and evolved into complex human religions. But they all contain the essence of mankind's thinking on the subject. The essence of the Folk and unknown/multiple gods religions including Hinduism and Buddhism and all their derivatives is:

Folk and unknown gods religions
- *The gods are mostly unknowable and uncommunicative with mankind*
- *Life is tough and the gods could care less*
- *The gods can be manipulated to help through rituals and sacrifices and intercessory shamans and gurus.*
- *The gods/spirit world demands perfection*
- *Your sins keep you from nirvana/heaven*
- *Your sins can make your next life (reincarnation) miserable*
- *The gods/spirit world provide NO direction for achieving perfection and entering nirvana/heaven*
- *Gurus/shamans/priests provide a multitude of different approaches to perfection and entering nirvana/heaven*
- *Buddha's advice is to avoid everyone different from yourself and think perfect thoughts. but Buddhism also acknowledges the need to manipulate the unknown spirit world with rituals through a "set aside" monastic life.*

Human religion originally was intended to manipulate the gods to do mankind's bidding. Judaism and Christianity have taken a totally different approach. Human religions focus on mankind controlling or manipulating God while Judaism and Christianity focus on God teaching mankind how to live.

In Human Religions mankind pursues their gods, the Judaeo-Christian concept is of God pursuing mankind.

Principles of the Judaeo-Christian Theology and Philosophy
1. God is the all-powerful creator and mentor God
2. There is no "quid pro quo" where you have to do something to please God and if you do enough, he'll respond favorably.
3. There is no uncertainty about entering the afterlife. God is not holding any of your sins against you.(Judaism shares this truth with Christianity.)

4. God has provided a written Theology and Philosophy of Life text
    for Judaism, the Hebrew Bible or the Old Testament of the
    Christian Bible. Both Hebrew and Greek texts provide a
    foundation for translation into other languages. It provides the
    Philosophy and Theology and religious social constructs to
    separate Judaism from the many religions in the area. The
    Theology and Philosophy provides the keys to living a prosperous,
    shalom life.
5. God has designed and created a world that provides all that
    mankind needs.
6. Prosperity multiplies as more and more citizens apply that
    Philosophy of Life to their culture and individual lives.

The key to understanding how and why Christianity promotes
prosperity is to therefore see and understand the Judaeo-Christian view of
a true God, worship, and rituals. In Human derived religions rituals are
everything. Rituals are used to manipulate and appease the gods to do
humans favors. In the Judaeo-Christian view, God cannot be manipulated,
He does things for us according to His plans. The purpose of ritual is to
teach a lesson or principle about Theology or the Philosophy of Life, or
how God works with mankind, or to inspire us to follow Him.

The difference is that in human religion rituals are thought to have
intrinsic value on their own. Whether it is the sacrifice of children to the
gods or the lighting of a candle, that worship is thought to have value in
appeasing the gods and therefore manipulating them to do the bidding of
the shaman or priest. In Judaeo-Christian applications, rituals have no
actual value in causing God to move or take action. The intrinsic value is
in the principle the ritual is portraying, usually by a metaphor. Prayer is
slightly different, but not by much, it's often asking God for the kind of
help that's already part of His plan. And of course, lighting a candle can be
a form of prayer rather than an attempt at manipulation. It's all in the eye
of the beholder.

Christianity is an expansion of Judaism that drops the Jewish cultural
and traditional aspects and explains or fulfills the rituals, making Christian

Theology and Philosophy easily adoptable by any culture. And Christianity includes only one ritual, one that is a metaphor for living the Christian life. There is no value to performing the ritual itself, its value is totally in following the reality of the metaphor. (To be explored later.)

Human emotion is not excluded from worship. Emotional stimulation in the form of music was a big part of Jewish temple and synagogue services, as it is a big part of the Christian Church today. Music, art and architecture are the most prominent examples, but an elaborate church service itself is often designed to provide an emotional or spiritual response to God.

> **Jewish music traditions** *The history of religious Jewish music spans the evolution of cantorial, synagogal, and Temple melodies since Biblical times.*
>
> *The earliest synagogal music of which we have any account was based on the system used in the Temple in Jerusalem. The Mishnah gives several accounts of Temple music. According to the Mishnah, the regular Temple orchestra consisted of twelve instruments and a choir of twelve male singers. The instruments included the kinnor (lyre), nevel (harp), tof (tambourine), shofar (ram's horn), hatzotz³rot (trumpet), and three varieties of pipe, the chalil, alamoth and the uggav. The Temple orchestra also included a cymbal (tziltzal) made of copper. The Talmud also mentions use in the Temple of a pipe organ (magrepha), and states that the water organ was not used in the Temple as its sounds were too distracting. No provable examples of the music played at the Temple have survived. However, there is an oral tradition that the tune used for Kol Nidrei was sung in the temple.*
>
> *After the destruction of the Temple in 70 AD and the subsequent dispersion of the Jews to Babylon and Persia, versions of the public singing of the Temple were continued in the new institution of the synagogue. Three musical forms were identified by scholars of the period, involving different modes of antiphonal response between cantor congregation: the cantor singing a half-verse at a time, with the congregation making a constant refrain; the cantor singing a half-verse, with the congregation repeating exactly what he had sung; and the cantor and congregation singing alternate verses. All of these forms can be discerned in parts of the modern synagogue service.*
> *https://en.wikipedia.org/wiki/Jewish_music*

And then there is "Fiddler On the Roof". An emotional response to music is human and its objective is to energize God's people to follow the theology and the philosophy, to promote prosperity for themselves and their neighbors. God does not respond to us based on our emotions, he does not do things for us because we become emotional. But emotion is part of the good life and music and art are sources of emotion that inspire good people to do good things. And as in "Fiddler On the Roof", there's often wisdom found within the stories themselves.

Truth is The Meaning behind the Parable or Metaphor

The purpose of using Biblical references and stories is to present the key elements of belief that guide and drive Christians toward that prosperous shalom life. The Truth of the Bible is more than the exact literal translated words used but in the meaning of the collective words, the truth the words are intended to communicate. That truth is considered to be the simplest, most logical interpretation based on a principle of logic called Occam's Razor. Thus the meaning of any passage may come from both the original language and from a realistic or a metaphorical interpretation, justified by context and other passages. We don't expect God to trick us with outlandish, contorted explanations being the message He intended.

Occam's razor, *Ockham's razor, or Ocham's razor (Latin: novacula Occami) in philosophy is the problem-solving principle that recommends searching for explanations constructed with the smallest possible set of elements. It is also known as the principle of parsimony or the law of parsimony (Latin: lex parsimoniae). Attributed to William of Ockham, a 14th-century English philosopher and theologian, it is frequently cited as Entia non sunt multiplicanda praeter necessitatem, which translates as "Entities must not be multiplied beyond necessity", although Occam never used these exact words. Popularly, the principle is sometimes inaccurately paraphrased as **"The simplest explanation is usually the best one."***

This philosophical razor advocates that when presented with competing hypotheses about the same prediction, one should prefer the one that requires fewest assumptions and that this is not meant to be a way of choosing between hypotheses that make different predictions. Similarly, in science, Occam's razor is used as an abductive heuristic in the development of theoretical models rather than as a rigorous arbiter between candidate models.

In the scientific method, Occam's razor is not considered an irrefutable principle of logic or a scientific result; the preference for simplicity in the scientific method is based on the falsifiability criterion. For each accepted explanation of a phenomenon, there may be an extremely large, perhaps even incomprehensible, number of possible and more complex alternatives. Since failing explanations can always be burdened with ad hoc hypotheses to prevent them from being falsified, simpler theories are preferable to more complex ones because they tend to be more testable.
https://en.wikipedia.org/wiki/Occam's_razor

This principle was explained at the end of the last chapter concerning this verse where Paul explains exactly how metaphors express truths.

1 Corinthians 9:9-10 (NASB) *For it is written in the Law of Moses, "YOU SHALL NOT MUZZLE THE OX WHILE HE IS THRESHING." God is not concerned about oxen, is He? 10 Or is He speaking altogether for our sake? Yes, for our sake it was written, because the plowman ought to plow in hope, and the thresher to thresh in hope of sharing the crops.*

That is, free enterprise and capitalism are what God considers morally right, all the way back in Moses's time, and was understood from the time of Adam.   It is this free enterprise that has contributed greatly to our prosperity.

The first Judaeo-Christian Theological Metaphor

The overall message of the faith of Abraham becomes, "live life with gusto", and "be all that you can be" but, "do no harm to others", a message he learned directly from God. Abraham's faith lies in God to take care of what is beyond his control, but, as a formal religion, Judaism does not become fleshed out in written or practiced form until the Exodus where Moses leads the Hebrews out of Egypt and into the Promised Land, in the 1,500 BC timeframe.   The pre-Judaic simple religion was not without something to hold its beliefs together, however. The early introduction of a simple sacrifice to acknowledge God came from the Cain and Abel story in Genesis. It would take 2,500 years or so to bring Judaism and its complex set of rituals and customs into the picture.

Cain and Abel

Genesis 1:2-8 Again, she gave birth to his brother Abel. And Abel was a keeper of flocks, but Cain was a tiller of the ground.

So it came about in the course of time that Cain brought an offering to the LORD of the fruit of the ground.

Abel, on his part also brought of the firstlings of his flock and of their fat portions. And the LORD had regard for Abel and for his offering;

but for Cain and for his offering He had no regard. So Cain became very angry and his countenance fell.

Then the LORD said to Cain, "Why are you angry? And why has your countenance fallen?

If you do well, will not your countenance be lifted up? And if you do not do well, sin is crouching at the door; and its desire is for you, but you must master it."

Cain told Abel his brother. And it came about when they were in the field, that Cain rose up against Abel his brother, and killed him.   NASB

Now there are three significant points to this Genesis story of Cain's sacrifice and the consequences that deal with the beginnings of religion. Mankind created the idea of an offering, God didn't say make me an offering, it was mankind's idea for an offering or sacrifice.   God then evaluated the two offerings from Cain and Abel and indicated a preference for Abel's sacrifice. God was saying, "If you're going to make an offering, I like Abel's way better." Now God knew this would happen, just as we parents know or can anticipate what our kids will do, but the story is told from the children's perspective, they always think they surprise us.

Cain rightly complains that he worked just as hard for his offering so God's not being fair and Cain, representing mankind's approach to religion, believes that he, Cain has a right to create religion and ritual to his liking. And consequently, God should sit down and shut up and accept what Cain wants. But God has other plans, ones that will include an offering like Abel's as a sign of both Judaism, (the Passover lamb and the temple ritual on the day of atonement) and Christianity, (the Lamb of God sacrificed on the cross), thousands of years later. So God, in effect, humors Cain a bit by just chiding him about it. But God is thinking ahead, that's what He does, and He wants to use Abel's sacrifice as a token ritual for a simple pre-Judaic religion of Faith to carry mankind through the times of Abraham and his descendants.

But Cain wants control of God and religion, the worship aspect of it, so badly that he kills Abel, thinking he's sending a message to God that he, representing mankind, will be in charge of religion and will tell God just what kind of offering/sacrifice He will get.   This is typical of human thinking about the gods, they are little gods, ones they can manipulate and control, and it works for the little gods because they are silent.

Mankind's view of Religion is that he can control God by rituals he both devises and performs.

No matter what you call the account, or whether you believe the exact dialog took place, or that it is a parable or even just a story created by the writer, this account of the earliest religious rituals sends the message of a God-sanctioned ritual that establishes a simple religion that can easily be followed without all the trappings of a grand musical production and show, without the need for shamans or human intermediaries.

For the most part, the Genesis stories are the early historical accounts of local tribal encounters and conflicts.   Indeed the story of Noah and Abraham is in that timeframe, as is the story of Sodom and Gomorrah. Life at this time was dangerous, there seemed to be little in the way of a civilized society. The powerful city-states were just beginning to emerge to tame the lawlessness.   The reference to Melchizedek does add a small reference to a priest of God and at least a ceremonial serving of bread and wine to guests, perhaps a foreshadowing of Christianity.

> *Genesis 14:18-20: And Melchizedek king of Salem brought out bread and wine; now he was a priest of God Most High. 19 He blessed him and said,*
> *"Blessed be Abram of God Most High,*
> *Possessor of heaven and earth;(NASB)*

The animal sacrifice of Abel seems to be the only ritual used by the prototype Hebrew people from the time of Abel until the formation of Abraham's Hebrew dependents in Egypt, some 1,500 years or so later. And they did this despite the full-fledged development of mankind's religions all around them. Two other stories in Genesis relate to human nature, the tower of Babel and Noah's Ark and the flood. You might put these stories in the same category as the Adam and Cain and Abel stories, as parables. What they do is to help focus two ideas or guidance the prototype Hebrews could carry with them.

The Noah story reiterates the level of violence and corruption that can come from mankind when they get together and that at some point the gene pool was becoming so bad that there were too many bad genes being passed around and too many bad people creating problems for everyone. So God had to adjust the gene pool by eliminating those people with really bad genes and bad behaviors. But don't fear God doing it again. The message was also that mankind has a very evil and destructive side, a sinful nature so to speak, that does need to be controlled, especially if you want to be able to live the good life. When evil is left to freely develop it can create a very bad environment for everyone and it has to be kept in check.

The tower of Babel story (Genesis 11:1-9) comes time-wise after the Noah flood. People have a common language and movers and shakers of the time are getting together to build a city with a tower that reached into the heavens. This has signs of religion in mind, reaching up to God in heaven, but also the creation of a mega tribe with power ambitions because they sought to make a name for themselves. God heads this off immediately by scrambling their languages because a giant monolithic group leads to, or promotes "group think" and free will be restricted.

Mega powers had to await the Greeks and Romans who would establish great nations that relied on the free thinking of people to successfully develop effective management and control of large sectors of a political area. And it also allowed competition of ideas and counterbalances to power.

People in Noah's time were not ready to create world powers or governments, consciousness and malevolent evil thinking were too strong. It would crush dissent and create a unified but destructive worldview. This is a warning to us from the distant past. Be wary of any group that seeks to create a monolithic monopoly of thought and control the thinking of the rest of us. And especially dangerous are those groups with religious connections and motives.

These two parables, Abel's sacrifice and the Tower of Babel give us two pictures of conscious human nature. Cain displays a sizable arrogance to tell God what he should do and kills Abel to stick his finger in God's eye. With the Tower of Babel, mankind is manipulated into a blind group action of worship to reach God, possibly to try and directly control Him, but that thinking will not stop from trying to control all thinking.

There is a modern-day novel that paints a picture of how easily evil, through enforced groupthink, can envelop a society. It's told from the perspective of children representing a naive group susceptible to groupthink, who can easily be influenced to become evil and set up an evil society.

> **Lord of the Flies:** *A 1954 debut novel by Nobel Prize-winning British author William Golding. The book focuses on a group of British boys stranded on an uninhabited island and their disastrous attempt to govern themselves. Themes include the tension between groupthink and individuality, between rational and emotional reactions, and between morality and immorality.*
> *https://en.wikipedia.org/wiki/Lord_of_the_Flies*

The Lord of the Flies is just fiction, but it tells the story of the ease with which mankind can create disaster through irrational and enforced group thinking. Examine the rise of Hitler in Germany or the communist revolutions in Russia and China, or the 2022 Covid lockdowns in Shanghai, China, a city of 25 million people locked in their apartments by the government and unable to come out to get food or medicine for fear of spreading Covid. Groupthink comes easily when manipulative people control the government, we've seen this in our lifetimes where authoritarian governments have controlled and eliminated dissent and debate on policies, and bad decisions are made.

From Adam through Abraham and his offspring, living as slaves in Egypt, religion is very simply based on Faith in God to manage life and disasters. The Hebrews will be built into a nation dedicated to promoting this All Powerful Creator God.

1896 illustration: Moses receiving the commandments

Bishop John H. Vincent, D. D. - My Mother's Bible Stories
Illustrated plate from the book, page 37   Public domain, via Wikimedia Commons

14. The Exodus: The Creation of Judaism

The stories about the Tower of Babel and Noah, and others in Genesis served as guideposts for the pre-Hebrews through Abraham, Isaac, Jacob, and Joseph to journey off into Egypt to evade a famine and form the Hebrew population that would become the Exodus generation. But the simple animal sacrifice of Abel would shield them from the human religions all around them for 1,500 years, and would then play a major symbolic role in the Exodus, and as a symbol for Judaism of God's faithfulness.

This may seem rather remote from having any effect on your prosperity but we've covered many related aspects which are stepping stones across a raging river of human emotions and genes.   You are a product of your genes, consciousness, environment, and your culture, which is predominately determined by your family's religion. If you are a product of the Western World then Christianity is the most likely religion. And Christianity is born out of Judaism so the decisions by thousands of nomads in the middle east who resisted the folk religions are speaking directly to you. They followed a simple tribute to God for 2,500 years and camped out in Egypt for another 400 years before becoming the Exodus Generation. These nomads of thousands of years ago have brought you to this place and time where you are surrounded by prosperity and opportunities, just waiting for you to understand how to navigate through life and make use of them. Abraham is the key figure during these 2,500 years from Adam and Eve to the Exodus and the creation of Israel and formal Judaism. He is credited as being the father of both the Jews and the Arabs. Abraham sets the standards at that time abiding in a relationship with God based on faith in God to do the right things, as necessitated by God's purposes, for Abraham. The story proceeds from Abraham to his son Isaac, to his grandson Jacob, and then to great-grandson Joseph.

This is a well-known series of stories to both Jews and Christians. Joseph ends up in Egypt as a slave, and through hard work and humility, is later promoted as a prosperous member of the Pharaoh's court. A famine in the land occupied by Abraham's descendants, now called Hebrews, especially Joseph's family leads to many of them coming down to Egypt and they end up there for 400 years as working-class slaves to the Egyptians. These Hebrew people form the core group for the founding of Israel as a nation.

Hebrews

The terms Hebrews (Hebrew: עָבְרִים / עבריים, Modern: ʿĪvrīm / ʿĪvriyyīm, Tiberian: ʿĪḇrīm / ʿĪḇriyyīm; ISO 259-3: ʿibrim / ʿibriyim) and Hebrew people are mostly considered synonymous with the Semitic-speaking Israelites, especially in the pre-monarchic period when they were still nomadic. However, in some instances it may also be used in a wider sense, referring to the Phoenicians, or to other ancient groups, such as the group known as Shasu of Yhw on the eve

of the Bronze Age collapse, which appears 34 times within 32 verses of the Hebrew Bible. It is sometimes regarded as an ethnonym and sometimes not.
https://en.wikipedia.org/wiki/Hebrews

Because of Joseph's rise from a slave to a respected cohort of the Pharaoh's court, his family and many others who came to avoid the famine had a reasonably peaceful life in Egypt. The Hebrews spent the next four hundred years in prosperous slavery until Moses arose to take them out of Egypt and turn the Hebrews into the nation of Israel. Their lives as "slaves" were not so horrible however that they didn't sometimes wish to be back in Egypt, and this plays into the Exodus story. This was an experience that was not always appreciated by all who left with Moses. Many of the Exodus generation considered the conditions back in Egypt as slaves, to be better than life in the desert as free people. There's a story here worth examining.

The Exodus is more than a blockbuster movie, it is the story of a 40-year-long boot camp to teach the Hebrews the all-powerful creator God philosophy. It is where the Hebrews are built up into a tightly bound culture that maintains their sense of identity and fends off being overwhelmed and assimilated into the various emerging city-states and then later by the Nation states that follow. The story is told in the four books of the Bible that follow Genesis, the books of Exodus, Leviticus, Numbers, and Deuteronomy. It presents the story of the Hebrews over multiple years and significant transitional events.

The Exodus: Key Events
- Living in Egypt to avoid a famine in their own land
- Their transformation to slaves for four hundred years
- Their exodus from Egypt under the leadership of Moses,
- Forty years living in the wilderness, a boot camp to whip them into a cohesive culture
- The creation of Judaism with its traditions, yearly festivals and ritual sacrifices built around the original Abel animal sacrifice

This new religion has many of the trappings of other religions in tribes and city-states around them, perhaps to give the Hebrews some bragging rights, "my religion is just as good as yours" and to keep them from feeling inferior, and to further create a unique culture designed to endure for another 1,500 years.

During the Exodus, three significant events enforce the religious traditions of Abraham and the 1,500 years from Adam to the Exodus. These three events emphasize the basic principles of both Judaism and Christianity which lay the foundations for the shalom life, faith, or trust in God.

Note, it's not that if one follows some religious ritual their life will be prosperous, but the philosophy of life including who God is and how He works, the associated Theology, that opens the door for each individual to step out into life and make the best of it. And in doing so that individual will have shalom, the Good Life.

The Judaeo Christian philosophy, and more specifically for the Western World, the Christian philosophy, creates an environment that promotes prosperity wherever that philosophy is practiced, and to the extent that that philosophy is successfully followed.   One difference between Judaism and Christianity is that the historical timeframe dramatically changed as the world transitioned from a multitude of warring city-states into nations that control wide areas of civilized land. Don't let the middle ages with its city-states that re-emerged after the fall of Rome fool you.   They were transitory, the result of a temporary power vacuum after Rome.   And for a time Christianity filled in for the power vacuum.   We'll examine that story, from the viewpoint of the influence of Christianity on prosperity in Volume II.

The Exodus story provides a number of lessons for the Hebrews that serve to unite them and form a culture and belief system that will maintain the One All-powerful Creator God theology.

The Exodus Lessons

1.   FAITH: Belief that God exists and is engaged, and active. Faith or trust in God for living and eternity, the signature of Abraham, is the key entry point for believers. The initial ritual was the animal sacrifice of Abel which stood for about 1,500 years. It was modified by Noah after the flood to add a prohibition to how it was conducted. This adjustment was

part of an agreement by God that He would not bring another flood to ever again deal with the "bad seed" problem of mankind. The change was, "Don't drink, consume the blood of animals".

2. TRUST: Belief that God will do the best thing for you. The message, "stay away from the idols and idol worship of little gods found in the religions around them, the All-Powerful Creator God is much more than a silent block of stone or gold.

3. FOLLOW: Act upon Faith and Trust, and take to heart what God tells you, it's for your own good. A capsule of the philosophy of life to be followed is given in the Ten Commandments:
   • 1-5: Respect (love) the power and authority of God
   • 6-10: Respect (love) the humanity, rights, and property, of your neighbor

4. Stay Away from, Ignore the Little God Religions
   • The little gods of nature and idols which are part of the created world, are both silent and powerless.
   • Their followers beg, plead, and try and manipulate the little gods but fail.

FAITH, TRUST, AND FOLLOW: These three aspects of the Judaeo Christian relationship with God are all intertwined under the umbrella of Faith in an All-Powerful Creator God. All three are addressed in various ways in multiple stores related to the Exodus. These stories and variations are also repeated many times over throughout the Old Testament, insuring that the principle is not lost on the Hebrews. Likewise, the rationale, purpose, and objectives of human religions that were ubiquitous to the people that the Hebrews encountered, are meaningless. The little gods are mute and powerless.

All of this is wrapped up in the stories and events of the Exodus. There are three stories of immediate note as they address this differentiation between the little gods of the Hebrew neighbors and the All-Powerful Creator God of Abraham.

The Exodus and 40 years in the wilderness set the stage for the foundations of Judaism, and by extension Christianity. These principles are diametrically opposed to the view of the folk human religions. This includes Buddhism which while having some notable morality and principles for living, speaks of the isolation from everyone but a carbon copy of yourself, which means almost everyone. Buddhism also has roots in folk human religion philosophy.

NOTE: Buddhism is singularly pointed out here because it is the "go-to" religion for intellectuals in the West who "don't get" or "resist" Christianity because it's popular in general, and particularly with the working class who the intellectuals perceive to be inferior to themselves.

The first story from the Exodus deals with Abel's animal sacrifice which served as a basis for that religious belief system for 2,500 years. What we must first note is that there was a significant change to how this sacrifice was conducted following Noah's flood. After the flood, God promises Noah and the survivors that the flood will be the last time it will be used to cull the gene pool and get rid of generations of bad genes and bad people. Part of that promise, beyond the sign of the rainbow, is captured in Genesis 9:3,4.

> **Genesis 9:3-4 (NASB)** *Every moving thing that is alive shall be food for you; I give all to you, as I gave the green plant. 4 Only you shall not eat flesh with its life, that is, its blood.*

The animal sacrifices were normally eaten so this was a change to Abel's simplistic religious ritual. It surfaces again at the beginning of the Exodus in a sign to the Hebrews, the Passover, where the blood of an animal sacrifice carries a particular message of salvation.

The Passover

The context of the story is that Moses has been chosen by God to lead the Hebrew people out of Egypt, probably because he had risen to a high position in the Pharaoh's court and had access to the Pharaoh of Egypt. Moses was picked because he had all the preparation and training to lead the Exodus and was in the right place at the right time.

The Pharaoh of Egypt doesn't want the hard-working Hebrews to leave, however, so God puts the Pharaoh and Egypt through a series of plagues, which Moses foretells before they occur. These plagues occur in series, one after the other. The first nine are designed to lull the Pharaoh into thinking he's got this under control with the tenth designed to jerk him in the opposite direction and convince him to allow the Exodus. The tenth plague is a prophecy of a curse on the firstborn in the land, all shall die, and the prophecy alone does not dissuade the Pharaoh to let the Hebrews leave. All the other plagues are speed bumps compared to the tenth one, designed to get the Pharaoh's attention but something that could be dealt with, endured, or worked around. The tenth plague attacked the future. The firstborn were the future leaders of society, they received the primary family inheritance and expected to be the future of the society. This plague was a direct attack on the future generations by a threat of death, physically eliminating them from the future and therefore significantly hampering the future of society.

This dire outcome is not necessarily true, second sons can fill in of course, but it is the thinking and the symbolic concepts within both the Egyptian and Hebrew societies that are being challenged. For the Hebrews, it is the firstborn who will eventually lead them to the promised land so they are seen as immensely important to the future of the Hebrews. Remember that they still have Joseph's bones, which they carried with them in the Exodus. (Burial practices up to the time of Christ left the bones to be collected and preserved.) And Joseph died at the beginning of the Hebrew's tour of duty in Egypt some four hundred years before Moses came on the scene.

Moses is then told by God to tell the Hebrews to sacrifice a lamb and smear its blood above the doors of their homes as a sign that the plague should "pass over" those houses so marked. The tenth plague occurs, the Hebrew's firstborn are not harmed, and the Pharaoh relents, permitting them to leave.

Once the Hebrews leave Egypt and enter the wilderness there is a continued celebration of the Passover event, but there is a change. The lamb is slain at the front door of the Tabernacle, a portable temple, set up as a prototype of the future Jewish temple, that would host the initial temple rituals.

From the time of Noah the blood is not to be consumed, an adjustment to the animal sacrifice of Abel which was a primary guidepost for the Hebrew's relationship with their God for a thousand years. It is now introduced in a new ritual as the spiritual life force within mankind and giving it a saving nature. Not just any saving nature but saving the culture and civilization of the Hebrews.

Under the new Judaism documented by Moses during the Exodus, symbolic blood is again used in a new tabernacle /Temple ritual called the Day of Atonement, where the blood of the sacrifice is sprinkled on the altar. This new ritual ceremony presents the idea of a lamb without blemish being sacrificed for the sins of the people, that is, they are sinless and now qualified for heaven. The Passover becomes a major celebration in Judaism and The Day of Atonement becomes the holiest day of the Jewish year, Yom Kippur.

The two holiest days in the Jewish year of celebrations take their beginnings from the Passover lamb's blood saving the firstborn from the 10th plague of the Exodus story. The symbolic blood saves the future generations, preserving the culture, in the Passover metaphor, and Yom Kippur saves each individual in terms of a future with God in heaven. Both these rituals/celebrations deal with faith in the All-Powerful Creator God to save his people from disaster. The Passover from harm in life, Yom Kippur for cleansing of and forgiveness of sins and thereby being qualified for heaven.

The animal blood, which represents the animals' only life, a physical life, becomes a metaphor for human life and especially mankind's spiritual life which gives him a connection directly to God. This analogy of blood and a human spiritual life is further expanded in Christianity.

Note that this spiritual connection, especially in heaven, is the very things Hindus and Buddhists work so hard to gain. They strain and work tirelessly to achieve what the Jewish God freely gave to his people, what the human religious world is striving for all their lives and well into their second and third lives, for that matter. But what is worse is that they seek perfection which is not even defined. The more they strive, the more they suffer with even minor failures. One of mankind's most powerful negative emotions is guilt from some kind of failure, real or imagined, significant or minor. This is brought to light in the Garden of Eden story. Adam and Eve are full of guilt from the consciousness-induced realization of their nakedness and their sexual pleasures, having been tricked by the serpent, and from having disobeyed the command not to eat from the tree of knowledge of Good and Evil. We, humans, can carry this guilt of failure for decades, and for a lifetime and it is a burden in life and living. So it is significant that Judaism offers redemption, the forgiveness of sins by their God, demonstrated every year. For many people however, even that is not enough. They are incapable of forgiving themselves, and that is as much the cause of distress as anything else. This is perhaps why Christianity makes a big issue out of getting beyond your own sins and moving on with life.

Two typical stories emerge in literature that represent the extent to which this burden of guilt can lead us. In one story an individual continues to fail in various ways in life. It can be from alcohol, drugs or just being a nasty human being in general that everyone else despises. But through a series of events the lost person comes to see errors of his ways and turns his life around. The alternative story is where that same despicable character never recovers and self-destructs violently, his actions and life reforming those left behind.

Guilt drives the two individuals in different directions. Not everyone may have these feelings of guilt, but those that do can let themselves be driven into a helpless, immobile life where the individual withdraws from life altogether. There's even a lesson in the Old Testament about a prophet that does this because the people are not listening to the instructions God has given him to pass on to the people, and he goes and sits under a tree and pouts. God rebukes him for even unjustly feeling like a failure and tells him to get back to work.

For the All-Powerful Creator God to forgive mankind all of their sins and failures, frees mankind to shrug off the guilt and take up being a creative and valuable member of the community again. Knowing that one has God's forgiveness for one's errors, is a very freeing and inspiring aspect of life.

The story of the 2,500 years from Adam to Moses is one built on Faith in the All Powerful Creator God in the sense that He is managing their life for His purposes and will take care of their needs along the way. That's all the God of the Hebrews asks of his people. Along the way, they are writing the stories of their successes and failures as a testimony on how to live the good life for those who follow.   There is no burden on life from sin (excluding crime of course) so everyone is now free to devote all their energies to living, and some of this energy can be toward enjoyable projects that provide satisfaction, improved quality of life with neighbors and shalom that extends out into the community.

Yom Kippur (/ˌjɒm kɪˈpʊər, ˌjɔːm ˈkɪpər, llll-/;[1] *Hebrew:* יוֹם כִּיפּוּר, *romanized: Yōm Kīpūr, IPA: [ˈjom kiˈpuʁ], lit. 'Day of Atonement'; plural* יוֹם *הכיפורים, Yom HaKipurim) is the holiest day of the year in Judaism. Its central themes are atonement and repentance. Jews traditionally observe this holy day with a day-long fast, confession, and intensive prayer, often spending most of the day in synagogue services. The High Holy Days comprise both Rosh HaShanah and Yom Kippur.*

Yom (יוֹם) means "day" *in Hebrew and* **Kippur (כִּפּוּר) is translated to "atonement".** *The common English translation of Yom Kippur is Day of Atonement, however, this translation lacks precision. The name Yom Kippur is based on the Torah verse, "...but on the 10th day of the seventh month it is the day of kippurim unto you..." The literal translation of kippurim is cleansing. Yom Kippur is a Jewish day to atone for misdeeds and become cleansed and purified from them.*

Rosh Hashanah and Yom Kippur: *Yom Kippur is "the tenth day of [the] seventh month" (Tishrei) and is also known as the "Sabbath of Sabbaths". Rosh Hashanah (referred to in the Torah as Yom Teruah) is the first day of that month according to the Hebrew calendar. Yom Kippur completes the annual period known in Judaism as the High Holy Days or Yamim Nora'im ("Days of Awe") that commences with Rosh Hashanah. The ten days from Rosh Hashanah to Yom Kippur correspond to the last ten days of the 40-day period Moses was on Mount Sinai receiving the second set of tablets.*

https://en.wikipedia.org/wiki/Yom_Kippur

This concept of forgiveness is then taken into Christianity as a general statement of the Christian life, a starting point that expands into all manner of life circumstances.   It represents a foundation for living that eliminates that striving to perfect one's self and avoid starting all over again. Becoming a better person here offers a better life, a shalom life.

A second Exodus story involved the Hebrews falling apart when Moses goes up to Mt. Sinai to get the tablets containing the Ten Commandments.

He's gone for 40 days and the Hebrews fear he won't come back so they hassle Aaron, the second in command, to make them an idol, a golden calf, similar to the idols of bulls found in cultures around them. Aaron collects all the gold he can find from jewelry and creates the idol and the Hebrews have a big party to celebrate their new "little god" and worship him at an altar constructed for that purpose. When Moses returns he's not happy, and he breaks the first set of tablets containing the Ten Commandments. He melts down the idol, turns it into powder, mixes it with water, and forces the people to drink the mixture.

Subsequently, Moses has to go back and get a second set of tablets. This second set of Tablets, contains what we call the Ten Commandments and they are placed in a gold chest called the Arc of the Covenant, a most sacred relic of the Israelites and one that mysteriously disappeared during the Babylonian captivity which began in 587 BC with the destruction of Jerusalem.

The significance of the Ten Commandments is that they form the foundation for the spiritual approach to God and the moral approach to fellow mankind for both Judaism and Christianity. And they set the standard for how God speaks to His people, through the written word, encompassed in the writings in the Bible. There is now no need for God to speak individually to anyone, but He does through various prophets as the Old Testament writings are compiled and thus create a running narrative of the Judaeo-Christian philosophy of life that leads to shalom. When the Old Testament is completed the Jews have a completed document of God's will, purpose, and directions for Judaism.

The third story from Exodus involves two almost identical stories dealing with "no water" situations, a real threat to life in the desert. The Devil is truly in the details. A connected set of two stories some years apart but dealing with probably the most urgent problem facing a group of people living in a desert wilderness, the availability of water. These two stories occurred at different times and locations. They are almost a carbon copy of each other, but there were two different messages conveyed to the Hebrews as part of the Judaeo-Christian Philosophy. In both cases there is the idea that God will take care of difficult and life-threatening situations, especially when He leads you there.   The second message deals with leadership itself.

The first "no water" situation occurs about a year into the 40-year escape from Egypt.   Water is critical for life, so as they search for water they come to a site at a rock and Moses is told to strike the rock with his rod or walking stick.   This location is probably not too far from Mt Sinai. When Moses leaves them for a while to go up to Mt Sinai to get the Ten Commandments, they forget the lesson and fall apart, and maybe that's why it will take 40 years.   The Hebrews are not exactly happy to be out there in the first place and begin to think they were better off back in Egypt.   They are not yet exhibiting much faith in God at this moment, it is a test of their adjustment to living under the power and influence of the All Powerful Creator God who has brought them to this place for a reason.

The First No Water Situation

Exodus 17:1-7 (NASB) 1 Then all the congregation of the sons of Israel journeyed by stages from the wilderness of Sin, according to the command of the LORD, and camped at Rephidim, and there was no water for the people to drink. 2 Therefore the people quarreled with Moses and said, "Give us water that we may drink." And Moses said to them, "Why do you quarrel with me? Why do you test the LORD?" 3 But the people thirsted there for water; and they grumbled against Moses and said, "Why, now, have you brought us up from Egypt, to kill us and our children and our livestock with thirst?" 4 So Moses cried out to the LORD, saying, "What shall I do to this people? A little more and they will stone me." 5 Then the LORD said to Moses, "Pass before the people and take with you some of the elders of Israel; and take in your hand your staff with which you struck the Nile, and go. 6 Behold, I will stand before you there on the rock at Horeb; and you shall strike the rock, and water will come out of it, that the people may drink." And Moses did so in the sight of the elders of Israel. 7 He named the place Massah and Meribah because of the quarrel of the sons of Israel, and because they tested the LORD, saying, "Is the LORD among us, or not?"

Moses is commanded to strike the rock and God tells him that water will come out.   He does and it does, the lesson is completed.   There are at least two principles being made to the Exodus generation here.   The first is that God will handle the tough things in life and the second is to demonstrate that Moses is in control as their leader and works for God. One extended message for us perhaps is that good leaders take action and make good decisions in crisis situations.

The second "no water" situation is now almost 40 years later, near the end of the Exodus trek in the wilderness. It presents an almost identical situation to the first story, 39-plus years later the Hebrews are again searching for water and still grumbling about leaving the great life back with the Egyptians. This time however God gives Moses different instructions. Moses is not told to strike the rock with his staff, but to speak to the rock and water will come out.

The Second No Water Situation, The Water of Meribah

Numbers 20:1-8 (NASB) 1 *Then the sons of Israel, the whole congregation, came to the wilderness of Zin in the first month; and the people stayed at Kadesh. Now Miriam died there and was buried there.*
2 There was no water for the congregation, and they assembled themselves against Moses and Aaron. 3 The people thus contended with Moses and spoke, saying, "If only we had perished when our brothers perished before the LORD! 4 Why then have you brought the LORD'S assembly into this wilderness, for us and our beasts to die here? 5 Why have you made us come up from Egypt, to bring us in to this wretched place? It is not a place of grain or figs or vines or pomegranates, nor is there water to drink." 6 Then Moses and Aaron came in from the presence of the assembly to the doorway of the tent of meeting and fell on their faces. Then the glory of the LORD appeared to them; 7 and **the LORD spoke to Moses, saying 8 "Take the rod; and you and your brother Aaron assemble the congregation and speak to the rock before their eyes,** *that it may yield its water. You shall thus bring forth water for them out of the rock and let the congregation and their beasts drink."*

The Hebrews are about to enter the promised land, the land of milk and honey, so God no longer needs to prop up Moses as the leader. Once they leave the wilderness and enter the promised land they will need to transition to reliance on the Word of God as the Philosophy of Life. This is the path to prosperity as the nation of Israel. This time Moses is to speak to the rock. Speaking is the new dynamic for the revelation of the truth. But Moses is highly upset with all this grumbling after all these years. He gets mad and strikes the rock with his staff, not the instructions he was given. Water comes out anyway, God provides when needed despite our bad behavior, but God is not "happy".   It is vitally important that the Hebrews get the point that what God says is extremely important.

> *Numbers 20:9-13 (NASB)* 9 *So Moses took the rod from before the LORD, just as He had commanded him; 10 and **Moses and Aaron gathered the assembly before the rock. And he (Moses) said to them, "Listen now, you rebels; shall we bring forth water for you out of this rock?" 11 Then Moses lifted up his hand and struck the rock twice with his rod; and water came forth abundantly**, and the congregation and their beasts drank. 12 **But the LORD said to Moses and Aaron, "Because you have not believed Me, to treat Me as holy in the sight of the sons of Israel, therefore you shall not bring this assembly into the land which I have given them."** 13 Those were the waters of Meribah, because the sons of Israel contended with the LORD, and He proved Himself holy among them.*

So as a lesson to all the Hebrews, Moses is denied entrance into that promised land for disobeying God. Perhaps this clears up concerns that God's forgiveness of sins doesn't mean there are no consequences to those sins. In this case, God directly intervenes with the consequences. In most cases, however, the consequences are the direct result of the sin. In all cases however God forgives and we are to move on with our lives, perhaps being able to mitigate the impact on others. But never to despair and sit on a rock and mourn over it for days or weeks or years. Key messages from the story are:

No Water Lessons
1. God will give them imperfect leaders to carry them through tough situations
2. Good leaders know how to make things happen.
3. God will provide instructions and lessons for good life decisions which must be followed precisely as stated
4. When we or our leaders fail, for whatever reason, God will handle what we can not
5. Failure to follow God's advice has consequences personally and that can equate to national consequences

Moses is traditionally assumed as the writer of the Bible from Genesis through the Exodus events. The remaining portion of the Old Testament is added by prophets and leaders up until about 400 BC when the last book is written. Later dates are attributed to many passages based on later-dated language constructs, but these can easily be the result of rewrites for current language clarity. We are all familiar with this change from the King James (1611) translation of the Bible through all the modern translations in the last 100-plus years. So to put a date on any original text in the Bible based on language use is questionable at best. And don't let modern copy-write law confuse the issue. It didn't exist in the time of writing or copying either the Old or New Testament. Those who copied old documents, i.e., rewrote them by hand, probably thought little about clarifying the text, certainly under the guidance of language experts, during this pre-Christian Era. The other key factor is that this issue with document dating does little to change the impact of the document on those who take it as the Word of God. Even if the stories are parables, the philosophy of life built into these stories contains the best philosophy to provide the user with peace, prosperity, and happiness, the Shalom life as promised by those same words.

So, for the Hebrews and the follow-on Jews, and Christians, the lesson can not be lost that when God speaks, and He speaks to them through the words in the text, He means what he says. And even Moses must pay the price, especially because he is the leader and his failures are highly observable when he directly disobeys God's direct instructions. Why, because this is probably the biggest lesson the Hebrews can get, pay attention, listen up, get what I'm telling you through the word. This is the urgent message that is important for the lives of the Hebrews standing beside the rock, but also for the sake of Judaism over the next 1,500 years. There's both personal and far future truth at stake. The rest is history. The Hebrews enter the promised land and through trials and tribulations develop and maintain Judaism for about 1,500 years before giving way to Christianity.

What is perhaps as amazing as any other story in the Bible is that the generations from Adam to Abraham managed to keep themselves disentangled from the folk religions that sprang up around them. They maintained a simple Faith in the all-powerful creator God, they trusted God to provide their necessities, and they followed God and the simple animal sacrifice to lead them in the right direction. This isn't a mantra adopted by the Hebrews or the Jews in any official way but it summarizes the thinking that took place from Adam to the Exodus and to Christ. It's an imagined bumper sticker or community mantra. Perhaps the local folk religions were still pretty primitive and simplistic during this time. We don't know, but certainly, the Egyptian religion was fully formed while the Hebrews were in slavery for 400 years, so that must have been some temptation to at least dabble in it. Or perhaps the Egyptian religious tradition of making the Pharaoh a god was enough to keep them uninterested. Certainly, Joseph being a member of the Pharaoh's court meant that he knew more than enough stories about the Pharaoh's human characteristics to demonstrate that he, the Pharaoh, was not a real god.

Judaism Documented by Moses

Not all succeeded as the Exodus generation can attest. Only a few from that generation survived the 40 years in the wilderness and entered the promised land. The others were all second-generation Hebrews, having persevered after some tough training in the wilderness. They are no longer fearful of every event and decision in life, nor so worried about tomorrow or eternity that they are too petrified to take action. Now as Moses writes down the stories of the evolution from Adam to the Hebrews to Jews, he lays out a more precise regimen to follow, Judaism. Included are a multitude of instructions for life and the creation of a Jewish culture tied to Judaism that will hold them together for another 1,500 years. The common morality of the Ten Commandments teaches them to trust and rely upon each other through difficulties and come out the other side with a better life for everyone.

The Conditional Promise of Prosperity

The commandments given to the Hebrews as they are about to enter the Promised Land go way beyond the Ten Commandments however. Deuteronomy 27 proscribes a ritual "responsive chant" of a number of offenses that are condemned with the phrase "cursed is he who". Deuteronomy 28 immediately follows with the promise of great personal and national prosperity if the people follow God's commandments. Moses is trying to get them started in the right direction and that is to understand there are consequences to actions, cursing or blessings. This is the problem with conscious man, he's so motivated to satisfy his desires that he doesn't see the consequences of his actions.

Prosperity Promised

1. Deuteronomy 27 some immediate things that impact prosperity
2. Deuteronomy 28 The direct promise of prosperity, depicted initially here as economic prosperity to individuals and the collective society
3. The condition of prosperity, follow what God tells us, the Philosophy of Life, do's and don't do's.
4. This is a general promise to everyone
5. But there are some rules to prosperity, just like fishing
6. Learning the rules for prosperity requires training
7. Abraham had a general and nebulous understanding, but no specifics
8. God reveals his plan for mankind in stages, as the circumstances and man's capability to comply advance
9. Additional resources and solutions will be revealed as Judaism advances with the tabernacle and temple worship
10. Christ is the next big step in the plan, to follow Judaism

After forty years in the wilderness, Israel is now living in their promised land and is led first by a series of Judges and then a ruling kingship is established formally putting them on an equal footing with their neighbors. Two kings, David and Solomon create a very prosperous kingdom but that begins to fall apart under Solomon's successors and Israel is both divided through its politics and occupied by a succession of new powerful and warlike nation-states. Its citizens are shipped off into slavery and sometimes are freed to return to their own land, centered around Jerusalem. Religious rituals and worship are built around a temple in Jerusalem, built initially by Solomon, destroyed by the Babylonians and restored after returning from exile in Babylon, and rebuilt anew by Herod a few years before the time of Christ.

Israel's Historical Record

This story of Israel and Judaism is not a rags-to-riches story, but the story of a culture struggling to maintain its heritage through a number of failures. Beset often by bad rulers and decisions after David and Solomon, often overrun by powerful neighbors, with its people carried off into exile in foreign lands. This adversity creates a rich narrative documenting their history of trials and tribulations as well as observations and critiques by prophets on their successes and failures. Crucial to this story is the historical record of the life and times from Adam to the Exodus. All of this is compiled in the Hebrew Bible.

> *The Hebrew Bible or Tanakh[a]* (/tɑːˈnɑːx/;[1] *Hebrew:* תָּנָ״ךְ *Tānāḵ*),
> *also known in Hebrew as Miqra* (/miːˈkrɑː/; *Hebrew:* מִקְרָא *Miqrā'*), *is
> the canonical collection of Hebrew scriptures, **including the Torah, the
> Nevi'im, and the Ketuvim.** Different branches of Judaism and
> Samaritanism have maintained different versions of the canon, including **the
> 3rd-century BCE Septuagint text used in Second Temple Judaism**,
> the Syriac Peshitta, the Samaritan Pentateuch, the Dead Sea Scrolls, and
> most recently the 10th-century medieval Masoretic Text compiled by the
> Masoretes, currently used in Rabbinic Judaism. The terms "Hebrew Bible" or
> "Hebrew Canon" are frequently confused with the Masoretic Text; however,
> this is a medieval version and one of several texts considered authoritative by
> different types of Judaism throughout history. The current edition of the
> Masoretic Text is mostly in Biblical Hebrew, with a few passages in Biblical
> Aramaic (in the books of Daniel and Ezra, and the verse Jeremiah 10:11).*
> https://en.wikipedia.org/wiki/Hebrew_Bible

The period covered by the Hebrew Bible or Old Testament after the Exodus and the creation of Israel is from about 1,500 BC to about 400 BC. This is a very stressful time with warrior city-states turning into conquering nation-states competing for the same middle eastern territory inhabited by Israel. Yet throughout this time, the Bible maintains its focus on One All-powerful Creator God, a moral code and a philosophy of life that leads to a life of shalom. This philosophy of peace and prosperity continues as a promise of God in an environment that seems to say it can never happen. Numerous prophets also arose during the age of Israel who documented both the historical events and provided warnings to Israel when they were deviating from the traditions laid down by Moses. They also provided prophecy concerning both the results of their failures and prophesies concerning a future messiah who would restore the fortunes of Israel.

Together the moral code and the collection of year-round Temple rituals served as a rich new identity for the Hebrews. The rituals served as teaching aids and the Jewish priesthood as the coaches or teachers. The prophets became their conscience, continually reminding them to get back on the right track. The rituals and Temple sacrifices were a reminder of their God's promises and faithfulness and provided a visual and continuous collective identity, but it was the moral code that was transformational and significant in documenting the approach we, mankind, should take to both collective and individual prosperity.

So the moral code and the promise of shalom, and peace, remain a cornerstone of the all-powerful creator God philosophy for Judaism. That Israel could survive as a nation and even prosper is a miracle in itself. For 400 years, from 400 BC until the Christian Era, all the powerful nations around them have fallen to the power of Rome. This is also a silent period for Israel's prophets, yet their hope lives on that a Messiah will free them from oppression by foreign powers and their kingdom will be restored.

The prophecies of a Messiah are scattered through the Old Testament and are sometimes given in metaphorical terms and generally without any timeframe given. Many are in the book of Isaiah and a time-specific prophecy is provided in the book of Daniel. The Messiah was also predicted by astrologers (ancient astronomers) who envisioned future events from signs seen in the stars based on the movements and positions of the planets. Both the prophecies of Daniel and the astrologers were rather time specific, predicting the birth of a Messiah about 4 BC, give or take several years, The Jews and the astrologers saw the Messiah as a conventional King and new ruler over Israel. Both prophecies were apparently widely known enough to get the attention of Herod, the

Roman-appointed king of Israel (37 to 4 BC) so he tried to kill all newborn males around the prophesied years.

Since Daniel, in the 6th century BC or so, the Prophets have been silent. The religious establishment and those seeking a military solution to Rome's occupation are buzzing with excitement that a Messiah is coming, and the hope is to free them from control by Rome. High hopes for a small band of nomads who are but a blip on the Roman radar, a small mosquito, an irritating distraction.

There are a multitude of references to Judaism's Messiah, however, it is a two-edged sword for Israel. There are implications of a coming new age that opens up God's plan to the entire world, that is to the world of Gentiles. To the Jews, Gentiles represent everyone in the world who is not a Jew, and they see the hated Romans, so they become somewhat blinded to their own Torah. They focus on a Messiah only for themselves, a liberating Messiah. Their other problem is that the written Torah in either Hebrew or Koine Greek as the Septuagint, was not readily available to the general public. They couldn't look up passages on an iPhone, their only access was from hearing passages read in the Temple or in synagogues. So, like the internet, information, rumors, and misinformation had been flooding the populace, and the general consensus was that the Messiah was a warrior King.

Judaism deviated significantly from the other world religions in its approach to God. First of all it correctly saw God as an All-powerful Creator and Mentor God who was not subject to bribery and supported his creation as he deemed best. It put God on their side of life, rooting for them, rather than having to compete against a god who required their adoration and praise and was fickle and thin-skinned. The Jewish God was their coach and trainer, not some aloof and silent "Superman", and his offer to them was that their lives would be better if they followed him. Judaism had all the trappings of those other religions in terms of ritual, symbolism, and customs, but much of that was in the form of metaphors of greater truths that were to be revealed when the time was right. Principles of Living were embedded in the stories of the Hebrew Bible as guides to life and prosperity.

Israel as a Theocracy

The full Mosaic law served as the law of the land and thus Israel began life as a theocracy, where God's laws functioned as the law of the land. There was no other form of civic law. Initially, the country was ruled by a series of Judges who made decisions concerning matters of law. Once Israel had a king, the king usually made the final decisions but even that could be overturned by a vote of the people. Prophets rose to assist the kings and some lower courts of justice were established. Laws and punishments in the Mosaic Law were interpreted as precise and demanding, and appear cruel and unusual by today's standards. But by the standards of the time they were considered normal. Some may have been to head off very bad precedents and habits, not much different from today when we might delve out greater punishments for some offenses because they might be most devastating were they to become common practice. These hard laws and punishments were mitigated by other significant directions, however. "Love your neighbor" and surprisingly "an eye for an eye" which limited punishment to the limit of the offense. These harsh punishments were also destined to be changed as part of the transformation from Judaism to the Church.

Judaism was also to become confusing with multiple sources of religious text and oral traditions. The primary problem was a large body of work called the Mishnah, the Oral Torah, which was a collection of additions and comments on the Torah and Jewish culture and traditions. These were not written but learned by being passed down verbally and led to a whole new set of traditions that became religious law. These new traditions were roundly condemned by Jesus which led him to call the Pharisees, who promoted them, "whitewashed tombstones". That is the oral traditions were used as a "quick fix" to give one the appearance of righteousness, as opposed to following the written law which was much more demanding.

> **The Oral Torah: The Mishnah or the Mishna (/ˈmɪʃnə/; Hebrew:**
> מִשְׁנָה, "study by repetition", from the verb shanah שנה, or "to study and review", also "secondary") is the first major written collection of the Jewish oral traditions that are known as the Oral Torah.
> https://en.wikipedia.org/wiki/Mishnah

The oral Torah conditioned the Jews to rely on all forms of hear-say, following the easy way to being righteous. This is what we all do on occasion, look for and follow the easy way out of a situation.

Thus following the crowd and taking the easy way out by listening to the oral Torah became the quick solution to be seen as a true Jew. What was becoming lost was the detailed understanding of the Words of God that Moses had declared to be the path to prosperity. And along with it picking up popular views that the Messiah to come would be a military King or ruler who would free the Jews from the Roman occupation. Thus the path to rejecting the Messiah had been set.

It is perhaps, that this simple truth is a message in itself for Christianity. Shortcuts to learning how to live the Good Life only provide you with the appearance of the Good Life, not the reality. This was the condemnation of Jesus when he called the Pharisees white-washed tombstones Their daily rituals had all the appearances of living the Good Life but that appearance was all smoke and mirrors.

Daniel in the Lions' Den, c. 1615 By Peter Paul Rubens

15. Judaism Seeks Their Messiah

The exact relationship between Judaism and Christianity has been blurred for centuries by the antagonism over the crucifixion of Jesus and the superficial contrasts between the God of Israel and Judaism, and the Christian God of the New Testament. These contrasts ignore both the vast differences between the life and times of humanity and the vast changes and evolution of the revelations of God that took place over thousands of years. The times from Adam to Abraham to Moses and to Christ and even life in the Middle Ages was quite different in many ways from human society today.

So, why then are we surprised that God may have rightfully chosen to interface and act toward mankind per the nature of the beast that was humanity? Certainly, God has the knowledge, authority, and responsibility to interact with such vastly different people as He sees as fitting or just. Who are we to say how God should interact with these people or what rules he should choose to make with them?

The crux of the issue with the Hebrew God is that He may have occasionally acted harshly toward some lowly tribes encountered by Israel and may have seemingly acted harshly (capital punishment) toward Israel via the Mosaic Law over what we might consider relatively minor offenses. But God knew these people. He understands in much more detail than the simplistic genetic and consciousness-induced malevolent thinking of mankind we've discussed.

In fact, most of us have no way of conceiving of someone behaving like Charles Manson or Adolf Hitler or Joseph Stalin or their like-minded cohorts, which these tribes may have emulated. Nor can we easily comprehend the thinking of the drug addicts or homeless people living on the streets. God has a much better view and understanding of the future than we ever could, and He can and does take action to head off disasters when they matter. Israel was having to find its way through a wilderness of tribes who were no better than the drug cartels of Mexico. The Assyrians for example, randomly tortured and mutilated people to instill fear and compliance with their demands of acquiescence to their rule. They would skin alive opponents after a conquest, unleashing a reign of terror throughout the conquered lands. Only a miraculous interdiction was able to save Israel from such an outcome.

The true context of the capital punishment offenses was that they were destructive of the cohesive society needed for Israel to sustain itself from the Exodus until the time of the Messiah. Capital punishment became a severe warning to stay away from such activity. What is also missed is that other parts of the Mosaic Law mitigated the use of capital punishment in most cases so that it was little used.

The point is that God works with us based on who we are at the moment. He worked with the Hebrews and Israel one way and He works with Christians differently. Israel was a necessary step to prepare for Jesus and the advent of a spiritual kingdom on earth. Circumstances dictated a difference in dealing with Israel that comes across as a difference in policy where it is just a difference in tactics. The result is that a superficial view of Israel and the Church sees them as entirely different and disconnected events in time. The differences in tactics were necessary to advance God's plan for mankind.

What we want to address here is how the transition looked from the perspective of Israel and Judaism. In the next chapter, we'll address how the Theology, largely expressed in metaphorical rituals from Abel to the Pharisees of Jesus's time, merge directly into the story of the Messiah and the disastrous outcome of the crucifixion that seemed to be the end of the story, but was not.

There are two major views of the relationship between Judaism and Christianity within the Church. The first view is that Christianity is a natural continuation of Judaism's Theology and Philosophy of Life suitable for the Gentile World. The transition could not be smooth or easy, Israel was too embittered with the idea of a war of independence from Rome to see the coming changes. The second view is that the Christian Church, Christianity itself, is not connected to, nor is, a transition from Judaism but is a special age inserted in the middle of the Age of Israel. Judaism and Israel are still God's chosen people but they are under discipline because they rejected Christ, so the Church Age has been inserted as a temporary period until Israel finally accepts their Messiah.

This second view of Christianity as an afterthought, is like God seeing Israel reject and crucify their Messiah, and thinking "Oops, didn't see that coming, what to do now?" This idea of Christianity as an afterthought is a modern view that had much of its doctrines established in the 20th century. It began with a very literal interpretation of prophecies and an attempt to understand the exact timelines of every event prophesied. Because prophecies can be metaphorical and nebulous some prophecies given to Israel in the Hebrew Bible were considered to be prophecies of the Messiah's second advent and the millennium, when the Messiah will rule for a thousand years.

Ezekiel's Temple becomes a big example of this time-slipping interpretation.

The Book of Ezekiel is the third of the Latter Prophets in the Tanakh (Hebrew Bible) and one of the major prophetic books in the Christian Bible, where it follows Isaiah and Jeremiah. According to the book itself, it records six visions of the prophet Ezekiel, exiled in Babylon, during the 22 years from 593 to 571 BCE.
https://en.wikipedia.org/wiki/Book_of_Ezekiel

Ezekiel's Temple Features of the temple are described in detail in the book of Ezekiel, in the form of a vision given to the prophet. Physical characteristics of the multi-level wood-panelled structure such as gateways, outer and inner courts, side chambers and vestibules, archways, doors, windows, sanctuary and altar are described. Some furnishings are described. Details of decoration are given, for example cherubim and palm trees carved on the doors and walls. The purposes of the side chambers are given, for example, for robing of the priests, for consumption of the flesh of sacrifices by the priests, and for singers. Dimensions are given based on the cubit.

The fact that details of the temple are given in the context of a prophetic vision, gives rise to analysis and debate regarding the meaning, significance and purpose of the temple.

Some Christian interpretations of Ezekiel's temple are: it is the temple that Zerubbabel should have built; a literal temple to be rebuilt during the millennial reign of Christ; a temple that is symbolic of the worship of God by the Christian church today; or a symbol of the future and eternal reign of God. A number of Christian commentators also believe that this temple will be a literal fourth temple, which will exist during the Millennial Kingdom, following the destruction of a future temple that will be desecrated by the Antichrist.

Other theorists instead see Ezekiel's Temple as the New Jerusalem described in the book of Revelation; the bride of the Lamb (whose form and composite materials are similar to the Sanctuary); the Temple of God being the Christians themselves, where his Spirit will dwell in them (1 Corinthians 3:16).
https://en.wikipedia.org/wiki/Ezekiel's_Temple

What is obvious is that the rebuilding of the temple authorized by the Decree of Artaxerxes, King of Persia in 457 BC over a hundred years after the Babylonian captivity and Ezekiel's prophecy, began the restoration of the temple in Jerusalem and might be considered just a restoration of Solomon's temple. But there was another temple restoration yet to be built

Herod's Temple

The Second Temple (Hebrew: בֵּית־הַמִּקְדָּשׁ הַשֵּׁנִי, Bēṯ hamMīqdāš haššēnī, transl. 'Second House of the Sanctum'), later known as Herod's Temple, was the reconstructed Temple in Jerusalem between c. 516 BCE and 70 CE. It stood as a pivotal symbol of Jewish faith and identity during the Second Temple period. The Second Temple served as the central place of Jewish worship, ritual sacrifice, and communal gathering for Jews, attracting Jewish pilgrims from distant lands during the three pilgrimage festivals: Passover, Shavuot and Sukkot.

*The Second Temple replaced Solomon's Temple, which occupied the same location before its destruction by the Babylonians in c. 587 BCE.[1] Construction began under the auspices of the Persian King Cyrus the Great and was completed during the reign of Darius I, signifying a period of renewed Jewish hope and religious revival. **According to the Bible, the Second Temple was originally a relatively modest structure built by Jews who had returned from exile in Babylon** under the authority of Persian-appointed governor Zerubbabel, the grandson of Jeconiah, the penultimate king of Judah.*

***The Second Temple was refurbished and expanded in the first century BCE under the reign of Herod the Great, hence its alternative name, Herod's Temple.** The temple's transformation resulted in a grand and imposing structure and courtyard, including the large edifices and façades shown in modern models such as the Holyland Model of Jerusalem. **The Temple Mount, the platform upon which the Second Temple stood, was also significantly expanded, doubling in size to become the largest religious sanctuary in the ancient world**.*

https://en.wikipedia.org/wiki/Second_Temple

It is the expanded version of the Second Temple which comes close to matching the description of Ezekiel's Temple prophecy.   But this is ignored, maybe because it is not exact enough or maybe because since Herod's temple was destroyed by the Romans in 70AD, a restored Israel in our future needs a temple, and Ezekiel's prophecy can be applied to a new temple, in our current future being built for that purpose. Unfortunately, for that school of thought, Herod's Temple appears to have an uncanny likeness to Ezekiel's prophetic temple.   Compare the two pictures below. The point is that Ezekiel's prophetic temple just as easily fits with Herod's

Temple redesigned some 500 years later and before the first advent of Christ.

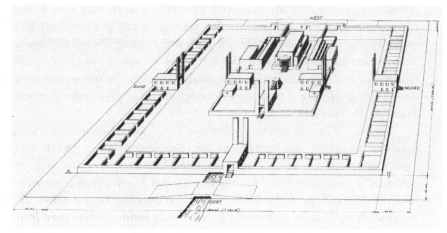

Schematic of Ezekiel's Temple drawn by Dutch architect Bartelmeüs Reinders, Sr. (1893–1979)
Public Domain. https://commons.wikimedia.org/w/index.php?curid=8007167

The Second Jewish Temple, Herod's Temple. Model in the Israel Museum C H Kirchner 2023

The Ezekiel Temple prophecy is a big driver for the future Restoration of Israel prophecy. A second big driver is that promises to Abraham, David, and Israel were considered unconditional covenants but were unfulfilled when the Messiah was rejected. As unconditional promises, they must still be coming in the future and this meant that Israel would have to be fully restored to power using a very literal interpretation. So Christianity is looked at as God's temporary solution until Israel and the Jews finally accept their Messiah. When that happens the Church age or the age of Christianity will end Israel and the Jews will again be God's favored people.

This second view of Christianity, as a temporary period, then has Israel and Judaism being interrupted, until the Church age and Christianity are phased out. Israel is then restored to its role as God's people in the future. This restoration includes a rebuilt temple and all of the Mosaic law, the rituals, and animal sacrifices, and puts Israel as the world ruler, in support of the future Messiah, who will rule the world. All the unconditional covenants or promises to Israel will be fulfilled at that time. Christianity was not what God wanted but came about as a temporary plan because the Jews rejected their Messiah when he first appeared.

Current Jewish beliefs are similar, they believe that their Messiah is in the future and that He will rebuild and restore the Temple and reestablish the sacrifices. They actually believe that their Messiah exists in all generations and is not manifest because of weaknesses in the Jewish community, or something similar. In this alternate second Christian view, the Messianic future for both Christianity and Judaism thus merge into the same future, both eagerly awaiting their Messiah, as a physical world ruler.

The first view of a natural and permanent transition from Judaism to Christianity is the view of several more traditional Christian organizations. This also seems to be a better fit with the Hebrew Bible's Messianic prophecies, and what the New Testament supports with its Theology. This view also provides a more logical match with the actual historical accounts of Jesus and the crucifixion and of Israel's rebellion and ultimate demise at the hands of the Romans. The connected view of Christianity as the evolutionary successor to Israel and Judaism, and to Judaism's Theology and Philosophy of Life seems to be the best match for both the Hebrew Bible prophecies, the explanations in the New Testament, and what actually happened. The biggest issue raised by the second view is about the unconditional covenants and perhaps Israel must be restored for those to be fulfilled. But both the Hebrew Bible's prophecies and New

Testament passages actually solve this dilemma as well and this will be addressed shortly.

The Jewish educated and religious community was fully aware of the prophecies concerning the Messiah but they were so focused on a King who would free them from Roman control that they overlooked much of the meaning of the Old Testament passages. One particular prophecy even foretold of a great change in God's plan, the Jews and Judaism were to be replaced as God's people. This is found in Isaiah Chapter 65. The entire text is included below because of the significance of a certain statement that is a most powerful prophecy and warning to the Jews of an end to the Jewish age. The prophet Isaiah lived in the 8th century BC (700 BC era). There are two ideas prophesied that relate to the relationship between Israel and the Church that we've been discussing, the unconditional promises and the nature or permanence of the transformation to Christianity.

Isaiah 65: Judaism to be Replaced

Isaiah 65 (NASB) A Rebellious People

1 "I permitted Myself to be sought by those who did not ask for Me;
I permitted Myself to be found by those who did not seek Me.
I said, 'Here am I, here am I,'
To a nation which did not call on My name.
2 "I have spread out My hands all day long to a rebellious people,
Who walk in the way which is not good, following their own thoughts,
3 A people who continually provoke Me to My face,
Offering sacrifices in gardens and burning incense on bricks;
4 Who sit among graves and spend the night in secret places;
Who eat swine's flesh,
And the broth of unclean meat is in their pots.
5 "Who say, 'Keep to yourself, do not come near me,
For I am holier than you!'
These are smoke in My nostrils,
A fire that burns all the day.
6 "Behold, it is written before Me,
I will not keep silent, but I will repay;
I will even repay into their bosom,
7 Both their own iniquities and the iniquities of their fathers together," says the LORD.

"Because they have burned incense on the mountains
And scorned Me on the hills,
Therefore I will measure their former work into their bosom."
8 Thus says the LORD,
"As the new wine is found in the cluster,
And one says, 'Do not destroy it, for there is benefit in it,'
So I will act on behalf of My servants
In order not to destroy all of them.
9 "I will bring forth offspring from Jacob,
And an heir of My mountains from Judah;
Even My chosen ones shall inherit it,
And My servants will dwell there.
10 "Sharon will be a pasture land for flocks,
And the valley of Achor a resting place for herds,
For My people who seek Me.
11 "But you who forsake the LORD,
Who forget My holy mountain,
Who set a table for Fortune,
And who fill cups with mixed wine for Destiny,
12 I will destine you for the sword,
And all of you will bow down to the slaughter.
Because I called, but you did not answer;
I spoke, but you did not hear.
And you did evil in My sight
And chose that in which I did not delight."
13 Therefore, thus says the Lord GOD,
"Behold, My servants will eat, but you will be hungry.
Behold, My servants will drink, but you will be thirsty.
Behold, My servants will rejoice, but you will be put to shame.
14 "Behold, My servants will shout joyfully with a glad heart,
But you will cry out with a heavy heart,
And you will wail with a broken spirit.
15 "You will leave your name for a curse to My chosen ones,
And the Lord GOD will slay you.
But My servants will be called by another name.

First note in verse 9 that the Promises of God are addressed as "My Mountains", a fit description because one of the promises is of the Land to both Abraham and Israel. This is the Promised Land part two, a land of shalom prosperity where God's servants dwell. It is likened to a gift, but a gift can be passed down to descendants as an inheritance.

> **Isaiah 65:** 9 *"I will bring forth offspring from Jacob,*
> *And an heir of My mountains from Judah;*
> *Even My chosen ones shall inherit it,*
> *And My servants will dwell there.*

"My Mountains" as the promised land of God's people is indeed a metaphor for wherever God's people live. Remember that Christianity is now a spiritual kingdom on earth, no longer a physical kingdom such as Israel, therefore it exists wherever God's people exist. That is, there is no longer a specific physical location for God's people in the Christian Spiritual Kingdom.

Christ is the "offspring from Jacob", the Messiah. "My servants" as heirs to the promise are clarified in later verses to be those who accepted the Messiah and his message so Christians, either Jews or Gentiles, collectively can be considered as offspring and heirs. Christians as heirs to the promise are then addressed in the New Testament in Ephesians 3:6 and Hebrews 6:17.

> **Ephesians 3:4-7 (NASB)** *By referring to this, when you read you can understand my insight into the mystery of Christ, 5 which in other generations was not made known to the sons of men, as it has now been revealed to His holy apostles and prophets in the Spirit; 6 to be specific, that* **the Gentiles are fellow heirs and fellow members of the body,** *and fellow partakers of the promise in Christ Jesus through the gospel,*
>
> **Hebrews 6:17 (NASB)** *17 In the same way God, desiring even more to show to the heirs of the promise the unchangeableness of His purpose, interposed with an oath,*

Even more specifically, Christians are called descendants and heirs of Abraham and the Promises in Galatians. Clearly, the promises or unconditional covenants can be passed down to the heirs of the original promise and that heir is the Christian Church and its members.

> **Galatians 3:27-29 (NASB)** *For all of you who were baptized into Christ have clothed yourselves with Christ. 28 There is neither Jew nor Greek, there is neither slave nor free man, there is neither male nor female;*

*for you are all one in Christ Jesus. 29 **And if you belong to Christ, then you are Abraham's descendants, heirs according to promise.***

Secondly, note in Isaiah 65: 15 two prophecies concerning the replacement of Judaism, hard times for the Jews, and a new name for God's servants, his chosen people.

Isaiah 65 (NASB):15 "You will leave your name for a curse to My chosen ones, And the Lord GOD will slay you.
But My servants will be called by another name.

The implication is that there will be animosities between the new group of God's people and the Jews. At least the horrible Roman wars, or perhaps even a view into the general hard times of the Jews living in a totalitarian Christian nation, Russia and Germany for example, or under Islam. The other name could refer to "Christian" or it might also refer to "Gentiles" becoming God's servants under Christianity.

The Jews did see the many references to the Messiah elsewhere in their Bible and also perhaps understood that God would eventually want the All-Powerful Creator God story carried to all the people of the World. But they thought that they, the Jews, would be the vehicle for that to happen, and in order to do that Israel would have to be freed from Roman rule. Thus their Messiah, as a great King, would be the one to take God's message to the World. And perhaps all the world would become Jews. Just to be clear the wording here is a prophecy of the life of Jews as a result of rejecting their Messiah. It means that circumstances will slay Judaism, and Jews, not God personally. Events will happen, that God will allow, which will cause the tragedies. And perhaps tragedies are a necessary learning experience so that we might avoid repeating the same mistakes again.

Note also the transference of shalom prosperity from Judaism to the new group of chosen ones. Not all Jews are to be outcasts however, much of Christianity began with the help of many Jews who joined Christianity at the beginning and were very instrumental in its growth.

Israel's and Judaism's dream of conquering the world for God was not the plan, as Isaiah explained in Isaiah 65 however, because the Jewish leaders as well as the people had not been faithful to the three primary lessons from the Exodus; Faith, Trust, Follow. This passage in Isaiah is but one of many where Israel is called out for deviating from the Judaism handed down by Moses. It's not that Israel has not been warned. Israel is prophesied to cease to exist and a successor will carry forward God's plan.

What must be equally galling to Jewish religious leaders is that Isaiah 65 also foretells that God's people, with a new name, will carry God's word to the world and they now will be blessed with prosperity as a result. This is stated in the form of a new heavens and a new earth, that replaces the old configuration.

There will also be a new Jerusalem, a replacement Jerusalem, not a rebuilt Jerusalem, to be the symbolic focal point for God's new people. Jerusalem is the symbolic focal point of Judaism so metaphorically the new Jerusalem is a different place and how ironic that that new Jerusalem could be Rome, the capital and namesake of their bitter enemy. That is, the symbolic focal point of the replacement of Judaism is none other than the capital of the Gentiles and a recognized focal point for Christianity. Isaiah 65:16 and following then prophesies a great shalom prosperity will follow for God's people. Keep in mind this was written in the 700 BC era and prosperity is defined in 700 BC terms.

> *Isaiah 65:16(NASB) "Because he who is blessed in the earth*
> *Will be blessed by the God of truth;*
> *And he who swears in the earth*
> *Will swear by the God of truth;*
> *Because the former troubles are forgotten,*
> *And because they are hidden from My sight!*
> ***New Heavens and a New Earth***
> ***17 "For behold, I create new heavens and a new earth;***
> ***And the former things will not be remembered or come to mind.***
> ***18 "But be glad and rejoice forever in what I create;***
> ***For behold, I create Jerusalem for rejoicing***
> ***And her people for gladness.***
> ***19 "I will also rejoice in Jerusalem and be glad in My people;***
> *And there will no longer be heard in her*
> *The voice of weeping and the sound of crying.*
> *20 "No longer will there be in it an infant who lives but a few days,*

Or an old man who does not live out his days;
For the youth will die at the age of one hundred
And the one who does not reach the age of one hundred
Will be thought accursed.
21 "They will build houses and inhabit them;
They will also plant vineyards and eat their fruit.
22 "They will not build and another inhabit,
They will not plant and another eat;
For as the lifetime of a tree, so will be the days of My people,
And My chosen ones will wear out the work of their hands.
23 "They will not labor in vain,
Or bear children for calamity;
For they are the offspring of those blessed by the LORD,
And their descendants with them.
24 It will also come to pass that before they call, I will answer; and while
they are still speaking, I will hear.
25 The wolf and the lamb will graze together, and the lion will eat straw like
the ox; and dust will be the serpent's food. They will do no evil or harm in all
My holy mountain," says the LORD.

The Prophet Isaiah *(US: /aɪˈzeɪ.ə/*
or UK: /aɪˈzaɪ.ə/;[5][6] Hebrew: יְשַׁעְיָהוּ,
Yəšaʿyāhū, "God is Salvation") was the
8th-century BC Israelite prophet after
whom the Book of Isaiah is named.

Jesaja (Isaiah) Michelangelo
Sistine Chapel Ceiling i1508 to 1512,
Public Domain, https://
commons.wikimedia.org/w/index.php?
curid=2776989

Within the text of the Book of Isaiah,
Isaiah himself is referred to as "the
prophet", but the exact relationship
between the Book of Isaiah and the actual
prophet Isaiah is complicated. The
traditional view is that all 66 chapters of
the book of Isaiah were written by one
man, Isaiah, possibly in two periods
between 740 BC and c. 686 BC, separated
by approximately 15 years, and that the
book includes dramatic prophetic
declarations of Cyrus the Great in the
Bible, acting to restore the nation of Israel
from Babylonian captivity. Another widely
held view is that parts of the first half of the

book (chapters 1–39) originated with the historical prophet, interspersed with prose commentaries written in the time of King Josiah a hundred years later, and that the remainder of the book dates from immediately before and immediately after the end of the exile in Babylon, almost two centuries after the time of the historical prophet.
    https://en.wikipedia.org/wiki/Isaiah

A comprehensive summary of all the Biblical Old Testament references to the Messiah and this new age is found in a document created by a Russian Orthodox Priest, Bishop Alexander (Mileant)

The Document is called "The Old Testament Regarding the Messiah" and can be found in its entirety on this website.   It documents and explains over 60 Old Testament references.
https://www.fatheralexander.org/booklets/english/ old_testament_messiah.htm

Bishop Alexander (Mileant)

Bishop Alexander *(secular name Alexander Vasilievich Mileant, Russian: Александр Васильевич Милеант; 22 July 1938, Odessa, Ukrainian Soviet Socialist Republic – 12 September 2005, La Cañada Flintridge, California) was Bishop of Buenos Aires and South America of the Russian Orthodox Church Outside Russia.*

Bishop Alexander is well known for his missionary leaflets. From 1985 to 2005 Bishop Alexander published a total of 763 brochures: 300 in Russian, 192 in English, 168 in Spanish, and 103 in Portuguese.is taken to the entire world
https://en.wikipedia.org/wiki/Alexander_(Mileant)

Daniel's Prophecy of the Messiah: Daniel 9

Another somewhat obvious prophecy of the Messiah appears to give Israel an "out", an opportunity to recover and be aligned with the Messiah, but also forecasts directly the end of Judaism. In other words, Israel can become part of this new world with the Messiah, it's a possibility, but Judaism will end and the principles of the All Powerful Creator God and His philosophy for a prosperous life will transition to a new people, the

Gentiles. This is the prophecy in Daniel 9 that also aligns with Isaiah 65. Daniel was written in the 536 BC timeframe, although some scholars place it as late as the second century BC, still well before the advent of Jesus. The prophesy itself can be aligned accurately to specific years and as such provides a rather accurate and dramatic picture of the Jews. It's not clear that the historic calendar that we know today was as clear back at the time of Christ, however. We'll examine Daniel 9 shortly.

The history of Judaism, as well as Christianity, as portrayed by the Hebrew and Christian Bibles is two steps forward and two steps back, that is, progress or advancement in understanding is slow and also negative at times. Over the 1,500 or so years from the Exodus to about 30 AD has seen the growth of a priesthood infiltrated with human religious ideas. Volumes of rules have been added to the original guidelines laid down by Moses for Judaism. These new rules came about as second guesses about what would please God to gain His favor, (the thinking behind mankind's human-created religions). These rules became so cumbersome however that everyday Jews had a hard time understanding just what a Jew must do as he experienced the diversity of everyday life. Every decision required determining just what the Rabbi would do. Out of this convoluted thinking came several Jewish sects, each extrapolating a different approach to Jewish religious and secular life.

The Jewish drift into human religion's thinking, that man could manipulate God to his benefit, and at the same time make himself more righteous and thus more favored by God, is well documented in the Old Testament, the Hebrew Bible, so we're not making any derogatory claims against a religion that they don't already have documented in their own books. The only caveat to that is that Jewish thinking today may dismiss their own Biblical texts as only the writer's view and not the view of God. The Book of Isaiah would certainly fit in this category. And thus it was, and is left for either the local Rabbi or the individual, to sort out what God really wants.

This Jewish tradition of multiple additional rules for specifying how to obey the words of God, the Ten Commandments and follow the ritual traditions laid down by Moses became the focus of the teachings of Jesus, who came on the scene with the message that many of the Jewish laws were philosophical and general in nature, designed as principles to be applied as inspiration and motivation to real life rather than being amplified to hundreds of additional specific rules for every occasion. And further, the key point was that the rituals and directed laws of behavior were for tradition, to bind the culture together, and had little value in improving or maintaining a relationship with God. The rituals do have value in that they may teach or be a teaching aid to a principle or concept of valid Theology or Philosophy but they had become rituals without reality, rituals performed without any sense of the point or objective they were intended to portray.

> NOTE: Calling Gods Word as suggestions seems directly counter productive. If God says it, then do it, which can absolutely be true. But everything is not so absolute, or situations can make them less so. Jesus used the Sabbath day as the example and that is perhaps the best example of this "suggestion" idea. The sabbath day of rest is a law that requires some common sense being applied rather than doubling down on the wildest of applications.

Thus Jesus called the Pharisees Whitewashed Tombstones because they emphasized following all the additional oral traditional rules laid down over the 1,500 years. Jesus's point was that they kept all the little rules to appear righteous and favorable to God while they forsook keeping the meaning, intent, or philosophy of the law. The best example of this was the oral tradition Sabbath Laws which, for example, forbid harvesting crops including picking a single grain of seed, even if you were hungry. All the while the intent of the Sabbath law was to demonstrate that God had provided everything mankind needed in the design of the earth (Genesis paraphrased - God rested on the 7th day of creation because His work was done - not because he was tired). Secondly, He would also take care of provisional problems caused by locusts, floods, or years of famine.

The "no work" rule has also been adapted for modern life. One example is that hotels in Jerusalem have at least one elevator that does not require pushing a button, i.e., doing work, on the Sabbath day. The elevator automatically stops at each floor in a continual cycle so that you never have to push a button to summon it or select the floor you want. It

stops at the bottom floor, goes all the way to the top floor, and then stops
at each floor on the way down. It only goes in one direction, down, from
each floor. So if you want to go from the 5th floor to the 6th floor you
would first ride the elevator down to the first floor stopping at every floor
on the way down. Then you would take the elevator straight up to the the
top floor and then back down, stopping at every floor until you reach the
6th floor. Riding one of the regular elevators you control is forbidden by
the sabbath laws. There are still regular elevators available for all the non
Jews staying at the Hotel. But Jews can also go over to the stairwell, open
the door manually, and carry their bags up 5 flights of stairs to the 5th floor
without violating the sabbath laws.

The objective of the Sabbath day commandment is to assure you that
God is still in control of life and that life is designed and programmed to
allow us some free time to rest, recover, and be creative. Therefore you
could rest one day a week and not have to be fearful that you might lose it
all if you took the day off. That is, God was in charge of the world and
wasn't going to let his people down, a philosophy quite different from all
the surrounding religions. This was also a day that represented shalom, a
day of peace, freedom from worry, and freedom to enjoy the fruits of your
labor. So it didn't do a disservice to that principle to feed the cow or take
care of emergencies or grab a lunch of grains from a field on the Sabbath if
circumstances dictated the necessity.

Christianity is not immune. Many denominations have human-
derived rituals and practices that they believe are required for things such
as; entry into heaven, having faith, or being a good Christian. It is a sign of
human thinking and human religious ideas.

Guilt over our sins makes it difficult for human beings to believe that
God would ever forgive them, or make things simple or easy. We're stuck
on the "eye of the needle" or "the way is long and narrow", misapplied or
"made up" metaphors, to tell us we're not good enough. And even the
Pharisees were victims of this thinking.

So while the Pharisees included all the oral traditions and rituals,
hoping to salvage God's approval, they were opposed by the Sadducees
who dismissed major portions of the Jewish Bible as well as the oral

traditions and rules and claimed the ability to revise the rules and standards on the fly, based on their opinions at any given time.

The Pharisees and Sadducees

The Pharisees (/ˈfærəˌsiːz/) were a social movement and a school of thought in the Holy Land during the time of Second Temple Judaism. After the destruction of the Second Temple in 70 CE, Pharisaic beliefs became the foundational, liturgical and ritualistic basis for Rabbinic Judaism.

Conflicts between Pharisees and Sadducees took place in the context of much broader and longstanding social and religious conflicts among Jews, made worse by the Roman conquest. Another conflict was cultural, between those who favored Hellenization (the Sadducees) and those who resisted it (the Pharisees). A third was juridico-religious, between those who emphasized the importance of the Second Temple with its rites and services, and those who emphasized the importance of other Mosaic Laws. A fourth point of conflict, specifically religious, involved different interpretations of the Torah and how to apply it to current Jewish life, with Sadducees recognizing only the Written Torah (with Greek philosophy) and rejecting doctrines such as the Oral Torah, the Prophets, the Writings, and the resurrection of the dead.

Josephus (37 – c. 100 CE), believed by many historians to be a Pharisee, estimated the total Pharisee population before the fall of the Second Temple to be around 6,000. Josephus claimed that Pharisees received the full support and goodwill of the common people, apparently in contrast to the more elite Sadducees, who were the upper class. Pharisees claimed Mosaic authority for their interpretation of Jewish Laws, while Sadducees represented the authority of the priestly privileges and prerogatives established since the days of Solomon, when Zadok, their ancestor, officiated as High Priest. The phrase "common people" in Josephus' writings suggests that most Jews were "just Jewish people", distinguishing them from the main liturgical groups.

Outside Jewish history and literature, Pharisees have been made notable by references in the New Testament to conflicts with John the Baptist and with Jesus. There are also several references in the New Testament to the Apostle Paul being a Pharisee. The relationship between Early Christianity and the Pharisees depended on the individual; while numerous nameless Pharisees were portrayed as hostile, New Testament writings make mention of several Pharisees, including Joseph of Arimathea, Nicodemus and Gamaliel, who are sympathetic to Jesus and Christians.
https://en.wikipedia.org/wiki/Pharisees

The Prophet Isaiah is unique in that he states in Isaiah Chapter 65 that because of Israel's failings, God's people will have a new name, indicating that there would be a new standard bearer for the God of Abraham. The 1,500 year reign of Israel under the laws and rituals laid down by Moses could come to an end. Israel could be replaced as God's people. Not all prophesy is definite or unconditional, often it is conditional based on the actions of the followers but Isaiah was not allowing that caveat in his prophecy which we previously cited, perhaps because that prophecy was apparently not conditional and came true two thousand years ago.

Another somewhat obvious prophecy of the Messiah does give Israel an "out" or a last chance, an opportunity to recover and be aligned with the Messiah. But it also forecasts directly the end of Judaism. This is the prophecy in Daniel 9. Daniel was written in the 536 BC timeframe. The prophesy has several clues as to the timeframe of the Jewish Messiah and the specific dates can be very closely aligned with the actual times and dates of Jesus's ministry on earth.

Daniel 9:24-27 (NASB) Seventy Weeks until the Messiah

The Old Testament book of Daniel prophesies two critical things about a coming Messiah that's been the subject of many passages in the Old Testament. The Messiah is prophesied to come 69 weeks after the decree to restore Jerusalem following the Babylonian captivity. The 69 weeks are considered to be 69 times 7 days or 483 "days" and a "day" is considered to represent a year in prophecy so the 69 weeks are considered to be 483 years. Note that this prophesy also notes the failings of the Jews to follow the tenets of Judaism that were set up at its foundation following the Exodus, and confirms Isaiah's description when he talks about Israel being replaced as the standard bearer for the All-Powerful Creator God. Daniel also mentions sealing up vision and prophecy and anointing the most holy place, the inner temple sanctuary where God was said to appear. This is an illusion of the objective of Judaism being the acceptance of the Messiah who was God's representative on earth.   (Even though many Old Testament prophecies predicted that the Messiah would NOT be accepted by the Jewish community)

Daniel 9:24 (NASB)

24 "Seventy weeks have been decreed for your people and your holy city, to finish the transgression, to make an end of sin, to make atonement for iniquity, to bring in everlasting righteousness, to seal up vision and prophecy and to anoint the most holy place.

> **Weeks:** h7620. שָׁבוּעַ šâḇûa'; or שָׁבֻעַ shabuan; also (feminine) שְׁבֻעָה shbu'ah; properly, passive participle of 7650 as a denominative of 7651; literal, sevened, i.e. a week (specifically, of years): — seven, week.
> AV (20) - week 19, seven 1;
> seven, period of seven (days or years), heptad, week/period of seven days, a weekFeast of Weeks
> heptad, seven (of years)
> (From Strong's Exhaustive Concordance included with the NASB)

Daniel 9:25 (NASB)

25 So you are to know and discern that **from the issuing of a decree to restore and rebuild Jerusalem until Messiah the Prince** there will be seven weeks and sixty-two weeks; it will be built again, with plaza and moat, even in times of distress.

The year the decree was established

Ezra 7:1-7 (NASB) Now after these things, in the reign of Artaxerxes king of Persia, there went up Ezra son of Seraiah, son of Azariah, son of Hilkiah, 2 son of Shallum, son of Zadok, son of Ahitub, 3 son of Amariah, son of Azariah, son of Meraioth, 4 son of Zerahiah, son of Uzzi, son of Bukki, 5 son of Abishua, son of Phinehas, son of Eleazar, son of Aaron the chief priest. 6 This Ezra went up from Babylon, and he was a scribe skilled in the law of Moses, which the LORD God of Israel had given; and the king granted him all he requested because the hand of the LORD his God was upon him. 7 Some of the sons of Israel and some of the priests, the Levites, the singers, the gatekeepers and the temple servants went up to Jerusalem **in the seventh year of King Artaxerxes.**

The Decree of Artaxerxes, King of Persia 457 BC

Ezra 7:11-18 (NASB) 11 Now this is the copy of the decree which King Artaxerxes gave to Ezra the priest, the scribe, learned in the words of the commandments of the LORD and His statutes to Israel: 12 "Artaxerxes, king of kings, to Ezra the priest, the scribe of the law of the God of heaven, perfect peace. And now 13 I have issued a decree that any of the people of Israel and their priests and the Levites in my kingdom who are willing to go to

Jerusalem, may go with you. 14 Forasmuch as you are sent by the king and his seven counselors to inquire concerning Judah and Jerusalem according to the law of your God which is in your hand, 15 and to bring the silver and gold, which the king and his counselors have freely offered to the God of Israel, whose dwelling is in Jerusalem, 16 with all the silver and gold which you find in the whole province of Babylon, along with the freewill offering of the people and of the priests, who offered willingly for the house of their God which is in Jerusalem; 17 with this money, therefore, you shall diligently buy bulls, rams and lambs, with their grain offerings and their drink offerings and offer them on the altar of the house of your God which is in Jerusalem. 18 Whatever seems good to you and to your brothers to do with the rest of the silver and gold, you may do according to the will of your God.

The Decree continued to include setting up the rule of law

Ezra 7:25-26 (NASB) "You, Ezra, according to the wisdom of your God which is in your hand, appoint magistrates and judges that they may judge all the people who are in the province beyond the River, even all those who know the laws of your God; and you may teach anyone who is ignorant of them. 26 Whoever will not observe the law of your God and the law of the king, let judgment be executed upon him strictly, whether for death or for banishment or for confiscation of goods or for imprisonment."

There is one other potential starting point that some Christians use, a passage in Nehemiah that talks about a different decree to rebuild the walls of Jerusalem. The Ezra reference above more accurately reflects the prophesy because it restores the city as a functioning city with laws and judges to administer city functions as well as rebuilding the entire city, not just the walls. The Nehemiah reference has a problem, it doesn't align with the time of the messiah, it's off about five years or so. The quick fix for this is to use a lunar, 12-month cycle for a year rather than a seasonal year, one where a year is the time from one season to the next, our traditional 365-day year. The claim is that people used a lunar calendar, but they still lived by when to plant and harvest which was the seasonal year. In any event the Ezra date matches the prophecy about as close as we can get to exact dates.

Daniel 9:26 (NASB)(69 weeks of years= 7 weeks plus the 62 weeks)
26 Then after the sixty-two weeks the Messiah will be cut off and have nothing, and the people of the prince who is to come will destroy the city and

the sanctuary. And its end will come with a flood; even to the end there will be war; desolations are determined.

Daniel 9:27 (NASB) And he will make a firm covenant with the many for one week, *but in the middle of the week he will put a stop to sacrifice and grain offering; and on the wing of abominations will come one who makes desolate, even until a complete destruction, one that is decreed, is poured out on the one who makes desolate."*

The sequence of events in Daniel 9

1. Judaism and Israel have 70 weeks of prophetic years (490 years) left for them to straighten up (follow their guidance from God) and accept the prophecies of their Messiah

2. Messiah, the Prince will appear at the end of the 69th week of years or 483 years from the decree of Artaxerxes in 457 BC

> NOTE: There is also an ambiguity in counting years, do you count the first year or only count additional years. For example when you become one year old it comes in the second year of your life. This makes the estimates of the Messiah's birth, when his ministry begins and the crucifixion vary by a year or two. We'll assume that the first year is counted in the number. The difference is only a year in time which is well within the accuracy with which we can place dates on events.

3. Messiah the Prince will appear in the year 26 AD (457 years to 1 BC and another 26 years to 26 AD. there's no "zero" year between BC and AD so the jump between 1 BC to 1AD is just one year.

4. This puts the birth of the Messiah in 5 BC.(26 years from 1AD to 26 AD) We're not counting the zeroth year here because we're addressing age, which has ramifications for when Christ would begin preaching.

   a. A Jewish prophet had to be 30 years old to begin a ministry and 5 BC is the birth date of a Messiah who begins his ministry at age 30, in 26 AD. (If Jesus was born in 5 BC he would not be thirty until 26 AD)

   b. 5 BC is also right in the middle of the timeframe (6 to 4 BC) for the best alternative for the Star of Bethlehem, which was a conjunction of planets in the night sky known /seen only by the Wise Men, astrologers, who read meanings into the locations of the planets and this particular conjunction of planets was the sign of the birth of a new king of Israel. This also aligns with Herod's order to kill all males 2 years old or less which would have come sometime before

Herod died in 4 BC (date in dispute) when Mary and Joseph would flee to Egypt with Jesus.

5. The Messiah's ministry therefore is to begin in the fall of 26 AD. The best estimate of the time of year is in the fall when the sheep are in the fields so the birth of Jesus is best estimated to be about October of 5 BC so Jesus would have been 30 in the fall of 26 BC.

6. Per the records in the New Testament Gospels of Jesus's ministry is over 3 Passovers, his ministry runs over three years and the spring of 30 AD would three and a half years.

7. The Messiah's ministry was to last into the 70th week,

8. (Daniel 9:26 "then '**after the 62 weeks', (plus 7 weeks or after the 69 weeks total)** the Messiah will be cut off and have nothing")

9. That is in the 70th week of 7 years, and 3 ½ years of ministry would place the end of the Messiah's ministry right in the middle of the 70th week of 7 years.

10. The Messiah's ministry is the first three and a half years of the 70th week and it comes to an end with the crucifixion at that time, precisely in the middle of the "week" the 4th year of Jesus's ministry,

11. The Messiah will put a stop to the sacrifices and grain offerings. The sacrifices and grain offerings, especially Yom Kippur, the Day of Atonement are symbolic prophecies of a future event, the crucifixion of Christ, the Messiah. Once that future event happens the symbolic rituals are no longer needed, their significance and purpose end. The crucifixion as the reality of Yom Kippur ends the value and purpose of the sacrifice and all other temple rituals.

> NOTE: If Jesus is the Messiah, his crucifixion is the fulfillment (puts to end their purpose) of the metaphor symbology of the temple sacrifices and most specifically the Yom Kippur Day of Atonement. In this sacrifice the Lamb without spot or blemish is sacrificed and symbolically pays the penalty for the sins of the second lamb, the scape goat, who represents the people of Israel, and is set free in the wilderness, never to be judged for sins again.
> PRINCIPLE: Once the reality of a prophecy or metaphor has occurred, there is no longer a need to continue that metaphor.

12. The crucifixion of Christ comes in the spring of 30 AD, the middle of the 70th week of Daniel.

13. Daniel's prophecy says that Israel has 70 weeks of years to accept the Messiah so they have another 3 ½ years after the crucifixion which occurred in the middle of the 70th week. The prophecy notes that the Messiah makes a covenant with the many for one week, the 70th week. This means that for that one week period of 7 years Israel will be the exclusive group to whom the apostles will carry the message of Christ. What we do know is that the initial instructions to Jesus's disciples was to go only to the house of Israel.

Instructions to The Twelve Disciples

Matthew 10:1-7 *(NASB) 1 Jesus summoned His twelve disciples and gave them authority over unclean spirits, to cast them out, and to heal every kind of disease and every kind of sickness. 2 Now the names of the twelve apostles are these: The first, Simon, who is called Peter, and Andrew his brother; and James the son of Zebedee, and John his brother; 3 Philip and Bartholomew; Thomas and Matthew the tax collector; James the son of Alphaeus, and Thaddaeus; 4 Simon the Zealot, and Judas Iscariot, the one who betrayed Him. 5 These twelve Jesus sent out after instructing them: "Do not go in the way of the Gentiles, and do not enter any city of the Samaritans; 6 but rather go to the lost sheep of the house of Israel. 7 And as you go, preach, saying, 'The kingdom of heaven is at hand.'*

The reason for this policy is obvious, the prophecy in Daniel that sets aside a specific period of time for the orthodox Jewish community (excluding the Samaritans for example) to accept their Messiah. This policy was enforced for the entire time of Jesus's ministry and there was nothing to change that direction after the crucifixion. So for the next 3½ years, this was what the disciples did. That is the only direction the Disciples have had all the way to the end of the 70th week. The period of an exclusive ministry to the Jews is then over, it's time to take the new reality of Judaism, the new or revised religion, to the rest of the world, meaning to the Gentiles or Romans.

What Christianity is not, is that it is not a new religion that's being put in place of Judaism because the Jews blew their opportunity to be God's chosen people. Christianity is not God's Plan B, the backup plan. We know this from Isaiah's prophecy. That prophecy was certainly claiming some bad results for Jews who continued to reject their own Messiah, but also promised prosperity for those who signed up for Christianity.

What actually happened was that there were a large number of Jews who became Christians because they could see that Jesus was not teaching a new religion but a transformed Jewish religion. The New Testament Book of Acts testifies to the difficulties the Apostles were having in launching a movement to follow the initiatives laid down by Jesus. One big question was how to deal with the Jewish rituals. Both Gentiles and Jews were converts and the question that perplexed the apostles was whether or not the Gentiles had to become Jews first, conform to the Jewish rules for conversion to Judaism in order to become a Christian.

The answer to this question would come over time as the realization came that many of the customs of Judaism were cultural phenomenon that had no meaning for Gentiles who were joining the Christian movement. Further the essentials of the Theology and Philosophy of Judaism as espoused in the Jewish Bible were included in Christianity either directly or in an extended form. Foremost of these was that Christ had fulfilled the Jewish most holy day ritual sacrifice and the need for the Temple rituals was no longer required. This understanding made it easy for many Jews and Gentiles to join together in this revised version of Judaism.

This is the period when Christianity establishes roots in the Roman world, roots so deep that it easily survives the persecution of Christians to come in a hundred years or so at the hands of various Roman emperors.

.

The Exhortation to the Apostles_-James Tissot

16. Christianity: Fulfilling The Mysteries of Judaism

The impression can be that the Jews fiercely resisted their Messiah and Christianity, considering it an aberration of the followers of just another Messianic imposter.   But that is not the reality of either the historical records or even the New Testament book of Acts, that documents the rise of Christianity. The fact is that many Jews, including Pharisees, who were religious scholars, became Christians. Then there were many Jews who had been living outside of Israel for tens to hundreds of years, yet kept their Jewish roots and traditions and helped form the initial clusters of Christians throughout the Roman World.

So while the Jewish leaders crucified Jesus, there were many Jews who heard the message and saw something different enough to begin to form the cadre of Christian converts. The reason for this was first of all, Christianity was not presenting them with a totally new or different religion, but a revision built on an expected Messiah and ties to the Jewish traditions.

The reality of Christianity is that it carries most of the Theology and Philosophy of Life of Judaism forward with connections that are perhaps subtle to us but were significant to many Jews at the beginning of the Christian era. Christianity did abandon many Jewish traditions and rituals which were cultural, derived from both written and the oral traditions, but some, such as the synagogue meetings, were used as models of the early church.

Christianity clarifies or explains some of the metaphorical rituals and traditions from a direct personal standpoint, one that made sense to the Jews going through their struggles with the Roman Empire. The fact that Christianity could provide reasonable explanations for Jewish traditions and metaphorical beliefs became an open door for a new beginning. When Jews looked forward into Christianity they could see the reflection of Judaism with changes that they could understand and accept.

The relationship between Judaism and Christianity.

1. The Theology and Philosophy of Life are the same
    a. God is an all-powerful creator and mentor God
    b. There is a "Holy Spirit" part of God that communicates directly with mankind
    c. God is not visible to humans but a human representative of God, a Messiah, is manifest for special purposes
    d. Directions are provided through the Bible in human literary styles capable of being understood in all periods
    e. The Theology and Philosophy are progressively revealed through the Bible in a suitable format for the historical timeframes
        • The Torah (first five books of the Old Testament)was verbally handed down from Adam to Moses and written down by Moses
        • Additions were made by Prophets and Leaders over the next 1,000 years

- The New Testament was written within two to twenty years of the events discussed, in the form of letters circulated among the early Christian Churches from about 34 AD to 90 AD. That is, it was written within the lifetimes of the people and events recorded

2. The steps or phases in time of revelations are:
    a. Adam to Abraham to Moses: Simple Faith, single sacrifice of Abel, minimal ritual of Melchizedek sharing bread and wine
    b. Moses to the Messiah: Judaism as a cultural and ritualistic rich tradition designed to keep Israel and Judaism intact during the evolution of city-states into nation-states ending with Rome
    c. Christ as the Messiah introduces:
        - an expanded spiritual relationship and
        - An expanded documentation set
        - A shift from a child to an adult lesson focus, more theories for general application, softer do's and don'ts.
        - A more direct presentation of the Theology and Philosophy
        - A simple ritual across all cultures, communion bread and wine that connects back to the past historical traditions from Abel's sacrifice to Melchizedek to Moses to Judaism to the Messiah
        - A culturally neutral and flexible tradition
3. The basis for a relationship with God is the same, by Faith or Trust in God
4. The basis for a heavenly future is the same, by Faith in God
5. The basis for shalom prosperity is the same, adopting the Philosophy of Life to the maximum extent possible

The six big changes from Judaism to Christianity are:

1. **Shift from Temple Centered to Church Centered.** The establishment of the Local Church as the local and culturally diverse center for learning both the Theology and Philosophy of Life. Judaism had already begun a shift from Temple worship to community synagogues due to the scattering of the Jewish population.

2. **A New Spiritual Kingdom.** A new Spiritual Kingdom will replace the earthly physical Kingdom of God formed by Judaism, the Jewish traditions and worship, and the Temple rituals. This is perhaps the hardest for the Jews to accept. Thus probably why both Jerusalem and the Temple had to be destroyed, to make that

transition more obvious and final. The destruction of the Temple is also the subject of prophecies in Daniel 9.

3. **Christians have a full-time spiritual connection to God** through the Holy Spirit. This is neither the full-blown connection in the Garden before consciousness nor up-front guidance such as given to Noah or Abraham but rather helps with difficult and complex situations and decisions in life.

4. **Christ fulfills or explains or demystifies the Temple sacrifices and Holy Days.** The ritual and temple worship of Judaism, especially Yom Kippur, the Day of Atonement, was a prophecy of sorts of the Cross and Christ atoning for the sins of all mankind. With the reality of the Cross, there is no need for the shadow metaphors of the Temple to continue. This simplifies the traditions and allows adoption by diverse cultures.

5. **Christianity amplifies the Theology and Philosophy.** Christians are considered adult sons, they are given adult lessons and logical arguments, and expected to make good judgments in life as examples to the world. This is compared to Judaism where Jews followed what they were specifically told to do through the rituals and traditions without explanation or logic as to why. Christianity provided that "ah hah" moment, "now I understand", about much of the mysticism, ritual, and traditions of Judaism. It then became obvious that Judaism was a placeholder for a broader and richer Theology and Philosophy that required a more civilized and mature world and human nature before it could be understood and accepted.

6. **Christianity does away with the Theocracy relationship of Israel and Judaism** In this sweeping change Christianity separates church and state and it turns civil law and enforcement over to Governments. This is an open door to the Gentiles and states firmly that Christianity is not seeking political power but an individual life-changing experience.

The shift from the Temple to a local Church format for teaching had already been taking place in Jewish Synagogues, (similar to churches) as places of local worship among Jews dispersed in foreign lands. The destruction of the Temple in 70 AD prompted a total shift into synagogues as Judaism was practiced in Israel. The changes regarding the believer's relationship to the Holy Spirit and the fulfillment of the temple sacrifices were both smooth transitions that were predicted by Old Testament Prophecy and confirmed by New Testament writings as a completion of God's plan. That is Christianity was not God's Plan B when Israel did not unilaterally accept their Messiah.   These two changes, the end of the Temple rituals and the local community congregations were planned from the beginning and set up to point back to Judaism and Jewish traditions as the origin of the new Christian-centered life. Jews who could see these connections easily accepted the new religious reality.

The genius of the Christian transformation was having a former Pharisee, the Apostle Paul, become the one to both explain the connections between Judaism and Christianity and to make good use of simplified metaphors of Theology as inspiration. Secondly Paul as a scholar also understood the importance of scholarship in grasping principles so we now have Christianity become a classroom for learning both the Theology and the Philosophy of Life, as the key to shalom prosperity.

The timing also sends a message to Israel, one only observable in hindsight. The time at the end of the 69 weeks of years prophecy, 26 AD, and for the next 40 years until the Jewish-Roman War of 66 AD was a quiet period in the Roman world that allowed Christianity to take root and flourish. From Israel's standpoint, 40 years was also the transition time for the Exodus generation to get their act together in the wilderness and form a cohesive society. The forty years is measured from the advent of Christ as the Messiah in 26 AD but you can also measure 40 years from the crucifixion in 30 AD to the destruction of the Temple in 70 AD near the end of the Jewish-Roman War. Israel is now spending an identical 40 years, again in the wilderness, having been cut off per Daniel's prophecy until the final blow with the destruction of the Temple. Symbolic relationships can sometimes speak volumes, and signs such as this were a big part of Jewish traditions.

Historically the Jews were certainly antagonistic toward Rome during this time but no big conflict emerged. The Jew's own internal "back fence" rivalries were just enough of a problem to keep Rome focused on the Jews and ignore the Christian growth closer to home. The destruction of the Temple and Jerusalem was not yet the end of Israel, that would take another 70 years or so, a story continued in Volume II.

The Passover and the Temple Sacrifice Connections

One of the primary connections the Apostle Paul was to make was the Messiah's connection to the two most significant Holy Days in Judaism, The Passover, and Yom Kippur. The Passover tells of a miracle escape from death that was the beginning of the formation of Israel and Judaism. Yom Kippur is the message, in a temple sacrifice format of God's forgiveness of sins which also has the subtle connotation of salvation from punishment for sins. The connection of these two most holy Jewish celebrations and their Messiah to Christianity was significant to the Jews who heard the message so it was perhaps far more acceptable to the Jewish people than to the Jewish religious leaders who saw Christianity as blasphemy against Judaism as well as a challenge to their authority.

Yom Kippur, the Day of Atonement

Yom Kippur, the Day of Atonement was the holiest day in Israel. The holiest event of Christianity is Easter, the crucifixion and resurrection of Christ, which is the embodiment of Yom Kippur, the day of atonement which occurs in September in the Jewish calendar. Christ sacrificed on the Cross pays the penalty for our sins, and paves the way for God to forgive the sins of the entire world, not just every Christian. This was the message of Yom Kippur, the innocent lamb was sacrificed, metaphorically paying the price for sins, while the second lamb, is freed into the wilderness, never to be judged again. That second lamb represented each individual Jew and metaphorically told each of them that God was forgiving their sins, their sins were paid for by the sacrifice of the perfect innocent lamb. Most likely they all understood this was a symbolic sacrifice. The sacrificed innocent lamb was symbolically paying the penalty for their sins. They didn't necessarily know what the symbology meant but they accepted the results as true. Old Testament passages strongly suggested that the Messiah would be a reality, but it's not clear that they connected the two. The message to Christians was that once the crucifixion of Christ occurred, in the middle of the seventieth week of Daniel's prophesy, the Temple sacrifice metaphor was no longer needed, the reality had occurred.

Yom Kippur in the Mosaic Law

Leviticus 16:7-10 (NASB) He shall take the two goats and present them before the LORD at the doorway of the tent of meeting. 8 Aaron shall cast lots for the two goats, one lot for the LORD and the other lot for the scapegoat. 9 Then Aaron shall offer the goat on which the lot for the LORD fell, and make it a sin offering. 10 But the goat on which the lot for the scapegoat fell shall be presented alive before the LORD, to make atonement upon it, to send it into the wilderness as the scapegoat.

The scapegoat

h5799. עֲזָאזֵל 'ăzâ'zêl; from 5795 and 235; goat of departure; the scapegoat: — scapegoat.

AV (4) - scapegoat 4;

entire removal, scapegoat refers to the goat used for sacrifice for the sins of the people

meaning dubious

Olive Tree Enhanced Strong's Dictionary Copyright ©1998-2022 Olive Tree Bible Software

What is interesting is that the translation of the Hebrew word as "scapegoat" comes from The King James Version (KJV) of the Bible, an English translation of the Christian Bible for the Church of England, which was commissioned in 1604 and published in 1611. The English definition and common usage of "scapegoat" however is of someone who is innocent, but blamed for what someone else has done and pays the penalty for it. In the Yom Kippur sacrifice, the innocent and blameless goat/lamb is the one sacrificed and the "scapegoat", the one set free, is the one who carried the sins but escapes punishment. So, there is a mixup in the terminology that originated in the King James Version and is carried into most all modern translations. The scapegoat released into the wilderness, never to return, is symbolic of the fact that once the innocent goat/lamb pays the penalty for the sins of the people, the people are never to be subject to being judged again. The scapegoat will never again find itself paired with another goat and lots tossed to determine which goat pays the penalty for the sins of the people. The metaphor says that once the sins are paid for, the All-Powerful Creator God will never require a second judgment of those sins personally on any individual, no matter how horrible those sins may be.

This is the message of Yom Kippur. But it is a metaphor that depends on the priests and Pharisees to correctly communicate the message to the people. We know from the writings of the Prophets in the Bible that this was not always done correctly so it's not clear that everyone, or any Jew in the first century AD, understood this correctly. The Mishnah or the first Oral Torah of Jewish traditions documents alternative versions of Yom Kippur. What is comical, in a way, is that the original Yom Kippur understanding by the priests was that the scapegoat represented the people who were never to return to face judgment again, sins paid for by the sacrificial goat. So, to ensure that happened they would take the scapegoat out into the wilderness and throw it off a cliff, ensuring that outcome. It couldn't come wandering back into the city to be judged again, it was dead. Fortunately, this was done in secret so the mixed message did not get back to the congregation, that both goats died. But given that it was impossible to hide that outcome the Priests changed the story. Instead the sins of the people were said to be placed on the scapegoat and scarlet threads were placed on it which were proclaimed to have turned white after being tossed off the cliff, indicating forgiveness of sins. (The revised story account is in the Mishnah on the next page.) The Oral Torah, the Mishnah, modified the Biblical intent. Human religious overthinking and manipulation at work.

> *The **Mishnah** or the Mishna (/ˈmɪʃnə/; Hebrew:* מִשְׁנָה, *"study by repetition", from the verb shanah* שנה, *or "to study and review", also "secondary") is the first major written collection of the Jewish oral traditions that are known as the Oral Torah. The Mishnah was redacted by Judah ha-Nasi probably in Beit Shearim or Sepphoris[4] between the ending of the second century and the beginning of the 3rd century CE[5][6] in a time when, according to the Talmud, the persecution of Jews and the passage of time raised the possibility that the details of the oral traditions of the Pharisees from the Second Temple period (516 BCE – 70 CE) would be forgotten. Most of the Mishnah is written in Mishnaic Hebrew, but some parts are in Aramaic.*
> https://en.wikipedia.org/wiki/Mishnah

Note that the Mishnah was redacted, developed from a collection of writings about 200 AD. The original sources can go back to as early as 5oo BC.

The Azazel or Scapegoat traditions revised by the Oral Torah

The Mishnah (Yoma 39a[14]) follows the Hebrew Bible text; two goats were procured, similar in respect of appearance, height, cost, and time of selection. Having one of these on his right and the other on his left, the high priest, who was assisted in this rite by two subordinates, put both his hands into a wooden case, and took out two labels, one inscribed "for Yahweh" and the other "for Azazel". The high priest then laid his hands with the labels upon the two goats and said, "A sin-offering to Yahweh" (thus speaking the Tetragrammaton); and the two men accompanying him replied, "Blessed be the name of His glorious kingdom for ever and ever." He then fastened a scarlet woolen thread to the head of the goat "for Azazel"; and laying his hands upon it again, recited the ...confession of sin and prayer for forgiveness:

This prayer was responded to by the congregation present. A man was selected, preferably a priest, to take the goat to the precipice in the wilderness; and he was accompanied part of the way by the most eminent men of Jerusalem. Ten booths had been constructed at intervals along the road leading from Jerusalem to the steep mountain. ..... When he came to the precipice he divided the scarlet thread into two parts, one of which he tied to the rock and the other to the goat's horns, and then pushed the goat down. The cliff was so high and rugged that before the goat had traversed half the distance to the plain below, its limbs were utterly shattered.

https://en.wikipedia.org/wiki/Azazel

The Passover - The Blood Metaphor: A Spiritual Connection

The second most Holy day in Judaism was the Passover. Here the significant sign or metaphor is the blood of the Sacrificial animal smeared over the doors of the homes of the Hebrews in Egypt which made their families immune from the plague that was to kill the firstborn in Egypt. This was the tenth plague, the one that caused the Pharaoh to allow Moses and the Hebrews to leave Egypt.

Exodus 12:1-13 (NASB) The Passover Lamb

1 Now the LORD said to Moses and Aaron in the land of Egypt, 2 "This month shall be the beginning of months for you; it is to be the first month of the year to you. 3 Speak to all the congregation of Israel, saying, 'On the tenth of this month they are each one to take a lamb for themselves, according to their fathers' households, a lamb for each household. 4 Now if the household is too small for a lamb, then he and his neighbor nearest to his house are to take one according to the number of persons in them; according to what each man should eat, you are to divide the lamb. 5 Your lamb shall be an unblemished male a year old; you may take it from the sheep or from the goats. 6 You shall keep it until the fourteenth day of the same month, then the whole assembly of the congregation of Israel is to kill it at twilight. 7 Moreover, they shall take some of the blood and put it on the two doorposts and on the lintel of the houses in which they eat it. 8 They shall eat the flesh that same night, roasted with fire, and they shall eat it with unleavened bread and bitter herbs. 9 Do not eat any of it raw or boiled at all with water, but rather roasted with fire, both its head and its legs along with its entrails. 10 And you shall not leave any of it over until morning, but whatever is left of it until morning, you shall burn with fire. 11 Now you shall eat it in this manner: with your loins girded, your sandals on your feet, and your staff in your hand; and you shall eat it in haste—it is the LORD'S Passover. 12 For I will go through the land of Egypt on that night, and will strike down all the firstborn in the land of Egypt, both man and beast; and against all the gods of Egypt I will execute judgments—I am the LORD. 13 The blood shall be a sign for you on the houses where you live; and when I see the blood I will pass over you, and no plague will befall you to destroy you when I strike the land of Egypt.

The blood of the Passover has the same origins as the Yom Kippur offering, the animal sacrifice of Abel that was used for 2,500 years. The metaphor of the blood representing human spiritual life (contrasted with animals with only physical life) was initiated in the time of Noah. A prohibition on drinking or eating animal blood was instituted because the blood was the physical life of the animal and metaphorically was tied to the life of mankind which is a spiritual life or connection to God that the animals didn't have. The prohibition on drinking animal blood was a metaphor depicting that a spiritual connection with God was broken. But restoration would come with the Messiah and a spiritual kingdom of God on earth.

> **Genesis 9:3-4 (NASB)** *Every moving thing that is alive shall be food for you; I give all to you, as I gave the green plant. 4 Only you shall not eat flesh **with its life, that is, it's blood.***

In the Exodus passover the blood (the spiritual life) is symbolically saving the future generations and the cultural future **and prosperity** of Israel and Judaism. Thus the Passover and the blood is symbolic of the beginnings of Judaism and the nation of Israel. The blood preserved the advent of the Jewish people and Israel, it allowed Judaism to become a reality.

Remember that when consciousness overtook mankind, the exit from the Garden, our day-by-day spiritual connection to God and life was lost. It wasn't quite lost as much as our consciousness overwhelmed our thinking and squelched that spiritual connection. Our human consciousness is a dominant factor in life, it's what drives us most of the time. So much so that when exiled from the Garden mankind could no longer hear that still small spiritual voice. In reality, certain prophets and rulers of Israel had temporary access to that spiritual voice. But it was never permanent. Thus David, for example, was distraught when that spiritual connection left him. David wrote of this in the Psalms praying,

> *Psalms 51:10-12 (NASB)*
> *10 Create in me a clean heart, O God,*
> *And renew a steadfast spirit within me.*
> *11 Do not cast me away from Your presence*
> ***And do not take Your Holy Spirit from me.***
> *12 Restore to me the joy of Your salvation*
> *And sustain me with a willing spirit.*

God probably didn't take away his Holy Spirit, it is mankind's consciousness that overwhelms the spiritual connection. The restoration of a better, or always available, spiritual connection then was what the new Kingdom of God, or Kingdom of Heaven that Jesus was proclaiming was all about. So, the Passover looks forward to a new spiritual connection with God, symbolized by the blood. This new age is prophesied by Jeremiah and it is called one of the unconditional covenants or promises to Israel.

Jeremiah lived during time of the Babylonian captivity. Nebuchadnezzar II, king of the Babylonian Empire besieged Jerusalem and finally capturing it and burning it down, including Solomon's Temple in 587 BC. Much of the population of Jerusalem and Judah, the Southern Kingdom were taken as hostages and deported to Babylon including Jeremiah and   Daniel, for which the Hebrew Bible's book of Daniel was named and where that definitive prophecy of the Messiah was written down. Daniel and many, most of the captives were apparently treated well while in Babylon. Captives were really hostages to insure that those back home would continue to pay tribute to Babylon. Jeremiah having been imprisoned and treated harshly by Judah's Kings, was treated better in Babylon, being allowed to choose where he would live.

> *Jeremiah[a] (c. 650 – c. 570 BC),[3] also called Jeremias[4] or the "weeping prophet",[5] was one of the major prophets of the Hebrew Bible. According to Jewish tradition, Jeremiah authored the Book of Jeremiah, the Books of Kings and the Book of Lamentations,[6] with the assistance and under the editorship of Baruch ben Neriah, his scribe and disciple. In addition to proclaiming many prophecies, the Book of Jeremiah goes into detail regarding the prophet's private life, his experiences, and his imprisonment.[7]*
>
> *Jeremiah is an important figure in both Judaism and Christianity. His words are read in synagogues as part of the Haftara and he is quoted in the New Testament.[8] Islam also regards Jeremiah as a prophet and his narrative is recounted in Islamic tradition.[9]*
>
> *https://en.wikipedia.org/wiki/Jeremiah*

The New Covenant

> ***Jeremiah 31:31-34 (NASB)*** *31 "Behold, days are coming," declares the LORD, "when I will make a new covenant with the house of Israel and with the house of Judah, 32 not like the covenant which I made with their fathers in the day I took them by the hand to bring them out of the land of Egypt, My covenant which they broke, although I was a husband to them," declares the LORD. 33 "But this is the covenant which I will make with the house of Israel after those days," declares the LORD, **"I will put My law within them and on their heart I will write it;** and I will be their God, and they shall be My people. 34 **They will not teach again, each man his neighbor and each man his brother, saying, 'Know the LORD,' for they will all know Me, from the least of them to the greatest of them,"** declares the LORD, **"for I will forgive their iniquity, and their sin I will remember no more."***

The New Covenant points forward to the new covenant with the Messiah. Three forward-pointing factors to Christianity are mentioned.

1. ***I will write my law upon their hearts.*** *An allusion to the new spiritual kingdom to come where the spiritual connection is designed to help us remember God's word and directions*

2. ***Everyone will know the Messiah.*** *Christianity takes over the entire Roman Empire, the story of Volume II*

3. ***I will forgive their sins.*** *The sign of the Cross and the fulfillment of the Yom Kippur sacrifice*

The Passover has a much deeper and complex connection to Christianity, however, one that requires examining the New Testament and fundamental principles in Christianity which promote a new way of thinking that drives prosperity. This connection will therefore await that discussion in Volume II.

Islam as the third Big God religion will round out the current discussion on the drivers of mankind's thinking that impacts the world.

Muhammad receiving his first revelation from the angel Gabriel, 1307

From the manuscript Jami' al-Tawarikh by Rashid-al-Din Hamadani, 1307
By Rashid al-Din Ṭabib - https://images.is.ed.ac.uk/luna/servlet/detail/UoEsha~4~4~60658~102846,
Public Domain, https://commons.wikimedia.org/w/index.php?curid=116545962

17. Islam: The Culture and Thinking

What is Islam??

Islam is a complex mix of politics and religion that requires delving into both historical and religious aspects to understand its values, ideas, and goals. These factors will serve to provide an understanding of the thinking and motivation of Islam and its followers and give us some insight into the motivation of the politics of Islamic nations. It is this thinking and motivation that directly affects both personal and national prosperity. We will begin examining Islam by looking at its historical beginnings as understood by Islam itself. Islam is thought of as an Arabic religion due to it's origins but Muslim populations are found in many other parts of the World. Maps of the Arab world and the worldwide distribution of Muslims are shown on the next pages.

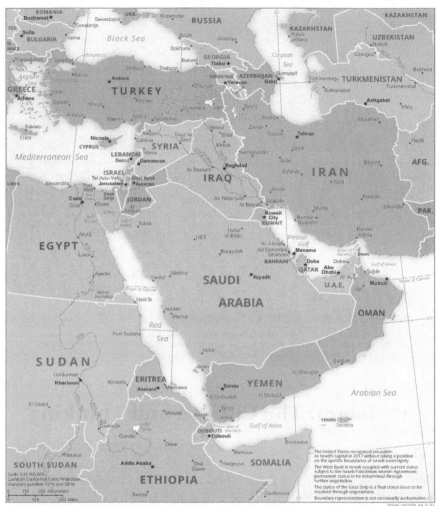

https://www.cia.gov/the-world-factbook/about/archives/2022/maps/world-regional/

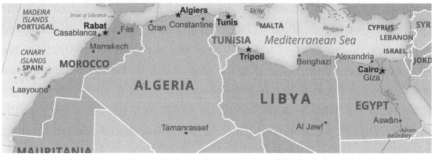

https://www.cia.gov/the-world-factbook/about/archives/2022/maps/world-regional/

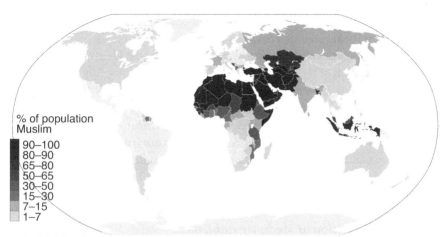

World Muslim population by percentage (Pew Research Center, 2014)
By M Tracy Hunter - Own work, CC BY-SA 3.0, https://commons.wikimedia.org/w/index.php?
curid=33660493

Muhammad

Islam's history is best explained by the life of Muhammad.

Muhammad's Life

The Prophet Muhammad (sometimes spelled Mohammad or
Mohammed) was born in Mecca, Saudi Arabia in the year 570 C.E. Muslim
tradition views Muhammad (c. 570 – June 8, 632) as the seal of the prophets
or the final prophet sent by Allah to reveal their faith to mankind. During the
last 22 years of his life, beginning at age 40 in 610 CE, according to the
earliest surviving biographies, Muhammad reported revelations that he
believed to be from God, conveyed to him through the archangel Gabriel
while he was meditating in a cave. The Prophet Muhammad was ordered by
the Angel to recite the words of Allah and he continued to receive revelations
from Allah throughout the remainder of his life. Muhammad's companions
memorized and recorded the content of these revelations, known as the
Quran.

During this time in the year 613, Muhammad in Mecca preached to the
people, imploring them to abandon polytheism and to worship one God and
that they should devote their lives to this God. Although some converted to
Islam, the leading Meccan authorities persecuted Muhammad and his
followers. This resulted in the Migration to Abyssinia of some Muslims (to the
Aksumite Empire). Many early converts to Islam were the poor, foreigners
and former slaves like Bilal ibn Rabah al-Habashi who was black. The
Meccan élite felt that Muhammad was destabilising their social order by

preaching about one God and about racial equality and that in the process he gave ideas to the poor and to their slaves.

After 12 years of the persecution of Muslims by the Meccans and the Meccan boycott of the Hashemites, Muhammad's relatives, Muhammad and the Muslims performed the Hijra ("emigration") to the city of Medina (formerly known as Yathrib) in 622. There, with the Medinan converts (Ansar) and the Meccan migrants (Muhajirun), **Muhammad in Medina established his political and religious authority.** *The Constitution of Medina was formulated, instituting a number of rights and responsibilities for the Muslim, Jewish, Christian and pagan communities of Medina, bringing them within the fold of one community—the Ummah.*

The Constitution of Medina established:

- *the security of the community*
- *religious freedoms*
- *the role of Medina as a sacred place (barring all violence and weapons)*
- *the security of women*
- *stable tribal relations within Medina*
- *a tax system for supporting the community in time of conflict*
- *parameters for exogenous political alliances*
- *a system for granting protection of individuals*
- *a judicial system for resolving disputes where non-Muslims could also use their own laws and have their own judges.*

All the tribes signed the agreement to defend Medina from all external threats and to live in harmony amongst themselves. Within a few years, two battles took place against the Meccan forces: first, the Battle of Badr in 624— a Muslim victory, and then a year later, when the Meccans returned to Medina, the Battle of Uhud, which ended inconclusively.

The Arab tribes in the rest of Arabia then formed a confederation and during the Battle of the Trench (March–April 627) besieged Medina, intent on finishing off Islam. In 628, the Treaty of Hudaybiyyah was signed between Mecca and the Muslims and was broken by Mecca two years later. After the signing of the Treaty of Hudaybiyyah many more people converted to Islam. At the same time, Meccan trade routes were cut off as Muhammad brought surrounding desert tribes under his control. By 629 Muhammad was victorious in the nearly bloodless conquest of Mecca, and by the time of his death in 632 (at the age of 62) he had united the tribes of Arabia into a single religious polity.

https://en.wikipedia.org/wiki/Islam#Muhammad_(610%E2%80%93632)

The significance of this account is that it acknowledges a number of characteristics of Islam that set it apart from past religions in terms of religion driving the politics and direction of politics. You could say it was not dissimilar to the Egyptian religion where the pharaoh was a god, and it certainly mimics Judaism in terms of moral authority. But Islam goes one level deeper. The interaction of Judaism with the surrounding people was generally a cooperative respect, live and let live. The biggest complaint against King Solomon was that he was too eager to allow idols from surrounding tribes to decorate the palace and be available in homes as well. There was no drive to turn all their neighbors into Jews. The drive to control everyone's religious beliefs through political force is unique to Islam.

We can assume that this brief description of the formulation of Islam is the Islamic correct version as Wikipedia is written by experts in the subject matter fields and its content is subject to peer review and change as those experts feel necessary. Islam then can be distinguished by the following features or characteristics.

The connection between the religious aspects of Judaism, Christianity and Islam is not mysterious as Islam follows Christianity by about 600 years. Muhammad is said to have received his first revelation in the Quran from God, Allah, around 610 AD and they continued until his death in 632 AD. During that time he was living in mixed communities containing both Jewish and Christian followers along with the Arabic mix of folk religions and agnostics. The city of Medina was actually noted for its strong Jewish community. Hence he was likely to have become familiar with many aspects of both Judaism and Christianity. The very short history from Wikipedia is illuminating as it reveals much the nature of Islam.

1. Muhammad desired to upgrade the religious thinking of the Arab tribes from the primitive polytheistic religions of early man to a belief in a single all-powerful creator God.
2. In doing so part of his desire was to upgrade the morality and fairness of the tribal customs and to meld the tribes into a much larger and therefore more stable political power.

3.Muhammad was exposed to Jewish teachings and was somewhat knowledgable of Judaism. There were also Christian communities in the region that contributed to Muhammad's modern religious knowledge as evidenced by the inclusion of Jesus into the Quran as a prophet of Allah.

4.The primary effort at unity in Medina however was political, the unifying agreement among all the tribes with different religions focused on political unity, not religious unity.

5.An Islamic nation is only considered complete where Islam is both a religion and a political power. That is where Islamic law is the law of the land for everyone, even those of other religions.

Islam is therefore a combined religious and political movement where its full implementation does not occur unless the Islamic political power is in force. Life in nations where Islamic political power rules are thus different than life where a more secular power rules. This occurs because Islamic moral and secular law is frozen from the time of Muhammad. That is, norms and standards come from the 7th century AD Arabic world and that code is especially frozen by the life of Muhammad because he is considered to have been without sin and thus everything he did is considered to be within the perfect life, and thus the model for life. Islam does morally and culturally include some Judaeo-Christian values which do contribute to improving life in the Arab world. They also ignore other basic Judaeo-Christian fundamentals that may undermine opportunities and prospects for prosperity.

Modern Islam might say that Western social freedoms and prosperity are Satanic, i.e., they tempt people to do bad things, which has more than a modicum of truth to it. And this is perhaps the motivation for political control. But that is also what happens in the Western Christian world where morality also enters common law as a legal deterrent to outrageous bad behavior.

Both Christian nations and Israel today have had civil laws that include some aspects of religious basis. The difference is that these laws are not dictated by the religious element of the country but come through a secular law-making body that is elected and answers to the population as a whole. This may seem like a small difference but it allows secular reviews and evaluations of all laws against standards of fairness and forces compromises between proponents of different views.   In strict Islamic countries religious laws are dictates of the religious leaders, and especially the top religious leader.   Iran has been an excellent example of this in action.   In other Islamic countries either a secular dictator or King rules or other religious views are strong enough to balance civil laws more toward a neutral religious flavor.

Pillars of Islam

Islam is also flavored by a number of ritualistic customs that are similar to those found in Judaism The fifth pillar, the Pilgrimage to Mecca is reminiscent of the pilgrimage of Jews to Jerusalem on the day of Pentecost and at some other holidays to pay tributes to the Temple. Differences between sects of Islam see the Pillars differently.

The five Pillars of Sunni Islam

1. *The Declaration of Faith*, the Shahada. *This is the ritualistic phrase that you might hear from a Muslim as the first statement is a speech. It is given in Arabic and states two principles of Islam. There is no god but Allah and Muhammad is the messenger of God. It is said five times a day during prayer.*

2. *Prayer, Salah*. *Prayers are done five times a day facing Mecca at dawn, noon, afternoon, evening and night. They are proceeded by ritual cleansing of hands, face and feet and involve prostrating ones self, bowing down from a kneeling position with 7 bones or points of the body touching the ground. The forehead and nose, two hands, two knees and two sets of toes.*

3. *Alms giving or charity*, Zakat. *This is giving about 2.5% of ones wealth to the local Muslim community.*

4. *Fasting, Sawm. The fast occurs from dawn to dusk during the holy month of Ramadan.*

5. *A pilgrimage to Mecca during the twelfth month of the lunar calendar while dressed in white sheets so that all look alike. There are specific paths that are to be taken in the sanctuary in Mecca and in an area outside.*
   https://en.wikipedia.org/wiki/Five_Pillars_of_Islam

Pillars of Shia Isalm

Shia Islam has 5 main beliefs which are called pillars and relate to tenants of faith, the oneness of God, God's justice, prophethood of Muhammad, succession of Muhammad and the day of judgement and resurrection.   In addition they have ten other practices that must be performed.

1. *5 daily prayers*
2. *Fasting during Ramadan*
3. *Zakat, alms giving*
4. *Khums, a 20% tax to the Imams*
5. *Pilgrimage to Mecca*
6. *Jihad, striving for the cause of God*
7. *Enjoining good*
8. *Forbidding wrong*
9. *Expressing love toward good*
10. *Expressing disassociation and hatred towards evil.*

Reference: https://en.wikipedia.org/wiki/Five_Pillars_of_Islam

Islam's religious books

Islam has not one but two religious texts that together define the religion.   The Quran or Koran is the book of Allah's words given to Muhammad during his lifetime.   The second book is the Hadith, a collection of the actions and sayings of Muhammad during his lifetime.

The Quran (Koran)

The Quran is the fundamental source of guidance and is considered the literal word of god, not just inspired by God. But Muslims do not rely on translations to extract meaning but rely on an expert and critical interpretation of the text.   That is the Quran is not easily read and understood even by a cursory reading of the original Arabic text.   This makes translations into other languages almost useless in understanding and makes it very difficult for non-Arabic-speaking Muslims to easily understand either the Theology or the Philosophy of Life within its covers.

Nature of the Quran

1. The Quran, which was dictated to Mohammad by an angel over Mohammad's lifetime, follows the flow of Mohammad's efforts and encounters with Arabic tribes and thus comments on that effort from two separate historical periods in Muhammad's life.
2. First his efforts to convert the tribes in Mecca by persuasion
3. Secondly his retreat to Medina and the subsequent military battles where he won over and unified all the regional Arab tribes.
4. The Quran is thus a book with two distinct approaches to the establishment of Islamic ideas, the use of persuasion, and the use of political power.
5. This division of approaches to Islam's founding is not physically separated in the Quran, chapters and verses are not in chronological order nor are the two phases of Islam's establishment separated into chronological parts. Chapters and verses are interspersed with portions from each phase. Each verse however is identified as to the period it comes from and is also associated chronologically with all the other verses from the same period.
6. Chronological order of Meccan surahs (chapters)
    *   One chronological order proposed by Abu al-Qasim `Umar ibn Muhammad ibn `Abd al-Kafi and considered the "traditional order" consists of 86 chapters, as follows:
    *   96, 68, 73, 74, 1, 111, 81, 87, 92, 89,
    *   93, 94, 103, 100, 108, 102, 107, 109, 105, 113,
    *   114, 112, 53, 80, 97, 91, 85, 95, 106, 101,
    *   75, 104, 77, 50, 90, 86, 54, 38, 7, 72,
    *   36, 25, 35, 19, 20, 56, 26, 27, 28, 17,
    *   10, 11, 12, 15, 6, 37, 31, 34, 39, 40,
    *   41, 42, 43, 44, 45, 46, 51, 88, 18, 16,
    *   71, 14, 21, 23, 32, 52, 67, 69, 70, 78,
    *   79, 82, 84, 30, 29, 83.
7. The reason for this tight control over time sequencing of verses comes from necessity in dealing with three significant Islamic beliefs.
    *   Each verse in the Quran is to be understood as real instructions or directions from Allah to each Muslim today.
8. There are no verses of purely historical information or parables where directions, events, and actions can be taken as informational and not directions from Allah.
9. There are different and conflicting direct commands of Allah for different periods of time that are resolved by believing that the latter commands take precedence over earlier commands to resolve these conflicting directions.
    https://en.wikipedia.org/wiki/Quran - https://en.wikipedia.org/wiki/Meccan_surah - https://en.wikipedia.org/wiki/Medinan_surah

The Quran (/kʊrˈɑːn/, kuurr-AHN;[i] vocalized Arabic: ٱلْقُرْآن, Quranic Arabic: ٱلْقُرٰءَان, al-Qurʾān [alqurˈʔaːn],[ii] lit. 'the recitation' or 'the lecture'), also romanized Qur'an or Koran,[iii] is the central religious text of Islam, believed by Muslims to be a revelation from God. It is organized in 114 chapters (pl.: سور suwar, sing.: سورة sūrah), which consist of verses (pl.: آيات ʾāyāt, sing.: آية ʾāyah, cons.: ʾayat). In addition to its religious significance, it is widely regarded as the finest work in Arabic literature, and has significantly influenced the Arabic language.

Muslims believe that the Quran was orally revealed by God to the final prophet, Muhammad, through the archangel Gabriel incrementally over a period of some 23 years, beginning on Laylat al-Qadr, when Muhammad was 40, and concluding in 632, the year of his death at age 61–62. Muslims regard the Quran as Muhammad's most important miracle, a proof of his prophethood; and as the culmination of a series of divine messages starting with those revealed to Adam, including the Tawrat, the Zabur (Psalms) and the Injil (Gospel).

The Quran is believed by Muslims to be not simply divinely inspired, but the literal words of God, and provides a complete code of conduct that offers guidance in every walk of their life. This divine character attributed to the Quran led Muslim theologians to fiercely debate whether the Quran was either "created or uncreated." According to tradition, several of Muhammad's companions served as scribes, recording the revelations. Shortly after the prophet's death, the Quran was compiled by the companions, who had written down or memorized parts of it. Caliph Uthman established a standard version, now known as the Uthmanic codex, which is generally considered the archetype of the Quran known today. There are, however, variant readings, with mostly minor differences in meaning. Controversy over the Quran's content integrity has rarely become an issue among Muslim history [iv] despite some hadiths stating that the textual integrity of the Quran was not preserved.

The Quran assumes the reader's familiarity with major narratives recounted in the Biblical and apocryphal scriptures. It summarizes some, dwells at length on others and, in some cases, presents alternative accounts and interpretations of events. The Quran describes itself as a book of guidance for humankind (2:185). It sometimes offers detailed accounts of specific historical events, and it often emphasizes the moral significance of an event over its narrative sequence. ***Supplementing the Quran with explanations for some cryptic Quranic narratives, and rulings that also provide the basis for Islamic law in most denominations*** *of Islam, are hadiths—oral and written traditions believed to describe words and actions of Muhammad. During prayers, the Quran is recited only in Arabic.* Someone who has memorized the entire Quran is called a hafiz. Ideally, verses are recited with a special kind of prosody reserved for this purpose, called tajwid. During the month of Ramadan, Muslims typically complete the recitation of the whole Quran during tarawih prayers.

https://en.wikipedia.org/wiki/Quran

Translation and Interpretation

- *Translating the Quran has always been problematic and difficult. Many argue that the Quranic text cannot be reproduced in another language* or form. *Furthermore, an Arabic word may have a range of meanings depending on the context, making an accurate translation even more difficult.*
- *The Quranic content is concerned with basic Islamic beliefs including the existence of God and the resurrection. Narratives of the early prophets, ethical and legal subjects, historical events of Muhammad's time, charity and prayer also appear in the Quran. The Quranic verses contain general exhortations regarding right and wrong and historical events are related to outline general moral lessons. Verses pertaining to natural phenomena have been interpreted by Muslims as an indication of the authenticity of the Quranic message.* **The style of the Quran has been called "allusive", with commentaries needed to explain what is being referred to** *—"events are referred to, but not narrated; disagreements are debated without being explained; people and places are mentioned, but rarely named."*
- *In order to extrapolate the meaning of a particular Quranic verse, Muslims rely on exegesis, or commentary rather than a direct translation of the text.*

https://en.wikipedia.org/wiki/Quran

The Hadith

A second primary source for Islamic truth is the Hadith.   This is a collection of the words, actions, and sayings of Muhammad, transmitted through various narratives. This is the source of most of the Sharia Laws and has different compilations based on different sects of Islam.   It is somewhat analogous to the Jewish Oral Torah.   The thinking of Muhammad, as these are reputed to be, was not written down during Muhammad's lifetime nor shortly after his death but was compiled in the 8th and 9th centuries, one to two hundred years later.   There are also different compilations by different sects of Islam, e.g., Sunni, Shia, etc. with varying degrees of acceptance as valid. There is therefore no uniform agreement on what constitutes Islam. The Quran is the only universally accepted authority but is recognized as difficult to understand.

Ḥadīth (/'hædɪθ/or /hɑː'diːθ/; *Arabic:* حديث, *ḥadīṯ, Arabic pronunciation: [ħadiːθ]; pl. aḥādīth,* أحاديث, *'aḥādīṯ, Arabic pronunciation: [ʔaħaːdiːθ], lit. 'talk' or 'discourse') or Athar (Arabic:* أثر, *'Aṯar, lit. 'remnant' or 'effect') refers to what most Muslims and the mainstream Islamic sects believe to be a record of the words, actions, and the silent approval of the Islamic prophet Muhammad as transmitted through chains of narrators. In other words, the ḥadīth are attributed reports about what Muhammad said and did (see: Oral tradition).*

Ḥadīth is the Arabic word for things like a report or an account (of an event).: For many, the authority of hadith is a source for religious and moral guidance known as Sunnah, which ranks second only to that of the Quran (which Muslims hold to be the word of God revealed to Muhammad). **While the number of verses pertaining to law in the Quran is relatively small, hadith are considered by many to give direction on everything from details of religious obligations (such as Ghusl or Wudu, ablutions for salat prayer), to the correct forms of salutations and the importance of benevolence to slaves. Thus for many, the "great bulk" of the rules of Sharia are derived from hadith, rather than the Quran. Among scholars of Sunni Islam the term hadith may include not only the words, advice, practices, etc. of Muhammad, but also those of his companions.** *In Shia Islam, hadith are the embodiment of the sunnah, the words and actions of Muhammad and his family, the Ahl al-Bayt (The Twelve Imams and Muhammad's daughter, Fatimah).*

Unlike the Quran, not all Muslims believe that hadith accounts (or at least not all hadith accounts) are divine revelation. *Different collections of hadīth would come to differentiate the different branches of the Islamic faith. Some Muslims believe that Islamic guidance should be based on the Quran only, thus rejecting the authority of hadith;* **some further claim that most hadiths are fabrications (pseudepigrapha) created in the 8th and 9th centuries AD, and which are falsely attributed to Muhammad.** *Historically, some sects of the Kharijites also rejected the hadiths, while Mu'tazilites rejected the hadiths as the basis for Islamic law, while at the same time accepting the Sunnah and Ijma.* **Muslims who criticise the hadith emphasise that the problems in**

the Islamic world come partly from the traditional elements of the
hadith and seek to reject those teachings.

Because some hadith contain questionable and even contradictory
statements, the authentication of hadith became a major field of study in
Islam. In its classic form a hadith consists of two parts—the chain of
narrators who have transmitted the report (the isnad), and the main text of
the report (the matn). Individual hadith are classified by Muslim clerics and
jurists into categories such as sahih ("authentic"), hasan ("good"), or da'if
("weak"). However, different groups and different scholars may classify a
hadith differently.

https://en.wikipedia.org/wiki/Hadith#

Hadith compilation

The hadith literature in use today is based on spoken reports in
circulation after the death of Muhammad. Unlike the Quran, hadith were not
promptly written down during Muhammad's lifetime or immediately after
his death. Hadith were evaluated orally to written and gathered into large
collections during the 8th and 9th centuries, generations after Muhammad's
death, after the end of the era of the Rashidun Caliphate, over 1,000 km
(600 mi) from where Muhammad lived.

"Many thousands of times" more numerous than the verses of the Quran,
hadith have been described as resembling layers surrounding the "core" of
Islamic beliefs (the Quran). Well-known, widely accepted hadith make up the
narrow inner layer, with a hadith becoming less reliable and accepted with
each layer stretching outward.

The reports of Muhammad's (and sometimes his companions') behavior
collected by hadith compilers include details of ritual religious practice such
as the five salat (obligatory Islamic prayers) that are not found in the Quran,
as well as everyday behavior such as table manners, dress, and posture.
Hadith are also regarded by Muslims as important tools for
understanding things mentioned in the Quran but not explained, a
source for tafsir (commentaries written on the Quran).

Some important elements, which are today taken to be a long-held part
of Islamic practice and belief are not mentioned in the Quran, but are
reported in hadiths. Therefore, Muslims usually maintain that hadiths are a
necessary requirement for the true and proper practice of Islam, as it gives
Muslims the nuanced details of Islamic practice and belief in areas where the
Quran is silent. An example is the obligatory prayers, which are commanded
in the Quran, but explained in hadith.

https://en.wikipedia.org/wiki/Hadith#

Islamic Foundations Drawn from Judaism and Christianity

Islam is a tribal Big God Religion in the mold of Judaism. Like Judaism it contains theology, philosophy of life, moral codes and cultural traditions and rituals. The objective of Muhammad was to break the desert nomads of their primitive gods and religions and, as with Judaism, create a strong cultural basis to give them a group identity which the nomads had not had. This made Judaism an easy model to follow, at least in principle. Islam also has a strong connection to Christianity as the timeframe is the 6th and 7th century AD and both Jewish and Christian followers, synagogues and churches, and books are available in the area.

The Quran includes a number of accounts from the Hebrew Bible (the Christian Old Testament). These include numerous Adam and Eve stories, Noah's Ark, Jonah and the whale, and numerous accounts of Abraham and his progeny connecting to Moses and the Hebrew exodus from Egypt. There are deviations from the Old Testament stories, such as Adam being the one tempted, not Eve, and also being tempted to eat from the Tree of Life rather than the Tree of Knowledge of Good and Evil. Thus they miss the whole Garden of Eden metaphor of mankind knowing God and then through consciousness, taking on humanity's malevolent nature by knowing good AND evil.

But in general, Islam appears to accept Judaism as a valid Big God model of religion. Islam counts, as its own, several prophets from Judaism including; Noah, Abraham, Jacob, Joseph, Moses, David, Solomon, Job, Aaron, Zacharias, John, Jesus, Elias, Ishmael, Elisha, Jonah and Lot. These prophets are all credited with bearing witness on the Day of Judgement as to who has rejected Islam. Another story from the Old Testament, that of Cain and Abel, is also retold, this time with a twist that appears to come from an extra-biblical Jewish account. (Per a nineteenth-century Quranic historian.)

> *Abel justly warned Cain that God only accepted the sacrifice of those that are righteous in their doings. He further went on to tell Cain that if Cain did indeed try to slay him, Abel would not retaliate and slay him because the God-fearing would never murder for the sake of envy. Abel then told Cain*

that in murdering him, he would carry the weight not only of his sin but also
of the sins of his victim. The victim, as a result, in suffering the injustice,
would be forgiven his own sins and the murderer, while being warned, would
consequently increase his own sin. Abel preached powerfully and reminded
Cain that the punishment for murder would be that he would spend the
afterlife in the fires of Hell.
https://en.wikipedia.org/wiki/Cain_and_Abel_in_Islam

Jesus, the Messiah, in the Quran

The Quran also refers to Jesus and his mother Mary as the only sinless people who have ever lived, but not to be outdone, Muhammad himself is added to that list by his followers per Islamic tradition. This is the basis for anything that Muhammad did during his lifetime as being not just legitimate, but the role model for Muslims to today, thus making many 7th century practices a model for living.

Jesus is also referred to as a prophet of Allah and as a performer of miracles. One of these miracles, bringing clay birds to life, comes from the extra-Biblical second-century book, the Infancy Gospel of Thomas. From this we can see that while Christianity had determined what books legitimately described Christianity several hundred years earlier, the books excluded were still in circulation, especially in the remote nomadic tribes of interest to Muhammad.

In the Quran, Jesus is described as the Messiah (al-Masīḥ), miraculously born of a virgin, performing miracles, accompanied by his disciples, rejected by the Jewish religious establishment, but not as crucified or dying on the cross (nor resurrected), rather as miraculously saved by God and ascending into heaven.

> *The Quran places Jesus among the greatest prophets, and mentions him*
> *with various titles. The prophethood of Jesus is preceded by that of Yahya*
> *and succeeded by Muhammad, the latter of whom Jesus is reported to have*
> *prophesied by using the name Ahmad.*
>
> *There is a variety of variable interpretations in Islam about Jesus Christ.*
> *Mainstream interpretations of the Quran lack the Orthodox Christian*
> *philosophy theological concepts of Christology regarding divine hypostasis,*
> *so to many it appears the Quran rejects Christ because in the Christian view*
> *of the doctrine of the divinity of Jesus Christ as God incarnate being a man,*

or as the literal Son of God in human flesh, as it apparently denies the doctrine of the divine humanity of Jesus as God in several verses, and also insinuates that Jesus Christ did not claim to be personally God (God the Father). Muslims believe that Jesus' original message was altered (taḥrīf), after his being raised alive. The monotheism (tawḥīd) of Jesus is emphasized in the Quran. Like all prophets in Islam, Jesus is also called a Muslim, as he preached that his followers should adopt the 'straight path' (Ṣirāṭ al-Mustaqīm). Jesus is attributed with a vast number of miracles in Islamic tradition.

In some views of Islamic eschatology, it is claimed that Jesus Christ will return in the Second Coming with Imam Mahdi to kill the Al-Masih ad-Dajjal ('The False Messiah'), after which with the ancient tribes Gog and Magog (Ya'jūj Ma'jūj) would disperse[citation needed]. After these creatures would miraculously perish, Imam Mahdi and Jesus would rule the entire world, establish peace and justice, and die after a reign of 40 years. Some Muslims believe that he would then be buried alongside Muhammad at the fourth reserved tomb of the Green Dome in Medina. These are apocryphal traditions related to hadith-based traditions.[citation needed]
https://en.wikipedia.org/wiki/Jesus_in_Islam

Islam's Future Messiah

Like Judaism, Islam has a belief in a Messiah that is worth addressing here.   Islam believes that they will have a Messiah (The Mahdi -transliterated from Arabic) come to them and leads Islam to conquer the world.   **Interestingly he is said to appear just before Jesus returns and the Mahdi supports Jesus.** The Mahdi is said to be the descendent of the eleventh Imam, who died in 874 AD. He is also said to have been born, but has been put in hiding by Allah until the time is right for his appearance (occultation). He is also called the twelfth Imam and has not been revealed because the Muslim world has not been faithful enough or prepared enough to take over the world. This idea is almost identical to the Jewish beliefs held in the first century AD about their own Messiah being reborn in every generation, but not revealed because the time was not right to overthrow Rome. One of the more well known believers in the Mahdi is Mahmoud Ahmadinejad, the only non cleric president of Iran from 2005 to 2013. He was an engineer and also a hard line Muslim who reversed some of the more liberal Muslim traditions in

Iran instituting a crackdown on women with "improper hijabs" and jailed and tortured political opponents. The Middle East Forum reference below gives a rather extensive discussion of the Mahdi which is a widely held belief in Iran.

https://en.wikipedia.org/wiki/Mahmoud_Ahmadinejad#Human_rights
https://www.huffpost.com/entry/ahmadinejad-the-mahdi_b_2131974
https://www.meforum.org/1985/ahmadinejad-and-the-mahdi

The Mahdi *(Arabic: المَهْدِيّ, romanized: al-Mahdī, lit. 'the Guided') is a messianic figure in Islamic eschatology who is believed to appear at the end of times to rid the world of evil and injustice. He is said to be a descendant of Muhammad who will appear shortly before the prophet ʿĪsā (Jesus) and lead Muslims to rule the world.*

Though the Mahdi is not referenced in the Quran, and is absent from several canonical compilations of hadith – including the two most-revered Sunni hadith collections: Sahih al-Bukhari and Sahih Muslim – he is mentioned in other hadith literature. The doctrine of the mahdi seems to have gained traction during the confusion and unrest of the religious and political upheavals of the first and second centuries of Islam. Among the first references to the Mahdi appear in the late 7th century, when the revolutionary Mukhtar ibn Abi Ubayd (c. 622–687) declared Muhammad ibn al-Hanafiyya, a son of caliph Ali (r. 656–661), to be the Mahdi. Although the concept of a Mahdi is not an essential doctrine in Islam, it is popular among Muslims. It has been a part of the ʿaqīdah (creed) of Muslims for 1,400 years. Over centuries, there have been a vast number of Mahdi claimants.

The Mahdi features in both Shi'a and Sunni branches of Islam, though they differ extensively on his attributes and status. Among Twelver Shi'as, the Mahdi is believed to be Muhammad al-Mahdi, son of the eleventh Imam, Hasan al-Askari (d. 874), who is said to have been in occultation (ghayba) by divine will. This is rejected by the Sunnis, who assert that the Mahdi has not been born yet.

https://en.wikipedia.org/wiki/Mahdi

Theology and sin

The view of sin in Islam is also viewed somewhat similarly to Judaism and Christianity. There are similarities between what Islam considers as the important sins, and the Ten Commandments, and teachings about morality are similar in many aspects. The big difference is in the nature of who has responsibility for God forgiving one's sins. In Judaism and

Christianity God is the one to take action and forgive the follower's sins through a mechanism that is totally outside of the control of the follower. The YomKipper Day of Atonement Temple sacrifice established that principle for Judaism. The crucifixion of Christ, the Messiah, on the cross, painted the picture of the event that would bring about the forgiveness of everyone's sins, totally apart from any action on the sinner's part.

In Islam, Allah forgives one's sins but there are actions and rituals that will aid in that forgiveness. And in the end, Allah determines just whose sins are forgiven, based on their life and ritual religious practices. Thus the Muslim believer is left in a state of uncertainty, never knowing and sometimes, or often, doubting that he will make it to heaven and escape punishment. This is why dying as a martyr in the service of Islam is so well thought of, it guarantees entrance into heaven and additionally has great rewards there.

Going to heaven is totally conditioned on Allah's judgment of the relative merits of a Muslim's good works vs his sins. As with most religions there are some suggestions for what the follower can do to enhance the probabilities of being found acceptable and thus eligible for heaven.

Sin, morality and repentance

Sins and good deeds are big issues for Muslims. Islam has tabulated 60 or so really bad sins and many more moderate sins. All sins against God are to be handled directly with Allah by repentance which includes repentance, remorse, and resolution to change one's behavior. Retribution is also required for sins against other people. There are also lists of good deeds that can offset sins. Smiling at someone can be a good deed that offsets some bad deeds. In terms of eternal punishment or rewards Allah weighs one's good deeds against one's sins and determines whether one is punished or rewarded.

1.   *Sin is an important concept in Islamic ethics that Muslims view as being anything that goes against the commands of God or breaching the laws and norms laid down by religion. Islam teaches that sin is an act and not a state of being.* **It is believed that God weighs an individual's good deeds against their sins on the Day of Judgement and**

punishes those individuals whose evil deeds outweigh their good deeds.[The Quran Surah Al-A'raf (7:8-9)

2. *The Quran describes these sins throughout the texts and demonstrates that some sins are more punishable than others in the hereafter.* **A clear distinction is made between major sins (al-Kabirah) and minor sins (al-Sagha'ir) (Q53:31–32), indicating that if an individual stays away from the major sins then they will be forgiven of the minor sins.** *Sources differ on the exact meanings of the different terms for sin used in the Islamic tradition.*
   https://en.wikipedia.org/wiki/Islamic_views_on_sin#Repentance_of_sin

Islam's Ten Commandments

There are two sources of direction for Muslims, the Quran, the words of God given to Muhammad and the Hadith, a collection of the teachings, deeds and sayings of Muhammad. These two books contain the directions for all Muslims with **the Hadith considered to be the body of norms to be followed in worship and in everyday life.** Muslim theologians claim the Golden Rule, "Do unto others" is implicit in both books and some have compiled a list somewhat equivalent to the Ten Commandments.

1. *"Worship only God," (17:22);*
2. *"Be kind, honourable and humble to one's parents," (17:23-24) ;*
3. *"Be neither miserly nor wasteful," (17:26-29);*
4. *"Do not engage in 'mercy killings' for fear of starvation," God will provide. (17:31);*
5. *"Do not commit adultery," (17:32);*
6. *"Do not kill unjustly," (17:33);*
7. *"Care for orphaned children,"(17:34);*
8. *"Keep one's promises:" (17:34);*
9. *"Be honest and fair in one's interactions," (17:35);*
10. *"Do not be arrogant in one's claims or beliefs," (17:36-37).*
    https://en.wikipedia.org/wiki/Morality_in_Islam

Major Islamic Sins (with examples, conditions, etc

1. *Shirk (associating partners with Allah)* **(I.e., the Christian Trinity)**
2. *Committing murder (killing a human being that Allah has declared (undefiled, unspoiled, etc) without a just cause)* **(per the Quran Jews and Christians are / can be inherently bad people for rejecting Allah and everyone else is of no value and always condemned rightly - ie, it's not murder to kill such people)**

3.   *Practicing black magic*

4.   *Leaving daily prayers (Salah)* **(5 times a day facing Meccah)**

5.   *Zakat evasion (not giving obligatory charity)*

6.   *Not fasting on the days of Ramadan (without an excuse)*

7.   *Not performing Hajj (while being able to do so)* **(the Pilgrimage to Mecca)**

8.   *Cutting off the ties of relationships* **(the Quran specifies exceptions, divorce, etc)**

9.   *Committing Adultery or Fornication (Zina)*

10. *Committing Sodomy (but you can have sex with a condom or birth control with your wife)*

11. *Taking or paying interest (Riba)* **(Islamic Banking has special rules)**

12. *Consuming the property of an orphan*

13. *Lying about Allah and his messenger* **(any criticism of Allah or Muhammad could be any discussion or explanation of Christianity)**

14. *Turning back when the army advances (running from the battlefield)*

15. *The unjust leader* **(Every government official will make sure the clerics approve of every decision before taking action)**...
Reference: https://en.wikipedia.org/wiki/Morality_in_Islam

Islam's Key Directive: You are your Brother's keeper

This is defined by two overall objectives each Muslim is to seek.

1. Make God's pleasure the objective of life

2. Instruct others on what is right and forbid what is wrong. This is based on Muhammad saying, "I was sent to perfect the ethical conduct." This second objective is a very strong and a direct command to Muslims.

Islam is full of morality issues derived from the Quran and the Hadith. These include many common points that Judaism and Christianity contain such as kindness to people and animals, charity, forgiveness honesty patience, justice, respect of elders, keeping promises, controlling one's anger, love of God, Muhammad and other believers.

Beyond all the morality, however, a Muslim is especially obligated to straighten out the erroneous thinking and actions of others, <u>even by physical force if possible.</u>

However, Quran is clear about the importance of Muslims taking action to "enjoin what is good and forbid what is wrong". Quranic verses 3:104, 3:110, 9:71, 9:112, 5:105, 31:17 all contain some variation of that phrase. A famous hadith quotes the Islamic prophet Muhammad as saying:

"Whoever amongst you sees an evil, he must change it with his hand. If he is not able to do so, then with his tongue. And if he is not able to do so, then with his heart, and that is the weakest form of faith".

(Mutazilite and Shia Imamis quote different traditions than this Sunni Hadith, but **all agree on the Quran and on "the existence of the duty" to command and forbid**.)

Reference: https://en.wikipedia.org/wiki/Morality_in_Islam

Human Nature, Fitra

This idea of the need to straighten out the religious beliefs of others is further strengthened by the belief that everyone was a Muslim at birth and if not a Muslim currently, they are in revolt of their basic nature.

Islam believes mankind's initial primitive condition was in a covenant with God, Allah, before they were born so that they could not plead ignorance of Allah at the Day of Judgement.   Basically they assume everyone is a Muslim from his nature at birth and if he disregards his nature, Islam is here to remind and help him see the light. This view gives them license to do just about anything to "restore unbelievers to their roots.   This also helps form the logic for instilling Sharia Law wherever Muslims form a majority and can control governments. Sharia is not only right for Muslims but for everyone who is a denier of their true Muslim nature.

Fitra or fitrah (Arabic: فطرة; ALA-LC: fiṭrah) is an Arabic word that means 'original disposition', 'natural constitution' or 'innate nature'. In Islam, fitra is the innate human nature that recognizes the oneness of God (tawhid). It may entail either the state of purity and innocence in which Muslims believe all humans to be born, or the ability to choose or reject God's guidance. The Quran states that humans were created in the most perfect form (95:4), and were endowed with a primordial nature (30:30). Furthermore, God took a covenant from all children of Adam, even before they were sent to Earth's worldly realm, regarding his Lordship (7:172–173). This covenant is considered to have left an everlasting imprint on the human *soul, with the Quran emphasizing that on the Day of Judgment no one will be able to plead ignorance of this event (7:172–173).*

Fitra is also associated with the divine spirit that God, according to the Quran, breathed into Adam (15:29, 32:9, 38:72). This means that the fitra represents the true essence of Adam, who was taught all the names by God (2:31). In the Quran, fitra is linked to the concept of hanif (30:30); a term that is often associated with Abraham but it also includes individuals who turn away from erroneous beliefs and instead embrace faith in the unity of God.

This teaching is echoed in prophetic traditions that reiterate the existence of intrinsic human nature at birth. Hence, in Islamic belief, humans are deemed blessed to have the ability to comprehend and affirm the existence of God. However, over time, people tend to disregard and overlook their innate nature, causing it to become obscured and deeply buried within them. In that vein, Islam is perceived as a means to assist individuals in rediscovering and reconnecting with their original nature, ultimately re-establishing their primordial relationship with God.
https://en.wikipedia.org/wiki/Fitra

The Quran states "fitra" this way.

According to Quran 7:172-173, God called upon all souls to witness His lordship before being sent to the world so that no one could plead ignorance on the Day of Judgment. ""Lest you say on the Day of Resurrection, "As for us, we were heedless of this," or lest you say, "Our fathers associated others with God before us, and we were their offspring after them. What, wilt Thou destroy us for what the vain-doers did?"". Some commentators, including al Razi, have argued that the inability of humans to recall the pretemporal covenant mentioned in Quran 7:172-173 implies that it is symbolic and therefore cannot be the basis of human responsibility. However, The Study Quran suggests that this event should be viewed within the wider context of the Quran and its prophetic history. According to the Study Quran, "this pretemporal recognition of God's Lordship can be understood as creating an innate disposition in human beings toward recognizing and worshipping God during earthly life and toward accepting the prophets and the messages they bring as "reminders" of what human beings already know inwardly, but have merely forgotten."
https://en.wikipedia.org/wiki/Fitra

Moral Law Applied: Sharia (Religious) Law

Sharia Law is the application of the rules identified in the Quran and the Hadith as if they were the secular laws of a nation. There are major disagreements about the application of Sharia Law. Some countries adopt modern human rights notions and European standards while other fundamentalist views are to apply it exactly like it is written. Often it is only applied in Family Law, disagreements between people in the community.

Sharia (/ʃəˈriːə/; Arabic: شَرِيعَة, romanized: sharīʿah [ʃaˈriːʕa]) is a body of religious law that forms a part of the Islamic tradition based on scriptures of Islam, particularly the Quran and the Hadith. In Arabic, the term sharīʿah refers to God's immutable divine law and this referencing is contrasted with fiqh, which refers to its interpretations by Islamic scholars. Fiqh, practical application side of sharia in a sense, was elaborated over the centuries by legal opinions issued by qualified jurists and sharia has never been the sole valid legal system in Islam historically; it has always been used alongside customary law from the beginning, and applied in courts by ruler-appointed judges, integrated with various economic, criminal and administrative laws issued by Muslim rulers.

Traditional theory of Islamic jurisprudence recognizes four sources of Sharia: the Quran, sunnah (a type of oral tradition narrated through a chain of transmission and recorded and classified as authentic hadith), ijma (may be understood as ijma al-ummah – a whole community consensus, or ijma al-aimmah – a consensus by religious authorities.) and analogical reasoning. Five prominent legal schools of Sunni Islam, Hanafi, Maliki, Shafi'i, Hanbali and Zahiri, developed Sunni methodologies for deriving rulings from scriptural sources using a process known as ijtihad. Traditional jurisprudence distinguishes two principal branches of law, rituals and social dealings; subsections family law, relationships (commercial, political / administrative) and criminal law, in a wide range of topics. Its rulings are concerned with ethical standards as much as legal norms, assigning actions to one of five categories: mandatory, recommended, neutral, abhorred, and prohibited.

Over time, on the basis of mentioned studies legal schools have emerged, reflecting the preferences of particular societies and governments, as well as Islamic scholars or imams on theoretical and practical applications of laws and regulations. Although sharia is presented as a form of governance in addition to its other aspects, especially by the contemporary Islamist *understanding, some researchers see the early history of Islam, which was also modelled and exalted by most Muslims; not a period when sharia was dominant, but a kind of "secular Arabic expansion".*

According to human rights groups, some of the classical sharia practices involve serious violations of basic human rights, gender equality and freedom of expression, and the practices of countries governed by sharia are criticized. The European Court of Human Rights in Strasbourg (ECtHR) ruled in several cases that Sharia is "incompatible with the fundamental principles of democracy".

In the 21st century, approaches to sharia in the Muslim world vary greatly and the role of Sharia has become an increasingly contested topic around the world. Beyond sectarian differences, fundamentalists advocate the complete and uncompromising implementation of "exact/pure sharia" without modifications, while modernists argue that it can/ should be brought into line with human rights and other contemporary issues such as democracy, minority rights, freedom of thought, women's rights and banking by new jurisprudences. In Muslim majority countries, traditional laws have been widely used with or changed by European models. Judicial procedures and legal education have been brought in line with European practice likewise. While the constitutions of most Muslim-majority states contain references to Sharia, its rules are largely retained only in family law. The Islamic revival of the late 20th century brought calls by Islamic movements for full implementation of Sharia, including hudud corporal punishments, such as stoning.

https://en.wikipedia.org/wiki/Sharia

Under an Islamic government, many of these Islamic major sins could or would become civil laws applicable to non-Muslims as well as Muslims. Even #15 in the list above of major sins, the unjust leader, could be applied to any member of the civil government for simple violations of Islamic laws. In Saudi Arabia Christianity can not be taught (outside the small Christian conclaves) or a written bible printed, because that becomes an attack on Allah or Muhammad, a major sin. In effect sins and laws are determined by the religious leaders much the same as the Jewish communities depend on the Rabbi to determine what is the right and wrong thing to do about complex matters. The difference is that the Rabbi's opinion is just his opinion while the Islamic Cleric's view IS the law in truly Islamic-ruled countries.

Loaning Money, Riba

A specific example of Islamic Law in today's secular world deals with borrowing and lending money, that is financial credit. In the Muslim world borrowing and lending money where interest is paid to the lender is a crime if not frowned upon. The Muslim world thus has to do some very precise tip-toeing and develop some convoluted practices to allow some forms of credit to exist.

Although Islamic financing contains many prohibitions—such as no consumption of alcohol, gambling, uncertainty, etc. -- **the belief that "all forms of interest are riba and hence prohibited" is the idea upon which it is based.** *The word "riba" literally means "excess or addition", and has been translated as "interest", "usury", "excess", "increase" or "addition".*

In the late 19th century Islamic Modernists reacted to the rise of European power and influence and its colonization of Muslim countries by reconsidering the prohibition on interest and whether interest rates and insurance were not among the "preconditions for productive investment" in a functioning modern economy. Syed Ahmad Khan, argued for a differentiation between sinful riba "usury", which they saw as restricted to charges on lending for consumption, and legitimate non-riba "interest", for lending for commercial investment.

However, in the 20th century, Islamic revivalists/Islamists/activists worked to define all interest as riba, to enjoin Muslims to lend and borrow at "Islamic Banks" that avoided fixed rates. By the 21st century this Islamic Banking movement had created "institutions of interest-free financial enterprises across the world". Loans are permitted in Islam if the interest that is paid is linked to the profit or loss obtained by the investment. The concept of profit acts as a symbol in Islam as equal sharing of profits, losses, and risks.

https://en.wikipedia.org/wiki/Islamic_banking_and_finance

In the Western world, banking is a big business and finances homes and cars for most of us, giving us a real leg up on the quality of our lives. The difference is the two radically different religious moral views. One allows individuals to engage in such business deals with their personal property, the other restricts such business deals. Other religions have restrictions of various natures but most are moral imperatives rather than legal.

Now, this approach to the loaning of money is a very specific difference and there are many other examples of differences between religions that might be laid down as rules that can affect prosperity. But there is also an overriding enforcement of religious beliefs that sets up an environment to generate these kinds of specific laws and rules.

The Dancing Girls of Iran

A typical example of this rule by Islamic Clerics was examined in a video by a news organization examining life in Iran in the 2018 timeframe. Part of the video examined the life and restrictions on women in the performing arts, especially dancing. The video commentary was not trying to cause a problem but simply document, in the video, the state of dancing as a performing art in Iran, and in particular, a woman in the Iranian dancing world. Several trial versions were produced with local television stations to determine just what was acceptable to put on a video of a dancing Iranian woman, trying to ensure that they would capture what was acceptable to show on a video so that it could be shown in Iran itself. As different Iranian TV producers examined the example dancing videos, different opinions and views of what was acceptable were provided. No consistent set of rules resulted and ultimately the question was posed to local Clerics. A similar wavering of what was acceptable resulted, with comments on movement, skin coverage, and appearance being subjects of discussion. The result was that the videographers were left with no real understanding of what was acceptable.

From the New York Post, this short article reports on a second female dancing conflict in Iran that has a similar problem with interpretation.

Iran continues to arrest young women for dancing videos

By Laura Italiano, nypost.com., November 1, 2019

- Iran is continuing to arrest and jail young women for the "crime" of posting videos of themselves dancing.
- At least three women were detained earlier this month, according to the French news site France24

- Each had tens of thousands of followers on social media and had posted images of themselves "shuffle dancing," described as a club dance featuring repeated shuffling of the feet inwards and outwards.
- State media reported that the three were among a larger group of women being prosecuted for "obscene content creation."
- The three, Sahra Afsharian, Sara Shariatmadari and Niloufar Motiei, were being held in the notorious Qarchak Prison near Tehran.
- YouTube footage from 2017 shows Afsharian dancing and twirling joyfully while fully clothed and wearing a head scarf.
- None of the other images of Afsharian dancing posted by France24 shows her exposed in any way remotely obscene.
- In the past, women arrested after posting images of themselves that officials found offensive have been forced to make public "confessions" of their "immoral behavior.
- In September 2018, two actors were detained for mixed-gender dancing during a theater production in Tehran of Shakespeare's "A Midsummer Night's Dream."
- In 2014, six young Iranians who videotaped themselves dancing to "Happy" by Pharrell Williams were sentenced to being lashed 91 times each for ignoring Islamic norms.
- The sentences were suspended, meaning they won't be carried out unless the defendants were found guilty of additional crimes within the next three years.

https://nypost.com/2019/11/01/iran-continues-to-arrest-women-for-posting-videos-of-themselves-dancing/

Motivation and Prosperity

Islam develops strong religious and organizational allegiance through its beliefs and religious practices that exercise both spiritual and secular controls over life. Basic values are shown in the table below. There is a strong orthodoxy built into those beliefs aimed at controlling heresies and deviations. But they also influence every individual's thinking about life and that impacts prosperity. The orthodoxy is enforced by the primary elements of Islamic philosophic beliefs. These elements are:

- The strong directive that each Muslim is his brother's keeper and has a responsibility to keep them from sinning
- the application of Cleric enforced Sharia religious Law;
- the large number of nebulous sins that defy specific descriptions
- The imposition of harsh punishments from the 7th century
- The difficulty for each Muslim to read and understand or know the rules
- The lack of forgiveness when a law is unknowingly broken
- The uncertainty of Allah's eternal forgiveness
-

Islam's Religious and Philosophical Characteristics	
God's forgiveness and Heaven	Allah's forgiveness and entrance to Heaven / escape from punishment is based on Allah's evaluation of one's **lifetime** of good works v.s. one's major and minor sins.
Neighbors	it is one's duty to prevent your neighbor from sinning, by force if possible, and necessary;
Religious Law	• Sharia Religious Law for everyone, • Right, wrong, and punishment defined by Islamic clerics as judge and jury.
Forgiveness	Only After punishment?, especially for major sins. Muslims are Allah's agent for punishment
Mandated rituals	• Daily prayers 5 times a day facing toward Mecca in a prescribed kneeling and bowed position • Fasting during Ramadan • Pilgrimage to Mecca
The Good Life	• The life and experiences of Muhammad in 7th century Arabia is considered to be the perfect life • Everything the Prophet did in life therefore becomes a role model for how a Muslim should live their life

The partial Legatum prosperity index on the next page shows where the Arab Islamic countries fall in this worldwide evaluation. Other Muslim countries are listed in the full tables beginning on page 101 and the GDP tables begin on page 35. Links to the sources are below.

https://www.prosperity.com/download_file/view_inline/4429

https://en.wikipedia.org/wiki/List_of_countries_by_GDP_(PPP)_per_capita

The table also lists export and population information showing that the top Middle Eastern countries have very small populations and that, with the exception of the UAE, oil dominates their economies. Another possible factor is that The top four have sizable Christian populations. UAE, 12.5%; Qatar, 14.2%; Bahrain, 14.1%; Kuwait, 17.3%: compared to Saudi Arabia, 4.4% (Pew Research Institute).

The UAE is the highest-ranking Arab country in the Legatum Prosperity Index and ranked number 41 in the world. It lies within the top third of the world's countries along with four other very small, population-wise, Arab states. While it shares this same Islamic religion with other Arab countries, it has some differences that produce different results.

2021 Middle East Legatum Prosperity Index (selected)

#	Country	Population	Percent Citizens	Number of Citizens	GDP 2021 per capita (US$ PPP)	Export 2021 Top Item	Export Top $ Billions	Export All $ Billions
9	Germany				$63,271			
13	United Kingdom				$55,301			
19	Japan				$48,814			
20	United States	331,900,000			$76,027	Oil (13.5%)	$220.0	$1,630.0
29	South Korea				$53,051			
32	Israel				$50,204	Diamonds	$9.1	$64.1
41	United Arab Emirates	9,282,410	11.6%	1,076,760	$78,255	Oil (19.7%)	$58.5	$296.0
46	Qatar	2,795,484	11.2%	313,000	$112,789	Oil	$57.2	$94.7
56	Bahrain	1,463,265	48.7%	712,362	$57,424	Oil	$4.3	$15.0
58	Kuwait	4,450,000	32.6%	1,450,000	$50,909	Oil	$40.1	$58.2
67	Oman	4,520,471	99.0%	4,475,266	$35,286	Oil	$24.2	$56.9
75	Saudi Arabia	32,175,224	99.0%	31,853,472	$55,368	Oil	$138.0	$256.0
81	Jordan				$11,861	Fertilizers	$1.2	$12.0
91	Morocco				$9,041			
93	Turkey				$37,488	Cars	$10.0	$234.0
96	Tunisia				$12,300			
107	Algeria				$13,002			
109	Lebanon				$12,035	Gold	$0.4	$4.8
121	Egypt				$14,978	Oil	$4.8	$44.5
123	Iran				$18,332	Ethylene	$3.2	$14.0
141	Iraq				$12,141	Oil	$72.0	$81.1
154	Libya				$18,345			
158	Syria				$6,374	Olive oil	$0.1	$1.0
165	Yemen				$2,078			

The United Arab Emirates *(UAE; Arabic:* الإمارات العربية المتحدة *,*
romanized: al-ʾImārāt al-ʿArabiyya l-Muttaḥida),[b] or simply the Emirates
(Arabic: الإمارات *, romanized: al-ʾImārāt), is a country in West Asia, in the*
Middle East. It is located at the eastern end of the Arabian Peninsula and
shares borders with Oman and Saudi Arabia, while also having maritime
borders in the Persian Gulf with Qatar and Iran. Abu Dhabi is the country's
capital, while Dubai, the most populous city, is an international hub.

The United Arab Emirates is an elective monarchy formed from a
federation of seven emirates, consisting of Abu Dhabi, Ajman, Dubai,
Fujairah, Ras Al Khaimah, Sharjah and Umm Al Quwain. Each emirate is an
absolute monarchy governed by a ruler, and together the rulers form the
Federal Supreme Council, the highest executive and legislative body. The
Federal Supreme Council elects a president and two vice presidents from
among their members; as of 14 May 2023, the president is Sheikh Mohamed
bin Zayed Al Nahyan and the vice presidents are Sheikh Mohammed bin
Rashid Al Maktoum and Sheikh Mansour bin Zayed Al Nahyan. In practice,
the ruler of Abu Dhabi serves as president while the ruler of Dubai is vice
president and also prime minister.

As of 2023, the UAE has an estimated population of 9.97 million. Emirati
citizens are estimated to form 11.6% of the population; the remaining
residents are expatriates, the majority of whom are South Asian. Islam is the
official religion and Arabic is the official language. The United Arab
Emirates' oil and natural gas reserves are the world's sixth and seventh-
largest, respectively. Zayed bin Sultan Al Nahyan, ruler of Abu Dhabi and
the country's first president, oversaw the development of the Emirates by
investing oil revenues into healthcare, education, and infrastructure. The
country has the most diversified economy among the members of the Gulf
Cooperation Council. In the 21st century, the UAE has become less reliant on
oil and gas and is economically focusing on tourism and business. The UAE is
considered a middle power. It is a member of the United Nations, Arab
League, Organisation of Islamic Cooperation, OPEC, Non-Aligned
Movement, World Trade Organization, Gulf Cooperation Council (GCC) and
BRICS. The UAE is also a dialogue partner of the Shanghai Cooperation
Organisation.

UAE Characteristics

- Its history has been as a British Colony
- Laws are a mix of British influence and Islamic values.
- It applies Sharia Law to family matters only
- and allows non-Muslim citizens to use their own form of family law.

- It does have civil laws against variant sexual preferences which are not rigorously enforced
- but women rape victims can be thrown in jail
- kissing in public is not permitted but holding hands is OK.
- It is also religiously tolerant and has a sizable Christian population of about 14% (Pew Research estimate) with 32 churches and also has a small Jewish population.
- There is also a Hindu population of about 6%.
- true citizens only comprise about 12% of the total population.
- There are a large number of foreign workers from undeveloped countries who have been characterized as slave labor.
- The finance and business economy is the source of most of the GDP
- tourism is also a big contributor.
- Dubai is the 5th most popular tourist destination in the world
- the Burj Khalifa in Dubai is the tallest building in the world.
- While Arabic is the official language, English is the most popular one used.
- The Government is totalitarian and autocratic, however, so freedoms of the press and speech are not respected.
- Internationally it has supported the war on Terror
- It was an original signer to the "Abraham Accords".
https://en.wikipedia.org/wiki/United_Arab_Emirates

Prosperity, both economic and mental outlook, comes first from a way of thinking about and living life. As we've discussed we also all have an internal battle with our genetic past and human consciousness that can easily make us self-centered and malevolent actors and that is the result of human nature coping with life. When life becomes tricky or difficult to negotiate, openness and a cooperative society deteriorate. Prosperity is built on a cooperative society, openness, and personal freedom. Islam's strong orthodoxy has consequences for prosperity both within the community and with external relationships beyond Islamic Societies.

The Legatum Prosperity Index, which captures the outcome and comments on the possible causes gives the best look at Islamic prosperity.

Observation, "Death to the infidels" is a long way from "Love your neighbor".

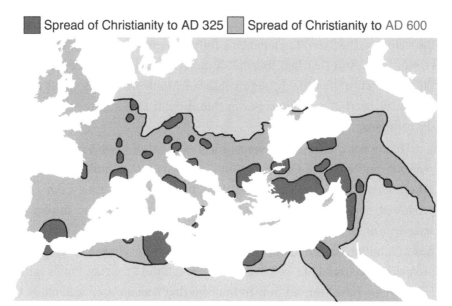

SECTION F: FORWARD TO VOLUME II

18. Intro to Vol II: The Abundant Life

We have only touched on the aspects of Christianity that have promoted the Western World's Prosperity. Volume II will provide added detail on the expansion and understanding of the full nature of Christianity and the Christian Philosophy of Life Basics. This will expand on the "Love your neighbor" concept.

Volume II is the story of Christianity expanding throughout the Roman Empire and eventually replacing Rome. It is the story of everyday people living in a primitive educational environment and being faced with a complex God and spiritual life. The complexity of Christianity is spelled out in the New Testament but many questions about the nature of God and Jesus abounded. Christianity came in and turned traditional religions and religious thinking upside down. The malevolent nature of natural mankind, when contrasted with Christian ideals, led to some outrageous attempts at living a Christian life. It would take fifteen hundred years for the value of the New Testament to fully explain Christianity to become recognized. And that had to await a major technology development and the appearance of a tough, argumentative Monk willing to stand on his beliefs, in front of a religious power that did not take kindly to heretics of the orthodoxy.

This is not a blow-by-blow historical account of what happened every year but the story of the key events of transformational thinking over many generations, developing a socialization based on Christian values, that promoted great advances in learning, education, the arts, music, and science. It is in the sciences where the giant leaps of technology and understanding of the nature of the world come alive and create the prosperous material life we have. It is through the Christian Philosophy of Life that we have learned how to manage that socialization and enjoy the fruits of this new world.

Volume II will begin with the historical account of Israel and Judaism's conflicts with Rome, and follow Christianity's spread across the Roman Empire. As Christian understanding expanded it promoted an explosion in a quest for knowledge, seeking first the mysteries of Christianity, and then expanding to a desire for education in general. This launched the University systems and then the Scientific Revolution. Technological advances, especially the printing press, created an explosion in knowledge on the scale of the Internet revolution today, opening the Reformation debate to the general population. Christianity expanded from its mystical nature into a true Philosophy of Life, as scientific advances carried us to our current level of technology, scientific knowledge, and prosperity.

This is a world of great prosperity and a world that again, based on the new scientific knowledge only available in the last 50 to 100 years points to God as the designer and creator of the Universe.

History is the story of mankind's conscious mind at work, the good and the bad. Prosperity is the story of the Christian spirit working behind the scenes.

Made in United States
Orlando, FL
23 September 2024

51843396R10186